The Sky *is on* Fire

The Sky *is on* Fire

One Woman. One Camel. Two Nomads.

Magsie Hamilton Little

First published in the United Kingdom in 2016
Published by Median, Max Press, London

10 9 8 7 6 5 4 3 2 1

Edition no 1

Text © by M Hamilton Little
Design and layout © by Median

ISBN: 978 1 906251 76 5

The author and publisher will be grateful for any information that will assist them in keeping future editions up-to-date. Although every reasonable care has been taken in the preparation of this book, neither the publishers, editors nor the author can accept any liability for the consequences arising from the use thereof, or the information contained therein. Some names of people and places in this book have been changed for privacy.

Printed and bound by CPI Group (UK) Ltd, Croydon, CR0 4YY

On the Desert

WILLIAM WENTMORE STORY (1819–1895)

ALL around,
   To the bound
   Of the vast horizon's round,
All sand, sand, sand,
All burning, glaring sand,
   On my camel's hump I ride,
   As he sways from side to side,
   With an awkward step of pride,
And his scraggy head uplifted, and his eye so long and bland.

   Naught is near,
   In the blear
   And simmering atmosphere,
But the shadow on the sand,
The shadow of the camel on the sand;
   All alone, as I ride,
   O'er the desert's ocean wide,
   It is ever at my side;
It haunts me, it pursues me, if I flee, or if I stand.

   Not a sound,
   All around,
   Save the padded beat and bound
Of the camel on the sand,
Of the feet of the camel on the sand.
   Not a bird is in the air,
   Though the sun, with burning stare,
   Is prying everywhere,
O'er the yellow thirsty desert, so desolately grand.

Not a breath
Stirs the death
Of the desert, nor a wreath
Curls upward from the sand,
From the waves of loose, fine sand,
And I doze, half asleep,
Of the wild Sirocs that sweep
O'er the caravans, and heap
With a cloud of powdery, dusty death, the terror-stricken
band.

Their groans
And their moans
Have departed, but their bones
Are whitening on the sand
Are blanching and grinning on the sand,
O Allah! thou art great!
Save me from such a fate,
Nor through that fearful strait
Lead me, thy basest servant, unto the Prophet-land.

Contents

Prologue   1

First light
I have nothing   6
In between   9
Wake up   18

Morning
Open your eyes   24
You're crazy!   29
I drank some tea   33
The day after   37
Beneath the palms   46

Towards midday
I return   52
She fell off the camel   63
The perfection of woman   67
A wonderful event   75
The goat jumped   80
Among the stars   91
Friendship   94
I cry when I remember   97

Hearts together, tents apart   104
Of the light   111

Noon
I feel the sun   118
The great desert   122
The sun does not take breaks   128
I'm in the fire   135
One branch does not make a goat pen   139
Snake!   145
The flies are on the wall   151
I wasted time   159
Let's unite   164
My friends, what have you got to say?   170
My heart is dry   177

Afternoon
My soul is thirsty   188
Underneath   195
Suffering and loss   201
Abandon your illusions   208
I went with the ardent wind   219
There is no certainty   226
Radiance   232

Sunset
Searching for freedom   238
That man   247

Death is here   255
A prisoner of the present   263
My heart cries out still   272

Dusk
I am ready to die   282
The dog leaves the doghouse   295
She runs to the house that is burning   303

Midnight
I do not understand   312
You can kill me or let me live   319
Afterwards   332

Dawn
I touched incandescence   338
I do not forget   346
Epilogue   350

Glossary   351
Acknowledgements   355

Prologue

Promises are tricky things. It's all about the delivery. We can offer anything in the world, but if we cannot remain true to our word, how can we live with that knowledge – or expect anyone to believe anything we say ever again?

I made a promise once. How little did I know then that it would change my life. The day it all began seemed so ordinary upon waking. There had been the usual quota of junk emails offering to sell me things that I did not want, update me with news that I had not asked for and invite me to events with which I had no connection. I scarcely registered the one from Afghanistan at first. It seemed so innocent and unobtrusive. And then I clicked it open. I stared at the ink and the spaces stared back. There was a wound in those words. It bled pound signs.

In search of air, along the drab, grey corridor, somehow my finger found the lift button. Goose-pimpled, dizzy-headed, I could hardly breathe. I could barely think. The charity I had founded in Kabul was in trouble. Families were relying on me. And I had given my word to children.

Going down from my apartment on the fifteenth and sixteenth floors always gave a sense of immersion, like a diver entering a pool. This time I saw only darkness. There was an impression of free fall; at the same time of breakage. I was aware of the heaviness of matter, the dragging of the curve of gravity, the spaces between the atoms.

At the bottom of the shaft the doors parted, the fissure of lead turned wax-white. My lungs took in the city.

The hum of the street was low, its rhythm sharp-edged, metallic. My steps followed its music, the soft roar of cars, the sharp tap of stilettos. A busker glowed with rush-hour happiness. Mobile phones danced with plastic carrier bags. Reflections of faces swirled on café windows.

In Kensington Gardens I collapsed on a carpet of grass, stretching out my toes beneath the arms of an oak. A speck of light floated off across the corner of my eye, up towards the leaves. It was precisely at that moment, as the dot drifted up between their bright edges, that the idea first occurred. I would have to think it over, I told myself. It would be unwise to rush.

Towards seven o'clock I made my way back.

Closing the front door is something of a metaphor, a symbolic gesture. We kick off our shoes and shut out the world for a while. I slammed mine that day. For good measure, I double-locked it.

The hot, frothy water of the bath did not stop my shivers. Afterwards, I lay motionless on the bed, my body inert, alien, without sensation. I shrugged off the duvet. Outside on the balcony the air frosted the eyelashes. A melancholy wind howled around the tower and there was no moon. Down below, black-bundled shadows crept like ants. A few murky shapes had taken form, as if the concrete and brick had uprooted themselves and laid siege in some dark fairy tale. But there were no brave knights and no white chargers here. This damsel was on her own.

I remember reading once that when we gaze up at the night sky we are looking at our history. The stars are just echoes of events that occurred light years ago in space and time. We are watching a fossilized snapshot of our past. Perhaps we too are a little like photographs, at times so obscured and at an angle. In the whirlwind of our society we can become so weighed down that it is hard to see ourselves and others as we really are. We have life at our fingertips, but it can so easily slip through our fingers.

Glancing out at the blackness of the horizon, it was as if I was regarding it for the first time, this dark place filled with vestiges of my own past. No matter how I squinted, I could see only the dry, shattered fragments of a life – the smiling faces death had torn from me, the many regrets and mistakes I had made.

The following day, I put my flat on the market. There was no other way to raise the amount of capital needed to keep my charity afloat. When my home was sold, the pain tore through my bones like glass shards. I closed the front door and threw away the key. Just like at a hot, crowded, sweaty party where everyone is absorbed in their own separate conversation, London did not notice me leaving.

First light
Ahal

· ⋮ · ‖

I have nothing
Ul lir haret

Sanctuary takes many forms. A home can be somewhere to rest, to escape fear, or to find ourselves. It gives us our identity. It calls to us, like a womb song. It follows our joy, our strife, and where it bears witness to sorrow it can feel as if the very walls are weeping. This sense of rooting lies deep within all of us, so what happens when, for whatever reason, the comfort blanket is ripped away?

With my home gone and most of my wealth discarded, some might have said I was free. And I was superficially. I had no ties.

But I was still in prison. Søren Kierkegaard might have called it angst – the state of collapse when everything has fallen. I cannot find words to answer the questions that plagued me because they lay beyond reasoned judgement.

Seeking out a refuge, I returned to Hertfordshire where I had grown up. There, I slept on a mattress on a floor in a small rented cottage. I went through boxes, unearthing the past, peeling away layers of time.

First came the wafting, chemical odour of mothballs, and now objects taking up space, paintings of landscapes all but forgotten – fluffy cashmere jumpers, silk skirts and sparkly shoes, a turquoise necklace – and a musical box, a hankerchief, the initials HL embroidered in silk, a fossilized dinosaur egg, a finger puppet even.

Some things I threw out, like a tired, angry old snake discarding its skin. Others I returned to their musty, tissue-lined dens, taking care to double-tape the boxes to prevent them leaking more grief. The rest were filled with tears. Those ones remained sealed.

I was a tortoise without a shell and now I retreated into one. Head clogged and cottony, with the curtains drawn, sapphire lights flashed before my eyes in silent migraines. Behind them nothingness slushed in a wave. Whatever was happening was my own fault. It was drowning me, this deluge called my past.

The memories, when they arrived, were hazy. I tried to distinguish memory from imagination, recalling elements, but not the detail. Scents, images drifted like flotsam on calm waters, or flashes, blurred at the edges, a negative reproduction of a positive image that had gone before. Is this all a life boils down to – a flick book of lost moments?

Seeking distraction, I revisited the Meccas of my youth – a common where wild harebells grew; a street where Morris dancers clanked sticks – and the rain kept falling, sucked down to the ground I had also been drawn to.

I walked, and the shadows of my past walked with me, filled with all those things I had done and had not done – past street lamps haloed in mist, my footsteps echoing to chimes of cathedral bells almost in tune, nearly in time. I re-trod the old lanes and avenues, my shadow twisted like an etiolated plant.

Flashes of beauty caught the imagination – the fast flight of clouds, a leaf that caught the light in the shadows, a Red Admiral on a yellow rose.

By the time the hares were boxing in the meadows, the charity in Afghanistan had recovered a little, although the problems faced by the Afghan people appeared to be no better. No sooner had British and American troops begun to withdraw from the country than the Taliban reclaimed their footing. Security in Kabul grew worse.

It took about three months before I managed to pull myself together. Then one day, through the branches of the trees, I spied a lapwing tumbling and falling. That was the one I was ready, when I gathered up the splinters of my heartbreak, tidied them away inside where they belonged, and bought a plane ticket.

A trip to the desert was everything I needed.

In between

Jer

Any journey is a state of suspended animation. Temporarily, we find ourselves holed up in an interim, that mysterious location that is neither here nor there. For a while we are boxed in. Our surroundings are boring, crowded places that do little for our blood pressure, but give time and space to think and ask questions. What is our real destination? we may ask. Hopefully, a deeper understanding. Am I heading in a straight line or stopping off en route? Or sometimes they prompt more practical concerns, such as in my case, did I remember to pack my toothbrush?

It was business as usual on the Air Algérie flight. The air conditioning was on the blink and there were sandwiches, curled up at the edges, entombed in plastic and apparently made from it. An odour emanated from the row in front, where an extended family were wedged into their seats like sweaty mozzarella cheeses. Water rationing had begun early, the half-filled cups dutifully handed out after take-off.

Dozing, I rested my head in the niche between the window and the seat, blotting out the choir of babies as they set each other off in antiphonal wails.

My dulled senses were stirring. I was suspended in that state of having left and not yet arrived, experiencing a moment pregnant with possibility, a time of anticipation and forgetting, of embracing the unknown. I longed for the peace and solitude of the desert, but there was more. I wanted to break with convention, to push my boundaries and dispense with the stereotype of what a woman should be doing with her life. I knew the risks, how to get around the reels of red tape, how to slip under the radar.

Fate would determine if I would return.

It was not the first time I had wanted to run away. On this occasion my destination was a small town of almost 50,000 people nestling at 4,000 feet in a fold of the Hoggar Mountains in the southern tip of Algeria.

Few places in north Africa are as remote.

Tamranasset is also the heartland of a people I yearned to know more about. The Tuareg, the Blue Men of the desert, or the Kel Tamahaq, as they prefer to be known in Algeria, number around two million and belong to no fewer than eight territorial groups. I would be meeting the Kel Ahaggar who live around the Hoggar and Tassil-n-Ajjer mountain regions. In this culture, it is men who wear the veil – the *chèche* or *tagelmust* – the faded length of indigo-dyed cloth wrapped about the head.

Although the Tuareg have played a huge role in the Sahara – as great as French colonization in the region – little is understood about what drives and inspires them in the modern age. In the past they established a complex society unprecedented in nomadic tribes, and with a sophisticated system of laws and hierarchies. In the modern age some speak of them with pity, as just another aspect of the planet laid siege to by a painful transition into the modern world, but this to me is a rather simplistic and naïve interpretation of the events that have taken place in central Sahara during the last twenty or thirty years.

Like many other nomadic groups, the Tuareg continue to be threatened by conflict, politics and the settled world's constant quest for pure, natural resources. Ostracised by successive governments and denied access to their ancient, historical homelands, generations of Tuareg have grown up displaced. Most have been forced to abandon the nomadic life and have turned to the cities to make a living, like so many wandering people – the Sami reindeer warriors of arctic Scandinavia who now live in houses and travel for brief periods to hunt or mark their reindeer; or the Inuits of Canada and Alaska, whose dog-drawn sledges have become mostly relics.

Soon I was on another plane, a small domestic flight. I had given up on the idea of watching a movie: the screen wasn't working, and someone had ripped out the pages of the in-flight magazine. The scenery below provided the entertainment. There, sand un-scrolled, huge and unimaginable as dreams, without edges, borders, brinks, limits or boundaries. Great mountain ranges sprawled like sleeping dinosaurs, scaly-skinned and gouged with dry rivers.

'At least you'll get a chance to practise your languages, darling,' my mother had said when I had told her I was off. The taxi had tooted. We had hugged and she had said no more. She hadn't fooled me.

Others I had not told. People are like places – some hold on to you, some egg you on. Others drive you away.

☂ ☂ ☂

It felt like I was the only person trying to enter Algeria. Everyone else was trying to leave. It didn't take long to deal with the documentation. Usually there were interminable queues, questions asked, items spread over long plastic tables, a visa scrutinized microscopically by men with giant moustaches who eyed my peppermint lip balm, moisturizing cleansing pads and super-strength headache tablets as if they concealed illegal substances. This time I sailed through unhindered, meeting with little more than puzzled stares.

The people who flocked the other way with their bundles and weary children had more difficulty. But they were the lucky ones. They had the money to flee the country by air, and they knew who to bribe to acquire permits to move to Europe. Thousands more were taking to the ocean in puny boats and rubber Zodiacs for the perilous journey across the Mediterranean from north Africa to Italy and Spain. War, unemployment, corruption and poverty were lethal ingredients in the cocktail that was the people trade in the region.

And they were just part of the greater refugee crisis that the world is facing today – one unlike any other in history, spawned not only by the wars in Syria and Afghanistan. Poor African migrants on epic journeys from Libya, Mali, Niger and further south in sub-Saharan Africa are loaded like cattle into trucks and dumped at coastal ports, where they are left to the mercy of so-called shipping agents. They risk their own lives and those of their children on choppy seas without food or water, escaping their pasts in the slender hope of building a future.

The customs hall was made of unplastered breezeblocks illuminated by flickering neon. In its thinning crowd tense faces bobbed like spring blossoms. A lone placard advertised adventure tours in seven languages, but there were no takers.

I scooped up my bags and edged tentatively towards the gate. At a kiosk I bought bananas, sweet, soft and redolent of Africa. I had read that the town – Ain Salah in Arabic – meant 'good well', but the sweet water had turned salty, so I passed. I switched on my phone.

A Tuareg named Samir was to be my tour guide. He came with impeccable references. The Consulate in London recommended him. We had spoken and we had emailed. We had even arranged a rendezvous. Now, as the ringtone beeped, the voice that answered was older, deeper. There was no mention of any meeting. The man hung up when he learned that I was travelling solo.

Perhaps it was only to be expected, I thought to myself. Cutting through paperwork, understanding that time has a different meaning in different parts of the globe, the minor shifts of accent – such glitches combine like a sequence of tests the traveller must pass.

Outside, my footsteps crunched in dust, the heat heavy on my head as if I were a shadow.

When travelling to a hot country we soon acclimatize, but that first blast of solar power alters the body's magnetic alignment. The senses tingle with new scents and sounds. The wind tastes different, feels different, arid and ancient as it sweeps over the skin as if to get a better look. At last, we can unplug.

I breathed it in, this country of dust, like a newborn.

☁ ☁ ☁

'You are visiting for how long exactly?' asked the bus driver.

I had escaped, although, it has to be said, not exactly into safety. My luggage disappeared into the hold of a filthy, battered specimen of a vehicle that by modern EU health and safety standards should have been scrapped decades ago, although for the locals it was not so much a bus as a miracle of modern engineering.

'Not long,' I said. 'Just a week or two.' I tried to sound cheerful, because at the rate I was going, just getting there was going to take up most of that.

'And you are going to… er… the *desert*?'

'Yes,' I said warily.

The driver called out again, as if it was my hearing that

was the problem rather than the deafening clatter of the engine. 'The desert is full of bad men. Why not go to Dubai? Dubai has shopping.'

He was ignoring the road, studying me in his mirror. I could make out his baffled gaze, the furrowed brow, the silvery swish of his moustache glistening in the sunlight.

'I like the desert.'

It was true. I believed at this point that the desert held a power. Far from cities and woodlands, I assumed life must be different there, purified somehow by the heat and sand, a symbol of constancy, truth and extremity.

'Why not just fly over it, get a good look and then… er… *go*?'

'But it might be interesting to… sort of *feel* it?'

As soon as I said this I sort of did – the seat appeared to have no springs, passengers being required to provide the suspension in their own bodies, and there were no seatbelts.

'It feels *hot*. And it has a lot of sand.' As he shook his head, I was left in no doubt as to what he was really trying to say: that the desert was no place for a foreign woman.

It was at that exact moment that a gentleman with a white beard tapped me on the shoulder and explained that going anywhere by bus in Algeria was against the rules for foreigners anyway.

Around me, old men gazed from withered faces. They had very little, but their curiosity remained. Perhaps it was their blurred reflections in the windows that surprised them the most, continuing on their own journeys into the region where they felt most comfortable, that of their shared roots. The elderly couple travelling from Biskra sitting in front of me remained impervious. Their own roots were back in the north. But they were glad to be away, drinking juice and playing cards. The husband knew all the little tricks, and his wife could tell when he was cheating. They were used to practising what all travellers on desert roads must practise: forbearance.

I wondered where they thought they were heading beneath the smokescreen of their years, and where they thought I was. They hooted their teenage laughter when I asked them this, waved their arthritis-nobbled hands and pointed up, towards the sky. They had no promises to keep. Their boxes were unpacked. They were going to see the desert, like I was. Afterwards they were planning to go shopping in Dubai.

We trundled across the rocky plain, united by discomfort. A sign warned of sand drifts and, as if on cue, suddenly sand was everywhere, eddying from the crests, slipping across the track, settling over the windscreen. Swathes of it spun across the landscape like sugar. Dunes mounted up along the side of the road, their errant particles threatening to engulf us.

We were lucky today, said the driver. Drifts building around the wheels were only to be expected when driving across the desert. Sometimes the grains were so fine they caused deeper slippage. Ramps had to be put down and vehicles coaxed out like frightened animals.

It was a good thing it wasn't an unlucky day. Perhaps those who hated the Sahara had a point when they argued that it was not about space, freedom, solitude or escape, but getting stuck, not to mention the poison from exhaust fumes, heat exhaustion and cigarette smoke.

The real desert is none of these things, of course. It is the planet in the raw, the earth's skin mashed to a pulp, burnt and scabbed. In its vastness human beings look like ants. Buildings are etched into the earth's surface as if part of it. Roadblocks melt into its haze like coagulating lava.

Alongside the misty peaks of the Tassili the dirt road

swung left. Gold canyons emerged dotted with palm trees and tamarisks. Small specks of Barbary sheep balanced like acrobats. For miles just the sweeping line of crisp dunes and low hollows fell upon a horizon the shade of ox blood.

Dusk fell, and with it the temperature. I huddled, dry-throated, in my inadequate cotton clothes, eyeing the bag containing the solitary sweater I had brought, which was beyond reach in the luggage rack several seats away.

It was dark when to everyone's relief we rattled into the *gare routière*. Some minutes later, I peered tentatively into the void, and strode into it.

☂ ☂ ☂

Word had it there were several not-too-bad lodgings for the few travellers who came to Tamanrasset, but apparently they were all miles away. Instead, I found a tumbledown establishment with a dimly lit façade that appeared to be in the process of refurbishment. In other words, it was a building site.

A firm knock produced shuffling sounds from within and the heavy front door squeaked open. A throat cleared its phlegm.

'*Shkoon?* Who is it?' said a man's voice. A hooked nose turned sideways in profile, then back again. Two beady eyes peered out, looking me up and down. '*Ruuh fi siteen dahya!* To sixty hells!'

'*Masa al-cher, andkumshee shambra faarigha?* Good evening, 'I was wondering if you might have any rooms?'

'*Anti dayie?* You are lost?' said the man suspiciously.

He didn't know how much.

'And you are travelling on your own?' he said, and an even greater look of mistrust crossed his face.

I nodded. '*Na'am*. Yes.'

'But you speak Arabic?' A heavy eyebrow lifted.

'*Shwe shwe*. A bit.'

'Two hundred dollar,' he sighed.

'*Meeteen*! Two hundred!'

A frown is the same in any language; his – and mine.

He scratched his cheek. 'OK. For you, one hundred.'

At last, the door opened. He was a large, egg-shaped man and, as he rattled his bunch of jailer's keys before me, picked one off and gave it to me, I thanked him profusely. Then the Demis Roussos *djellaba* swirled around and left, cursing and muttering.

Hot, out of breath, I struggled up the steep staircase to the tiny chamber. There was something familiar about this place, an echo – the rickety bed, its mattress still shrouded in the plastic cover it had arrived in to make it more appealing for the resale market; the bare bulb pitted with dead insects; the curtains that did not fit the window. Not forgetting the ceiling fan – for decorative purposes only.

Fortunately, the light switch did not illuminate the darkness beyond, or the hole from which an indescribable stench was wafting, which I was forced to conclude was the loo. There was no sprinkler on the shower, just the only-to-be-expected plastic tube grafted to a water pipe. Sand drifted across the floor in waves.

I opened the window and, just for a moment, I could smell the desert.

Wake up

Ebdadat

Things were looking up, although my eyes at the time were shut. Opening, then closing them again, red light exploded behind my eyelids, as if they had caught fire. Whispering names, I saw faces branded in burning iron. I opened my lids, blinked and they were gone.

Apart from the muezzin and the fly there wasn't a sound. Just for an instant, I felt the total cessation of everything. It cannot have been long before the rush of their return to my consciousness overwhelmed me.

Eventually I rose, leaned against the wall polka-dotted with insects and tried to weep – for those I had loved, for lost hope.

It was not the first time that I had worn the veil, although I am not Muslim. On this occasion, as I wound the material tight around my head, I wrapped my memories up in it. I pinned it so they wouldn't leak.

There are many subtleties to the meaning of the veil. Wherever it is worn, such nuances extend beyond religious dictate. It is an expression of identity. It is about respect, privacy and reserve. In hot countries it is also practical, protecting the wearer from the sun and dust, and helping to guard against dehydration. The *chèche*, worn by Tuareg men, conceals the mouth – that organ that gives away so much unconsciously, the area of the face that betrays feelings. It is so because it signals purity over impurity.

As I slipped past the desk and closed the door, there was no sign of the manager. I was not afraid. I did not intend to go far. I had learned to stride purposefully, to keep moving and to never ask for directions.

The street was a jumble of livestock, bicycles and carts all narrowly avoiding each other. Already the heat was high. I could smell the buttery, warm odour of sheep dung, spices, the heat crisping the skin and the harsh tobacco that thickens voices and dries throats. I plunged into the gaze of those who passed and they averted mine.

Men with covered heads bonded in whispers. Although sometimes it was possible to discern some minimal facial gesture, I could not penetrate the looks cast sideways. Nor could I yet grasp what kept people rooted to this dry, inhospitable land, why they gazed heavenwards or averted their eyes.

Algeria felt veiled, too, a country blinded by sunlight, yet at the same time dwelling in the shadow of everything that is missing, where even the sun makes zebra-striped patches, as if it is guarding secrets.

☼ ☼ ☼

The café bore no sign except 'Coca-Cola' in Arabic. From the tawdry exterior, you could just glimpse the floor within, dirty, bare, on which stood a few plywood chairs. Fly-infested sandwiches were air-drying in the window.

There was no sign of Samir. Perhaps I was in the wrong town, the wrong place at the wrong hour. My heart bucked like a just-caught fish. I sat down nevertheless.

Through the window I watched a small donkey pulling a load twice its size and three times its weight. I read a book without hearing the song of the words.

Time passes quickly while we travel, slowly while we wait, making time a mental construct that we live by as if it is some axiomatic truth, which, of course, it is not. The moon moves the tides. Nature progresses by seasons. Animals live by instinct. Only man is wedded to his own invention – and impediment – the clock.

I was about to give up my vigil when someone called my name. I looked up and smiled. He looked back, unable to imagine what, besides despair, could drive a person to this hot, arid, empty place.

There was something contradictory about his athletic build and dishevelled appearance. He was wearing yellow and he blended with the dust, as if he wished to be camouflaged by it. The only friendliness that stood out was his sudden white smile.

Our hello was formal, a symphony in which the same sentiment, give or take the odd variation, was offered repeatedly. Only then, having flogged to death the well-wishing, was the keynote of polite reciprocity cadenced with the inevitable round of Qur'anic invocations.

Grilled camel with chips looked interesting. I settled for *harira*, a soup with vegetables and spices, and Samir ordered goat.

We sipped tea from miniature glasses. It took little time to exchange news, since neither of us wanted to broach the subject of things best forgotten in our lives. We touched on our careers, and that took even less time. We brushed on politics and swiftly moved off it.

He cleared his throat, shifted one leg or the other. I should have guessed how difficult it was for him to work out the puzzle of who I was and what exactly I was doing here – an enigma, of course, that I was travelling by myself.

Sometimes culture, social attitudes and politics drift down from Europe like a cloud over Africa and the Middle East, entering people's minds in a hazy fog that is more confusing than enlightening. The five slow centuries of development that have brought the West computers and Kalashnikovs have, some say, still to take place in a few Middle Eastern societies, yet all these things can be found everywhere, along with a generosity of spirit born of the dictates of religion and cultural tradition.

Lunch looked like the bits you find in your pocket when it comes out of the washing machine.

We tucked in.

Samir seemed keen to practise the English he had learned giving tours. He was, in his own words, a forward-thinking Algerian, committed to guiding foreigners ignorant of ancient traditions so they might understand and appreciate the ways and customs of his people; and the desert which he loved and considered the best place on earth, a gift.

He smiled a lot, but I wondered if he was happy. He spoke of the *djinn* and their world that lay unseen around us, full of cities and mountains with great mosques and citadels. In turn, I told of the great cities and cathedrals of my country, whose bells chimed out of tune and not quite in time, and he found that hard to picture.

As a woman alone I expected to be thought easy prey. I was looking forward to an easy, uncomplicated trip, so I stressed that my family was Christian to throw him off course. It seemed to do the trick. He repeated his white smile, this time with a bewildered expression.

After that, we got on famously. He suggested trips we could make and people and places we might visit, although I understood it was so hot during daylight hours that it was unlikely we would do any of it. He had one thing in mind, he said, and that was to make my trip fun. I had one thing on my mind too. I wondered if he had an air conditioner.

It was late afternoon when he walked me back to my hotel through a labyrinth of alleys that constantly changed direction, not unlike our own strange, winding detours and impermeable defence mechanisms.

'I'll keep you safe,' he said. 'I promise.'

Morning
Tufat

+ ⁞ Ⱨ · +

Open your eyes

Aswadat

Strictly speaking, the speed of light is the only verifiable constant in our universe. Sunlight takes eight minutes and seventeen seconds precisely to travel from the surface of the sun to the earth, and yet daylight itself is not a fixed entity. Rather, each day is a process, and the amount of light emitted by the sun varies according to time, location, season and direction.

I knew light was the key to my own process, but I was unsure why. I was still at the beginning, and the speed at which I was travelling was erratic.

Two days had shot by and I had barely even noticed their passing, but already it felt as if a great curtain of gloom had been lifted. For a start I had changed rooms. The new one was less coffin-shaped, more a jam jar, and mercifully north-facing. There was a cot for a child in the corner, and for that reason it was called a family room.

Quickly I was discovering Tamanrasset. Grown out of a military outpost, the town was originally built to guard the silk routes on what was an abundant oasis. Today it provides apricots, dates, almonds, oranges, figs and cereals in spite of boiling temperatures. Linked to the north by the 1,200-mile artery of the Trans-Saharan, it is strategically placed on the crossroads of a network of ancient trading routes that stretch south towards Mali and east into Libya.

The oldest and most famous landmark is a small adobe fort that looks as if it belongs to the Foreign Legion, but was actually built by the scholar Charles de Foucauld, who moved here to live when it was little more than a nomadic encampment of straw *zeribas*.

These days it is very different. Connections with the outside world are limited. There is an unreliable postal service and no electricity, apart from the constant supply directed at the governor's residence.

The problems are both ecological and political, the complications religious. Frequent droughts exacerbate old enmities and create a general malaise throughout the central Saharan regions. Despite all these things, business prospects are hopeful, thanks to the encouragement of Islam and the real profits – from contraband.

It was easy to see why Saharans call Tamanrasset the new Timbuktu. It survives somehow against against violence, drought and famine. Shops are not empty and there is a marketplace, an arcade and even a cinema, but trees are almost as rare as rainfall and there is no telephone exchange.

Water is scarce. A central square bears cement columns complete with a fountain – brimming not with water but with rubbish. Those who can afford to do so survive on deliveries from private water companies that collect their supplies from far-off wells. The poor rely on street taps.

The car that picked me up that morning was part of this mixture. It was a Toyota Land Cruiser and it belonged to Samir. It seemed very new. I wondered how he afforded it, but as we climbed in he evaded my questions.

Instead, he practised that smile again, this time wryly. 'A lot faster than a camel, and less awkward,' he said.

He did not ask about my stay. Having been taught from a young age that all hotels were deviant places for sex and drinking, he did not approve of them.

In any case, he already regarded me as a fallen woman, although he did not understand the phrase. He thought it meant women who have fallen from the heavens on to men and hurt themselves.

I studied his *chèche*. It rather suited him, I thought. It was not indigo, as I had expected, but dark blue, and it was made of muslin. When it was dusty, he wore it high, so there was just a slit. At its lowest it was possible to see his whole face, which I had to admit was handsome.

We were about the same age, but so removed from each other. There was a vulnerability about him which I could not yet fathom. I wondered if I would ever understand him as well as he would have liked or as well as he allowed me.

He chose his comments carefully. 'I am so happy you have come to see our beautiful country,' he said. He was navigating effortlessly. His frown had gone and we were laughing.

'It's lovely,' I said, leaning into the hot wind that poured through the open window.

'Allah's country.'

'Like all Allah's countries.' I glanced over. Already my veil had uncoupled. I managed to put it on again, sort of.

He smiled too, but kept his eyes on the road. 'Just as it says in the Qur'an... an oasis... Paradise itself.'

We had descended from the city heading south and were following a rugged *piste* along the base of a valley. A cloud of dust swirled, hitting our faces in a hot blast. Samir didn't seem to notice.

Nowhere on earth does the wind's true force feel more unremitting than in the Sahara, where it disperses the clouds arriving from the ocean before they release rain and shapes the rocky plateaux, known as *tassili*. Sailors call it the trade wind. Saharan dust the colour of amber carried to great altitudes can rain down as far north as England.

A feeling of absence dominates everything in this landscape. Even the goats look puzzled, as if they wonder where everything has gone, as if they have coaxed their lives from the very dust, but haven't quite grasped them yet.

The truth of the desert is raw, massive, daunting. Rocks rise from the earth's crust organically, as if sculpted from the land in shark-toothed buttes and jutting crests. A dry riverbed, an *oued,* runs its ragged course at the edges of a plain littered with volcanic tuff and ferrous rubble. Then all these features disintegrate against the vast backdrop, melting into structures and patterns, like thoughts and feelings selecting pathways.

Specks of birds drift like snowflakes, as if they do not belong. Figures shimmer out of the heat haze before fading again, like tiny brushstrokes in an Impressionist painting, marching into infinity as if to the earth's core.

We passed a group of small boys dressed in bright rags, kicking their heels in the dust, while their young brothers and sisters went naked. This is what really takes root in the desert, near rocks, in the sand, in dust as soft and unyielding as pressed straw. Children have to fight for their survival here. They struggle on beneath the burden of everything they know. Like their dreams, they are little rubies and sapphires studding the beige.

'It must be good to get away and see the real world.' Samir looked pleased as he said this.

'Yes,' I said. 'It's very nice.'

'And how is your home country?'

'How do you mean, exactly?'

'You know.' He glanced over enquiringly, smoothly shifting gear. Even more dust swirled in our faces.

'Actually, there are children who suffer in my country too…' It was an unfair comparison and I knew it.

'I didn't mean that,' he said. 'I meant its reputation.'

'I'm not sure what you are suggesting,' I said.

'Well, morally speaking.'

'You mean, we are immoral?' I said.

Samir almost hit a donkey.

He was working on that puzzle: me, Europe, sex, our ill-defined roles as an unwed couple sitting without a chaperone in the front of his shiny car. I was hopeful that he was honourable. Honour, after all, was reputed to be a cornerstone of Tuareg custom, although so too were the unrivalled liberties afforded its young men and women, who could do as they pleased before marriage.

'For now, I am just happy to be here,' I said.

'And I am looking forward to showing you the desert, because it is our sanctuary…'

'Yes.' I looked out to the horizon and the blank canvas engulfed us, its wind now a lullaby.

A landscape's truth can only be suggested when it is first perceived. Like a new friend, it takes time before its lumps and ridges, uncertain in the initial moments of experience, take on clarity.

The eye catches hints that confirm what we believe we know about things. At that point we become aware of our foreignness. Like a disease it seeps from us, like air we breathe it out. Only, this time we are the one going by. We are the transitory glimpse.

Samir and I had glimpsed something else – the gulf of cultural and religious differences that we were both happy to let recede once again into the distance, like the solitary tree we had spotted there.

You're crazy!

Tessaded temdit!

In the centre of a square, men were seated, noses drooping like birds. Wool merchants touted dung-spattered fleeces and foul-smelling goatskins. Elders with leathery faces sat in tatty loincloths playing desert draughts and smoking pipes. Cattle herders from Niger chatted to farmers in Malian cloaks, while their wide-eyed lambs bleated. Voices were raised, heads shaken, battles fought over tiny amounts. The market was nothing short of an event, a chance to exchange news, above all, an opportunity to make money.

We parked in a sliver of shade below ragged palms and carved our way through the crowd.

A storyteller entranced his audience: 'And the wind turned the stream into a cloud…'

'A cloud, no less…' echoed the throng.

'And the cloud gave rain…'

'*Hamdul'illah,* rain…'

'Until the *djinn* drove it to the wind – who took it to the mountains…'

'Ah,' they sighed. 'The mountains.'

'And the cloud gave up its fruit, so the rain became a stream again…'

Stories bind us across borders of race, religion and culture, across time itself. The people who listened to this tale owned smartphones.

A stallholder beckoned me over. I was tempted to pay the extortionately over-inflated price he was asking simply to liberate the chicken.

'*Senorita, dame, masihi, gentille fille.*'
'*Vous voulez* gold, hashish, smack?'
'*Vous voulez? Tapis, cigarettes… alcohol…*'
'*Vous avez besoin? Voilà – garçons, filles, chèvres.*'

The scrum tightened around me. I struggled to get free – and ran. Too late did I realize I had been robbed. The travel purse that dangled around my neck was missing, the cord broken, and what remained of the body hung limply on its side. I would not have noticed had it not been for Samir, who, as he caught up with me, wondered if it was a new Western fashion accessory.

Luckily for me, my notes were in my pocket.

The pure air of the desert retreated behind a smog of diesel fumes, camels and human sweat. In the open back of a truck a young dromedary appeared to be floundering. It was frothing at the mouth, hump wobbling, body deflated. It was gasping for breath. There was no ramp for it to climb and no men to lift it down, just a boy. His stick fell hard on the scrawny rump.

The camel screamed. By writhing and pressing with its forelegs, it could push up its hind legs. Somehow it managed to stand.

A large crowd had gathered. No one offered to help. No one blinked They appeared to have forgotten the instruction in the Qur'an to be kind to animals, the creatures of Allah.

The nose rope wasn't working, the nostrils outstretched like a long rubber band.

The mob gathered closer.

Still, the creature did not move. Terror flashed in its big, watery eyes; and a dignity, an acceptance of fate perhaps.

I closed my eyes and listened to the bellowing. I had an impulse to end the thrashing there and then, but I was wary of imposing my ethics. In the West we think of animals as friends. We talk to them in confidence. They keep us company when we feel down. They are our family members. In Africa and the Middle East animals are the measure of survival.

Down came the stick. And again. And again. A frantic scrabbling began, toes on the hot, metal flatbed. In one clumsy movement, the camel toppled earthward. It sat, legs folded, head down. It did not move. It did not dare.

Together, we stood, Samir and I, helplessly staring at the great heaving mass, the shrivelled hump, the drooping neck. There was blood on the sand, in the mouth and on the guide rope. That was when I cracked.

Half an hour later my travel purse really was empty. Dazed and confused, I sat on the sand. The seller and the crowd had left long ago.

'Hello, girl.' Samir leant forward. He was whispering.

'It's a she, then? I thought so.' I could barely hear myself and, as Samir didn't answer, it was obvious he couldn't either. His gaze was upon the camel and he was listening, gauging her slow breathing. His arm moved.

The camel jerked. She gave a flick of her tail. She let out a groan. She shrieked.

It was still sinking in, this rash, crazy instant, a moment when what had been unthinkable became thinkable and the un-doable doable. I had been there once before. Responsibility, duty, call it whatever you may, had got me into trouble then. Now I had a charity *and* a camel to worry about. And I only had myself to blame.

I was on my knees as I was thinking this, one hand beside the long neck, now extended upon the sand, the other by the head. A bead of goo glistened on an eyelash, a white diamond in the rough.

Apart from the nostril, which was shredded, there were three gashes on her rump and a long cut on her neck that looked as if it needed stitches. There were ticks around her groin, ears and nostrils. Her fur was sparse. A few older wounds lay in latticeworks of cuts and scratches. Blood was still drying in small dotted lines.

But there was something else about the sad weariness of her form, slumped on the dry dirt, a defiance of suffering, a grace, even.

'She needs a name,' I said.

'*Miteuse*,' he said. It meant fleabag.

I raised my head, horror-struck. 'We can't call her *that*! She's beautiful.'

Samir was scratching his chin. He studied her again, her feet, her eyes, her tail, retreated into her stillness, her pain. He pulled up his veil.

There was something so calm and reassuring in that voice of his. It was hard not to wonder about the women that must have fallen for it. For now there were more immediate concerns.

'Do you know any vets?' I said.

'Perhaps.'

I was still wondering what exactly he meant by that when the camel began gathering herself. With much difficulty, in a sudden, jerking effort she stood up and hovered uncertainly. Balance came gradually, with more words of encouragement and the last few drops in the water bottle.

'Let's go,' said Samir.

Where I knew not. Against a gold sky with a new moon floating in it like a silver feather, we rounded the curve of the track to the gentle padding of camel feet.

I drank some tea

Iswegh attay

'Je ne suis pas Tuareg. Je suis Imohug.' The old genteman drew up his *chèche* as if I was malaria.

I had put my trust in Samir, and already it had gone wrong. I had not yet grasped that to call anyone Tuareg to their face was no better than calling them a savage.

We were standing in what felt more like a jungle than an oasis. Beneath tall palm trunks dead fronds littered the ground, where ants carried trophies twice their size on marathon journeys.

Beside an adobe camel shed sat a dozen or so dromedaries. Heads aloft, not one batted an eyelid.

At first I said nothing. It is better, it is said, to keep quiet and leave others suspecting that you may be a fool than to open your mouth and confirm their worst suspicions.

Samir stepped in. 'She's English,' he said apologetically, and the coin dropped.

At that moment, our camel, who had been very quiet, gave a grunt. I was not certain at which of us it was directed.

Gradually, words came to me. Inside them thoughts wandered, not knowing how to express themselves. There was a vast, shadowy verb I attempted to conjugate, tense past, mood subjunctive, before the sentence fell down.

'Haj,' I said at last. 'Please forgive me.'

The old gentleman bowed. Greetings were fired with aplomb and velocity. His name was Suleyman. I should have guessed he was Samir's father.

'Ah, it was you on the telephone!' he said, and then we all laughed.

He began pacing around the flanks. Three times he prayed, finally offering another *bismillah* for good measure. Only then did he lay his hand on the hump to divine the various messages and signals it gave him. He did not need a thermometer, he said. He could tell what was wrong by her dead eyes.

The elder's wizened features gave nothing away and, although I could not be certain, I hoped that we were in safe hands. Optimism consolidated my belief that a burst of cruelty in a hostile land could be matched by kindness.

He strode purposefully towards the shed, returning with a bucket. He placed it on the ground and the camel put her head in. A noise broke forth like an industrial-sized drain unblocking. She drank the water down in one.

Camels have naturally lugubrious faces, but hers was contoured in deeper lines of sadness. Flies collected on the patches of congealed blood and hummed over the wound on her neck. There was slight movement in her legs, as if she was testing her muscles.

Suleyman stroked his chin. Exclamations in Arabic gave way to steely observations in French and, at last, low utterances in Tamahaq, his own language, the one he felt at home with. At last he decided that what she needed was a sedative, a herb sweetened with dates to make it palatable. There seemed to be some uncertainty about the amount necessary, the dosage determined by hump size.

In the end, she swallowed her medicine and slipped down to rest, lips rubbery and floppy, eyes glazed, as if fascinated by the small insects crawling around her. Dribble fell from her jaws in molten stalactites. Seconds later, she was asleep.

Samir began the tea ritual, as was the custom, boiling the mixture over the flames. He tipped the tea from a great height into tiny glasses. The performance was impressive. This was the way it was done, moving the teapot further and further away so that the stream of hot liquid formed a twinkling arc as it filled the glass.

We drank three cups, each accompanied by the usual outbreak of well-mannered slurping. Only after this could the real conversation begin.

'As a matter of interest, how much did you pay?' asked the old man at last.

I approximated the figure and mumbled it inaudibly.

A cry rang out, and a barrage of invocations.

'Why didn't you buy two?' he cried. 'It would have been much less frightening for her.'

The tea was sweet and thick – and a distraction. I burnt my fingertips holding the scalding glass and avoided the temptation to lick away the heat. I sipped again. 'The problem is,' I said, trying not to sound defensive, 'I'm not really in a position to look after even one.'

'And she is totally ignorant about them,' offered Samir after some thought.

'And you bought a female!' added his father.

'So, will you help her?' I asked.

As the two men exchanged glances, I imagined I saw respect in their eyes: Samir for his father's vast store of knowledge, Suleyman for his son's awareness of the contemporary world and what that would mean for the Tuareg as that world closed in on them. There was also disbelief.

We sat for a while watching the play of light across the landscape, the rays dancing on the ridges and contours. As the colour disappeared, Samir pointed out star clusters – Amanar, the great desert warrior; Talemt and Awara, the female and baby camel; Azzeg Wille, which indicated the correct time for goat milking.

Suleyman's walnut face glowed pink in the firelight. Misty-eyed, he spoke about camels – those he had loved, those he had lost and those he had kept until they were so old that their teeth had worn out. Wistfully he mused that it had become impossible to find a good one any more. Like women, they tended to be too thin, old or unruly.

He owned only a small herd these days, he said, 'the strongest and fastest *mehari* in the Sahara'.

Fortunately, he also had his own shiny Land Cruiser, and since we had left Samir's behind, he loaned it to us to drive back.

As the time approached to leave we had done a deal. Suleyman seemed happy enough. It didn't surprise him that the seller had been Arab; there was great animosity between the Tuareg and their Arab neighbours, and after the disclosure it hadn't taken much to persuade him to offer his assistance. He saw it as his duty.

We parted amicably. Suleyman shook my hand the Western way. 'Don't worry,' he said, gathering up his *chèche*. 'If it doesn't work out, I can get a very good price for camel meat.'

The day after

Asal wa n'darat wen

'A *camel?*'

'Yes.'

'Not a dog this time?'

'Not a dog, no.'

'You mean…'

'Yes, I do.'

'One hump or two?'

'Just the one.'

'And where do you think we are going to put it, darling?'

It was one of those surreal conversations that one might experience in a dream, but this was not a dream. I had called my mother as soon as the intermittent reception allowed and she had remained astonishingly calm in the circumstances, offering her usual kind words, wry comments and thoughtful pauses. Tongue-in-cheek, she was talking stabling and livery, camel-milk marketing ideas and quirky Sunday afternoon pleasure rides around Redbourn village common.

Of course, it had never for one minute crossed my mind to take a camel to England. Fleabag belonged to the desert as the desert belonged to her. On the contrary, I had spent the night wondering what madness had possessed me. Trekking through the wilds of Afghanistan paled in comparison to the recklessness of a dromedary purchase, but, despite all reasoning, I could not see how it might ever have been otherwise.

It was getting on for noon when we next turned off the road that glowed white in the heat. Samir was driving his father's car, his dark eyes a little harder, eyebrows a little wilder, his smile a little broader.

As the high palms came into view, I saw the tall, gaunt figure of a man in a dark-blue robe and white turban. He was on his knees beside a camel, palms upturned. Suleyman was praying for Fleabag.

She came back to consciousness with a low, shuddering jolt. She raised her head and rolled drearily over, drawing her legs more tightly beneath her. Her head turned, she stiffened. The dead cast in her eyes was lifting, and I could just make out a faint glow of optimism in those big, dilated pupils.

Samir approached slowly. He tried to put the rope over her neck, but she twisted away. Somehow he calmed her and she managed to come up on all four feet without a fuss. Immediately she sat down again, her long neck laid on the ground, sides heaving with breaths that were almost groans. She had no energy.

Then she saw the water bucket. With all her strength, she rose, and it was as if new hope had been breathed into her. It still seemed as if her neck felt too heavy, but somehow she managed to lift it to drink.

Afterwards, she sat, shaded by the palm leaves, absorbing every ray of sunlight her painful body needed to heal itself. By now she had gained enough strength to wander into the shade and, as if this was a signal, numerous children appeared, flapping camel blankets at her. But she had a wise head on her young shoulders and remained where she was. The stick of course was forbidden.

When the vet finally arrived, he had a great deal to say about her condition, although much of it was in a dialect that was incomprehensible to me. As far as I could make out, there was good news and bad. The rupture around the nose was her most severe injury, though it could be treated. The problem was that she had been too young to be led with an *aghaba*, the rope looped around the lower jaw, and the hole in her nostril should not yet have been made.

There was also the dilemma of her brisket, the tough bit of cartilage covered by hard skin on her chest, behind her front legs and before her back ones, on which the camel sat. That was also damaged and would need regular washing with disinfectant and antibiotics.

Her general physical condition would improve with patience, good handling and good feeding. At some time in the future, it would be possible to make a *khurs* hole, a new peg, in the other nostril, the vet said, but not until the damaged nostril had healed. Only then would she be ready to begin carrying and being ridden. Once the new nose peg healed, it would be no more uncomfortable than a bit to a horse.

There ensued a detailed discussion about the ticks, fleas and worms. The vet looked me straight in the eye as he told me that biting fleas on a camel would hop effortlessly on to the nearest human, and that all those diseases that caused mild symptoms in camels could be passed on by eating infected meat, milk or coming into contact with other bodily fluids. *Surra* was a common disease suffered by camels, caused by small parasites known as trypanosomes, which live in the blood. A fever set in, the belly and legs became swollen and the hump usually dwindled in size. The vet was convinced that Fleabag had *surra*.

Much of what followed between the men was lost to me, but one thing was clear – the dollar signs clocking up in their eyes.

✹ ✹ ✹

In the Second World War, when General Eisenhower commanded the invasion of Normandy, he coordinated sea, air and land forces while negotiating unpredictable weather and juggling the political forces of Roosevelt, Churchill and de Gaulle. When asked about his success, he apparently admitted, 'Whenever I run into a problem I can't solve, I always make it bigger.'

Those words were with me now. I should not have been surprised that Fleabag was in a worse state than we had at first thought. Overnight it became clear that her nose was infected. The vet was called out a second time, the wound inspected, at which point pus was unearthed. She was sedated again, and a small operation took place.

Samir remained positive. 'At least she doesn't have the mange,' he said.

Surgery was followed by doses of antibiotic powders, as well as a special treatment for the common nasal bot flies. Vaccinations with what looked like a knitting needle were meant to protect against septicaemia, tapeworm and TB, the ailment, according to the Tuareg, that infested dogs and hyenas. During this process she was quarantined from the other camels, and while her nose was healing a jaw-line rope was used to tether her.

As the conventional methods were being completed, the unconventional techniques were only just beginning. By good fortune, Suleyman was well versed in the art of traditional Tuareg camel medicine and he began treating Fleabag with it. All the while, Samir assisted his father with diligence, with knowledge passed down for generations. It was an extraordinary gift. My family passed down china.

The Tuareg's use of desert trees and plants to treat illness is part of an ancient and universal tradition. The first written evidence of medicinal plants being used is a Sumerian clay slab from Nagpur, said to be around 5,000 years old and containing twelve formulae referring to fifty plants, including poppy, henbane and mandrake.

Pen T'Sao, the Chinese book on roots and grasses by Emperor Shen Nung, around 2,500 BC, mentions 365 drugs derived from plants, many of which we still use – ginseng, cinnamon bark, camphor. In India, the holy Vedas describe treatments with plants and spices, such as pepper, clove and nutmeg.

In the Middle East and Africa, nature's remedies are known from the tracts on plants attributed to Aristotle and mentioned by Nicholas of Damascus, work that was continued long after by Avicenna; in Roman times Pliny the Elder composed treatises on the use of plant medicines long before Galen. Pliny also once wrote that the only certainty is that nothing is certain.

Trust is needed, and faith.

That faith was required now more than ever.

When the two men whispered a prayer, I closed my eyes and said a silent 'amen'. When I found myself wavering, I did what we are expected to do when we find ourselves in a hot, arid country: I ate dates.

Some might argue that eating a date grown in the desert, where nothing is wasted from the palm, whisks us back on a culinary time machine. They taste of ambrosia, but are they really imbued, as the Tuareg maintain, with sacred properties? I remembered them as obligatory sticky things with a season at Christmas. Samir was convinced the male palm trees were the best.

I allowed him to go on thinking that.

There was a great deal to take in about leaves, barks and roots in general. Traditional Tuareg medicine uses around thirty-eight grasses and twenty-four trees and shrubs. All have powers of healing. All witness different states in our emotions and can restore balance and unification. All are thought to contain a blessing, or *baraka*.

Male and female camels are treated differently, as are men and women. Suleyman knew from experience the effect of each part of a plant on camel milk, its salt content and whether it caused bloating.

Always at pains to stress how important it was to give alms to a plant when he borrowed from it, each piece of bark was removed with a stone to avoid damage or contamination, and never with any metal such as iron, which was said to be particularly harmful to a tree. With some remedies he would say prayers, chant rites, blessings and Qur'anic verses. When making others, he would circle alms around the object of healing.

For males, roots were used, for females the entire grass. Sometimes for males the root of the doum palm and wild millet were employed, but not for females, whose barks were normally of reddish varieties. Medicines were prepared as teas or infusions, although on occasion they were pounded into pastes and applied liberally.

Tuareg belief holds that myriad camel diseases emerge through abuse, anger, cruelty and neglect. Fleabag seemed to be suffering from all of them.

The *shilim*, the ticks, were causing anaemia, so they had to be treated first. Then she had to be de-wormed, since her faeces were infested, and put on a diet of *gur*, molasses and clean water, to cure her indigestion caused from poor feed. *Tegare n tessa,* literally flying of the liver, was caused by the Evil Eye and Evil Mouth. She also had a skin complaint he called *kharfat*, for which he applied *hagar* leaves. To rid her of fleas, he combed her fur with a mixture of urine and salt (Pliny would have approved). The scratches over her flanks, rear and hump needed constant cleaning. This Suleyman did with the utmost precision, using his fingertips and salt water before applying neem pulp. For her torn, bleeding nose he used aloe.

Togerchet is an illness brought on by inconsiderate words that leave the mouth and have a physical effect, as is *karambaza*, a stomach disease caused by anger. It activates a malevolent force known as *tezma*, whereby rage flies from the heart to its victim and causes turmoil in the system.

As her body was torn and soft on the inside from these ailments, Suleyman used *takokiat*, a bark mixture. She had also been plagued by the *iskoki*, spirits of the wind that cause illness. For those she needed to have a *lisafe*, a major calculation in order to help resolve her most stubborn stomach afflictions caused by anger and foul words.

On top of everything else, she was afflicted by an 'unclean dust problem', for which the traditional cure is the sacrifice of a young, white male goat. The liver and intestines are cooked with a little fat in a pot over the fire, and consumed. The bladder and the contents of the intestines and stomach are discarded, and the meat eaten precisely three days later.

The evil spirits must have run wild at my horrified facial expressions in response to that one – some things do not require any translation.

Fleabag coped much better, however reluctantly she tolerated the stewed bark in water that was supposed to detox her liver. And she enjoyed dates. There was a spirit in her that I admired, a strength. But if she didn't like drinking something, she simply vomited, after which she lifted her head in the air, as if to say, 'Well, what did you expect?'

With courage, Suleyman persisted. As happens when we make friends with strangers, we were free of our social baggage, but weighed down by our cultural prejudices. Although it was difficult to contextualize the world of differences separating us, I respected him.

I watched, intrigued, as he encircled his patient with millet, offered prayers to dispel the bad spirits in her, and mixed pulps and pounded barks in his medicine pot, the *ten*, said by the Tuareg to constitute the universe in microcosm.

Often his *chèche* dropped and I caught sight of his face – the heavy eyebrows, the leathery patches of pigmentation on his forehead, the wrinkled leaf of his eyelids, the lines of experience that surrounded his mouth, revealing his joys and sadnesses. He spoke of dignity, *esshak moni*, and truth, *tidat*, values that mattered. He was of the noble Kel Rela, he said, a tribe that put honour above all else. I told him about my own noble tribe of Kensington and Chelsea, which valued those things too. He looked impressed.

Sometimes I returned to my fly-infested hotel room in awe of him, at others it felt the opposite. I remained sceptical when he blended industrial products with his concoctions. He applied brake fluid to open cuts, and used battery fluid as a base when preparing a poultice.

Samir helped me to stay positive. I loved to hear of his ancestors, those nomadic blue-veiled raiders and warriors of the central oases who belonged to the indigenous Amazigh, the free-born who lived in *akazam*, caves, and slept upon beds of leaves in *aza* trees to escape mosquitoes. I had heard they were opportunists possessed of great cunning, mercilessly raiding the richly laden caravans that passed through their homeland along the trade routes. And his unique interpretation of north African history certainly had spin. In return, I told him about my ancestors – Jacob Bee of Durham, who kept a diary from 1682 to 1706, and Thomas Thomson, a surgeon and botanist who helped to write the first volume of *Flora India*.

He wondered if Durham was in India.

Food proved to be a relatively safe conversation topic, though it was never easy to balance the infinite difference between this land of privation with the abundance of our supermarkets. We throw more food away each day than many families in poor countries have to eat in a week.

The grumpy hotel manager found my long absences alarming and grew even more suspicious of my bags full of dates. With increasingly shifty looks, he interrogated me. 'Either you are spying for your government,' he said, 'or you are smuggling dates.'

Beneath the palms

Daw tasdayt

It might have been said that the square mile of oasis was the perfect sanctuary for a recovering camel, located in an area of startling beauty. A long aisle of tall palms on the north side formed an effective barrier against the cruel desert winds. South and east, it ran into low inclines with sparse, erratic growths of shrub in a fertile, shallow layer of soil that was well irrigated where the ground lay burdened with melons. Going west, the levels became a little steeper, climbing into a series of broken steppes before plunging down into an orchard of pomegranate and almond trees.

Fleabag had good food to eat and fresh water to drink, and she had greenery. Sometimes she craved sunshine and stood basking in the golden light until she felt warm again, then ambled slowly towards the shade of the palms to cool off her hump.

With the passing of days, it felt as if some progress had been made. It was slow, but she was mending, and it was ancient knowledge as much as the vet's modern medicine that we had to thank for that.

As the sun beat down, it eclipsed the memory of those things I had for so long striven to forget. I shut my mind to the darkness and sat, sheltered beneath cool branches, my thoughts nourished by plants.

Squinting at the plain that extended far out to the horizon, it was easy to ignore the threats that lurked there. There, where no plant could survive, in the bright sunlight the senses might have been lulled into thinking there was no hint of menace or danger. Checkpoints manned by soldiers remained out of sight. Nomads passed by selling skins and cheese, heading into its oblivion without a care in the world. The thick black smoke rising into the sky from the oil and gas flares was hardly discernible.

I wanted to defy this landscape. I was daring it to do its worst, but with a limited exposure. I was testing myself gradually, dipping a little toe into uncharted waters. The ongoing sense of resignation, of giving myself up to my fate, had not left me, but wilful rebellion had given way to something else. I had a new cause now.

With fresh hope I watched the dash of the sparrows and songbirds resting on their migratory journeys. I took a book and hid in the shade of the tamarisk trees. Sometimes I read to Fleabag, and her ears and head lifted. I told her about a dog I once knew in Afghanistan. She too had been healed.

As was I.

The Tibetan word for yoga, *naljor*, means abiding naturally, just being. In the desert, just being has a quality unlike any other place. When surrounded by wilderness stillness, patience, the suppression of the self lend themselves to the discipline of meditation. Transference of energy in yogic *trongjug*, one of the *siddhis*, or feats of mind, is where the movement of thought ceases, allowing it to fuse with its object of concentration. To understand truth, the mind must be brought to the condition in which it is without movement, a vacuum where it has no impression at all.

The horizon held my own truth, of that I was sure, but for the time being it was far off. Frog-like, static, I practised *trongjug*. The object of my concentration was a camel.

And, for now, she was enough.

✹ ✹ ✹

It was the physicist Erwin Schrödinger who first used the word *Verschränkung*, a term he translated as entanglement, in a letter he wrote to Einstein. Entanglement holds that groups or pairs of particles in our universe interact in various, unpredictable ways that are co-dependent, at an atomic and subatomic level. They may even be separated by huge distances from each other, but remain connected.

I was entangled too – with a camel.

Every day I lay with my elbow on the ground, head propped up on my hand, gazing at Fleabag. I was a little more used to the mosquitoes that descended in black clouds at sunset, although not absolutely. By now I had discovered that burning dung and eucalyptus helped to disperse them. I didn't really enjoy the special herbal teas Suleyman gave me to drink for my health, but I managed to slip them down out of politeness.

On this occasion Fleabag fidgeted sideways. She lifted her head and looked down at me. She had reached the point where she knew the value of carrots.

I took a good look at her. Scabs were forming on the gashes on her back. Her cuts had stopped bleeding and the nose infection was well on the way towards healing. The daily routine of oats, grooming and a little light exercise had filled out her muscles. Good care had put a light sheen on her hump.

She had munched the carrot and she was sitting up, ears alert, as if she was listening. She knew and so did I that it was time. I told myself that it was for the best. It was going to be a fostering rather than an adoption, and certainly never parenthood. I had a life to get on with and I had to learn to put things behind me. Crucially, by now I had made the discovery that there were scorpions in this paradise.

That afternoon Samir, his father and I settled in at a dusty, boiling establishment. Seated on wooden benches, we came to what Samir described as an understanding. One thousand dollars was an extortionate price to look after a camel. Underneath, I did not feel they would break their word. My gut told me that I could rely on them. It had never let me down in the past.

Fleabag didn't seem to like goodbyes either. I sat down beside her, clasping my hands around my knees, and a wave of heat rushed over my body as I looked into the pools between her eyelashes. She even let me touch her.

I laid my cheek on her. I felt a slight tremor through her body, but she didn't flinch. As if no eye was on her, she reached out. I felt the soft muzzle against my back, between my shoulders. I turned and stroked her, and she didn't turn away. I put my mouth to her ear and made promises to her. I should have learned not to make them by now.

It felt a long time before Samir persuaded me away. Packing didn't take long. I handed in my key at the hotel and went to catch the ancient, honking bus again. Samir dropped me off at the bus station and this time, before my luggage was hurled into the hold, I made sure it didn't contain breakables.

'I promise I will write,' he said.

'Me too,' I said. What was it with me and promises?

I didn't imagine we would do so and was sure he didn't either. We said these things anyway. Some way on I looked back over my shoulder. Samir's face was now a small dot among all the other dots, his slim outline a sand-coloured smudge among the other sand-coloured smudges. Then the dot and the smudge merged.

When visiting a place for the first time, we leave behind so little of ourselves, as well as the illusion of our own problems, which we realize are minuscule compared with those who face genuine hardship. And what do we hold on to? Memories of a camel, two carrier bags full of dates and a talisman against the *tehot,* the Evil Eye, which, no matter how fast I ran from it, kept staring at me.

☀ ☀ ☀

England felt monotone upon my return. Expressions on faces turned inward. Matter was dusted with the everyday. I drowned in the grey skies, shadowy, viscous landscapes, felt constrained by the organized boundaries. I preferred the ones I had left behind that had sparkle and breathed light. I wrote songs, their words crisping at the edges like parchment. Now even music whispered regrets.

Of course, Samir did not write, just as I had expected. I tried contacting him, but the messages bounced back. The phone, when it was working, just kept ringing. I assumed that the money I had left for Fleabag's recovery had been spent on cigarettes. Such thoughts I packed, along with the memories, into the boxes of my mind.

Then one day it began raining, which meant it was a bank holiday. Torrents trailed down the windows like arteries. The email pinged, the subject in capital letters, its text full of mistakes and good humour. 'We are looking forward to giving you a hospital,' Samir had written.

It was the perfect excuse. I wrote back a one-liner, which turned out to be a one-worder: 'Yes.'

Then I punched the air in triumph. Somehow, Fleabag had survived.

Towards midday
Es terut

⸪ ☉ + ⸪ ◯ ⸭ +

I return

Yosa tamanyasat

At first sight it seemed doubtful this was Fleabag. Gone were the bruises, the chafes and abrasions. The hump was full, the flanks rounded, the gashes and cuts were no more. The brisket was back to normal, and that nose, once in tatters, looked intact.

'Are you sure it's her?' I said.

Coquettishly, the camel took a step. An indignant air emanated from her.

'Look at the nose scar,' replied Samir, a little defensively.

Approaching with caution and small steps, since I was hoping it might be less intimidating for her, I closed in.

As if on cue, the camel began defecating. There was no question that it was Fleabag.

Suleyman took a grip on the nose line, but she didn't seem to be taking much notice of him, because it was at this point that she clocked Samir. She began following his approach, eyes twinkling merrily. I could swear she was batting those long, furry lashes at him. She even seemed to be swaying slightly. With the utmost delicacy, she stretched out her neck and wiped his hand with her slimy snot. It was clear that she had taken a shine to him.

'*Suf, suf,*' he said gently. 'Now you try…'

'*Suf, suf,*' I echoed.

Fleabag turned away. I tried again, but no amount of *suf suf* seemed to persuade her, even as I dug out some sweets from the bowels of my rucksack and offered them up. This time an even more copious rain of stools shot forth, neat little pellets like rabbit droppings.

If I had been expecting an apology, I was to be disappointed. She just stood there, all hoity-toity.

'Does she always behave like this?' I said.

'What do you expect? She is a female.' Samir didn't need to say anything. His eyes said it all.

My eyes just rolled.

Fleabag was unimpressed. She opened her mouth and, without warning, she fired.

Proffering cloth rags made of unwound turbans, the two men tried to make me feel better. Throwing up cud was standard practice where camels were concerned. I just needed some *anawiak* with her. It meant 'one-on-one', to allow us to bond, although there wasn't any time for that, so we were *all* going to be taking part.

❃

It was midday and the sun was sweltering. A blue lake glimmered upon the horizon. In the warm shade, sharing a large, coarse camel rug, I cleaned off the worst of the cud with a towel. Samir produced a jug, while his father dug into his robe and pulled out some filthy-looking glasses, which he placed in front of us.

'The water is brown because it has oil in it. It is not just camels that need their vitamins,' he said as he poured.

I took a sip. I spluttered. I wasn't thinking straight. I was still reeling from the journey and my eyes were beginning to close. My limbs were like lead, as though they belonged to a dead person whose spirit couldn't float away.

By now Fleabag had moved off and was sitting with the other camels. She seemed to be consulting them. 'Serves her right,' they appeared to be replying. There was an emptiness about her, as if she had got it out of her system, which, of course, she had.

'Do you think she'll come round?' I said.

'She's a *camel*,' Suleyman said.

We sat in a long moment of silence. I imagined that to him she was just an isolated female surrounded by irascible bulls. I knew how she felt.

At first sight little had changed in the oasis since I had left. The palms were the same as I remembered – older, but I was older too, so the distance between us remained the same. Fresh dates still scented the air as well as the sweet smell of their decay, but fronds and leaves had been cleared and the oasis was filled with more flowers and fruit than before. There were other, familiar spots. That was where I had nursed Fleabag's sores. There was the *ten* pot in which Suleyman had mixed her plant remedies.

I looked up and saw in the coins of sunshine dancing objects that I had never seen before, to which I had been blinkered. Tiny sand beetles scuttled across the ground. A thin brown cow with a protruding pelvic bone appeared and slunk wearily into the distance without looking back.

The two men set about updating me while Fleabag and I eyed each other cautiously, maintaining a wide berth. She seemed happy to be with the other camels, but as she regarded lovingly her handsome foster parent, and as he gazed adoringly back, it was clear that in this *anawiak* only the two of them would be taking part.

It was a relief to see that her physical diseases had long gone and to hear more about her recovery. I was thankful that the trust I had placed in two men I had barely known had not been misjudged. A high-fibre diet – grasses and tree cuttings supplemented with plentiful quantities of palm sugar – had been used to build up her strength. She had also eaten crushed date stones, grains, beans and seeds mixed with water and extra minerals – a feast by any standards, albeit one that had already cost me hundreds.

Given her previous ill-treatment, it was unsurprising that she had hated training. As Samir put it, 'Camels always worry about what humans are going to do to them.'

The priority had been to win her trust, and that meant not asking too much of her. Suleyman had whispered to her to soothe her nerves, but when he had tried loading her, she had reared on her haunches and bucked violently. The pack had catapulted through the air and landed a good ten yards away. When the bucking had finally stopped she had stood remorsefully, saddle askew on her quivering belly.

To calm her, they had fed her grapes. Suleyman had groomed her flanks, gently stroking her skinny legs and accustoming her to having straps and bags on her back. At first her muscles had grown tense with fear and anxiety. Some camels have a habitual tendency to kick, and that is dangerous: one strike can break an arm or a rib. Fleabag was a gentler spirit. She would simply vomit over you.

'Why didn't you call me? Or email?' I said at last. 'I thought I had upset you.'

There was a glint in Samir's eyes that I couldn't fathom. It struck me that he was hiding something.

'I lost your address,' he said, looking downwards.

'But you emailed?'

'I found it again.' He played with his glass. He sipped.

'I see,' I said. I could imagine him, this young man, studying in Europe, unveiled, drinking lager in a college bar, distinguishable only by his exotic heritage, good looks and desire to please. His hands were without callouses, his teeth white and straight, and he could read well.

He was not marked by poverty, or eroded by age and sun like his father. Any apparent religious innocence he displayed belied a shrewdness that proved he was not afraid to embrace what he saw as the adventure of Western life. He didn't speak much about his friends.

Simultaneously, we all took another slurp of the foul water. 'So where do we go from here?' I said at last.

Samir returned an enigmatic Mona Lisa look. 'Actually, you owe us a bit extra, because of the complications.'

'What complications?' I gulped. It tasted like sewage.

'Well, she was a long time getting over that mange...' Suleyman grinned.

'Can she be ridden?'

'*You* have to ride her. She is *your* camel.'

'Can't you do it? It is obvious she prefers you.'

'Absolutely not,' laughed Samir. Perhaps, after all, there was nothing awry. He hadn't changed at all, with his long hair and loud laughter.

'We have to prove that a stranger can ride her,' insisted his father.

I lowered my head, feeling guilty for abandoning her. 'And if I succeed, then she will be healed?' I said.

No one seemed to have an answer.

Suleyman tamped down the tobacco. I didn't quite catch exactly what he was trying to say as he had lapsed into Tamahaq. I caught only the word '*marabout*', a term that I recognised as meaning holy man or saint.

Samir sighed. 'She needs to see someone else,' he said. ' 'An expert is needed to give her *baraka*.'

'I thought you were the expert?'

'She needs another expert. A better one.'

'But I thought she was doing well. She's much better.'

'There is still more work to be done,' said Suleyman,

shaking his head and murmuring.

'Right,' I said, trying not to sound disingenuous. 'But I don't understand why you can't give her *baraka*, Suleyman? You are a herbalist. Is there no bark that can help her?'

He sighed wearily. He lit his pipe. He puffed. 'Only a *marabout* can give *baraka*.'

'No need to be worried,' said Samir. 'It is only a short trip.'

'A trip? Can't he come here?'

They sucked their teeth and shook their heads.

'Why don't we give it a few days… see how she goes?' I said.

Shoulders crumpled.

Suleyman began to mumble again. From what I could gather, time would be needed to gradually ease her in, and in the meantime patience would be our ally. Naturally, he didn't say who 'her' was.

Fleabag had begun chomping *jisrif*, but she was not the only one who had bitten off more than she could chew.

※

The light was dazzling as we turned down the twisting track. It was filled with the voices of children. Barefooted and wide-eyed, they stampeded out of the door and careered towards us. Behind them stood elders in white gowns. History overflowed in their faces, in the lines and crevices gathered over time.

'*Merharba, amidi!* Welcome, friend!' they all chorused. Like the mountains, their names had meanings: Amalu, the shadow, Anamar, the happy, Gwazila, son of the plain, Igider, the eagle, and Yattu, the large, a man with sparkling, energetic eyes.

Women dressed in long wraparound skirts and bright

embroidered blouses waved hennaed hands. According to custom, they did not introduce themselves.

The house was modern by local standards. It lay in a village near Abalessa, not too far from the palm grove. It almost had elecricity, or rather, splayed wires dangling like exotic spiders over bare earth floors. It contained several rooms, a yard for livestock, even a toilet, complete with floating cigarette butts, and a tap which emitted more brown water, and which was perfect for washing off camel vomit whenever the occasion required. Great swords hung on the adobe walls that were relics of the past, for ceremonial use only.

To Samir and Suleyman, this was home, although it was not like in the old days when they lived in a group of straw *zeribas*, or huts, and moved around. 'How can you expect the sand and the wind to stay within borders?' was their way of putting it.

That evening, as the green fell from the palms and the orange sun died, in the small front room we sat in a circle of colourful cushions, Suleyman, Samir, various elders and I, our words spinning like butterflies. French mingled with Arabic; when the conversation turned to Tamahaq, Samir translated for me. How did we blow our noses where I came from? How did we placate our camels? Snatches of conversation in Tamahaq passed in a blur. It didn't matter. There were shared smiles, spontaneous gestures.

Soon a prodigious array of dishes began to appear. Aunts, sisters and cousins brought tea glasses, cloths and water for washing hands.

I felt honoured to have been invited. It was a relief not to have to stay at a hotel and I much preferred to offer Samir the dollars for my lodging. It was also arguably safer. Hotels are targets for kidnappers.

Of course, no one mentioned the matter of security. None of them could have imagined why I would place myself in such a vulnerable position.

In any case, Tuareg hospitality is intrinsic. It is no different to in other hot countries. In my experience, the harsher the landscape, the more generous-hearted the people. In societies where people have little, sharing is a way of life. It is not just because of the dictates of religion.

In Tamahaq there are no exact words for 'to give', 'to receive' or 'to owe'. When food changes hands, people say 'it travels'. Feeding others is as feeding themselves.

The food itself is simple. Dairy from camels and goats, salty and unpasteurized, is a staple. *Tagela*, desert bread, sweet and tasting of charcoal, is cooked in embers and eaten with a tomato sauce. Meat is a rarity. Goat's cheese is freshly made, as is a porridge called *eghajira*, made of camel milk with dried dates. Couscous is reserved for special occasions only.

After supper tobacco was squeezed into pipes. Old men in long robes saw how times changed. In Western terms they had very little, but what they did have were their values, their hospitality and, above all, their dignity.

Yattu had heard of my country. 'It rains there often,' he said eagerly, rain being as precious as gold here.

I thought of the long, dark days of pouring, miserable drizzle that I had longed to avoid. 'Yes,' I said.

The men began debating – about the high price of rice, about the old days, and the advantages of white over red camels. The women, who ate supper separately from the men, listened in. They preferred goats. They were more efficient than camels and could have four kids in a year, each one fully grown for mating within twelve months. Camels gave birth only once every two years, but at least they were less belligerent than their husbands. The men should count themselves fortunate to have goats, and they had wives blessed with much better manners; they did not pick their noses or, Allah forbid, slurp their tea like their husbands did.

They laughed as they made light of their hardships. They did not seem desperately poor, unlike so many of the pastoral Tuareg who live in tents and tend goats, make butter and grind millet to survive, walking for miles to retrieve water from a well. Still, I had no illusions about how difficult their lives were.

My room was next to the back yard and the scent of livestock drifted through the doorway. That night I lay awake thinking through what had been said earlier. I avoided the army surplus bed Samir had provided because the canvas that was stretched over its metal frame was smaller at the bottom than at the top. If I rolled over, I would be tipped out and the bed would land on top of me.

As they had raised their *chèches* out of respect, I wondered what the elders were really thinking. If they regarded it as unusual for a foreign woman to travel alone and admit herself to their home, they had been too polite to say. Experience told them to be on guard. What good had ever come from the West? Everyone who had ever come here had wanted something.

I was not so much a guest as a representative of my country. Worryingly, since none of them had ever been there or were likely to go, I was what they assumed was its epitome. I hoped I had not offended. Western pragmatism is often thought to lack finesse. Dressing modestly, avoiding gazes, such things can be learned, but not the way we walk, our gestures, our skin and the inflections of our voice.

Apart from our earlier conversation, there had been no

further mention about the holy man. I wondered if perhaps he had been forgotten, since Samir's face had betrayed no affirmation or denial when I had enquired about him, just the same enigmatic smile I had seen on many occasions.

As I understood it, a *marabout* treats people. I couldn't see how or why we needed one for a camel, and I certainly could not grasp why Suleyman, with all his experience and knowledge, was so keen on the idea.

Samir put it thus: his father was a generalist and a herbalist, whereas the *marabout* was a specialist, although, like all herbalists, he had to know which trees cure which diseases, whether to use bark or root mixtures and when to use unscented or scented remedies, since some bad spirits apparently responded to good odours. There were other differences too. Whereas a herbalist cured with plant and tree medicines, a *marabout* evoked or wrote passages from the Qur'an for healing using a blend of religious and traditional methods.

Perhaps I was underestimating the strength of their conviction. *Marabouts* have always held considerable power in many central Saharan regions, where they often conduct marriages and funerals, act as judiciaries, teach the Qur'an and mediate in disputes. To hold the position of *marabout* is to enjoy a great responsibility in the community. Training takes time, for if a *marabout* tries to learn too many verses too quickly, it is said he attracts misfortune.

Baraka, the *marabout*'s speciality, is a blessing regarded with particular reverence. Like many people, my new friends believed that God is eternal and powerful, but that He is capable of destruction and punishment. *Baraka* is His grace – a benediction or holiness coming directly from Him. It can be possessed by a person, or located in places and objects, such as date palms, milk and good grazing pasture. It is ruined by impurity, that evil caused by the Kel Essuf and *djinn*, those invisible spirits who live and die like humans, but who are essentially wicked.

Baraka is regarded as a blessing so deep that it permeates every cell, an act so intense that it brings good fortune for a lifetime. Such is its power that it is said to heal afflictions and bring prosperity, granting forgiveness to the most wretched of sinners. In Samir's eyes it could even restore milk to the breasts of a dry woman.

Unsurprisingly, his father had not stated that particular fact. Then again, he had not mentioned the dire smell that was wafting through the doorway either.

I did not dwell on these things. For now I was happy. I had replaced luxury with authenticity, and in so doing had received my own strange blessing – a lumpy, warm feeling against my back as one of the goats attempted to eat my sleeping bag.

She fell off the camel

Oda fall emnes

Gravity, the natural force by which all things with mass are brought towards one another, has an infinite range. Its pull affects stars, planets, galaxies, sub-atomic particles and even light itself. I was gravitating towards a camel, and our mass and energy appeared to be on a direct collision course.

When atop a camel, it becomes clear why force is such an apt word. Fleabag and I demonstrated this effortlessly. We remained together because the only thing we could do was to try to decipher what we were doing together, and why our bodies would not dislodge. She could not help but give off an air of awkwardness, a sense that she might be at odds with her passenger; I felt the same.

A long way down, Suleyman's small dark face was peering up. His expression said it all: 'It's a foreign woman. What did you expect?'

Fleabag shifted uneasily. She had that glint in her eye, the one that seemed to say, 'What have I done to deserve this idiot on my back?'

Over-optimistically, I thought of William Cavendish, Henry VIII and all the other great men of history whose superb horsemanship gave them control of their steed and bestowed power, but neither of us was ready for manège.

'Don't you think we should give it more time, so we can get to know each other?' I said tentatively.

'She belongs to you. You have to show her who is boss,' he said, although it wasn't clear to whom he was referring. He grunted and, as another grunt sounded, this time from

Fleabag, it was clear that they were the ones who were communicating. Theirs was a language of collaboration and assurance that I would never be able to master.

On his own camel, Samir was trotting casually around us, no hands. Having grown up on the sands, as a child he had used no saddle, sitting in front of the hump, leg over the animal's left shoulder. There was nothing you could teach him.

'It must be your white toes,' he cried, and slid off his mount. With one little jump, he was up again.

'Rest the soles of your feet against her neck so you can feel and guide her. If you want to use the rope, tap the right side of her neck. To run, dig your heels in. To halt, pull.'

As Suleyman barked instructions, I guided, trotted and pressed my heels in. I pulled on the rope. I tapped Fleabag's neck. My *shalwar khemeez* was twisted and my veil had unhooked itself and was strangling me, but somehow I hadn't fallen off. Gravity in this case was a blessing.

Having done a couple of laps of the surrounding area, Samir and his mount blithely trotted back.

'Act friendly,' he said.

'Come on Fleabag, darling,' I said. With a cool blast of confidence I gave her the lightest tap on the rear. I should have known this was asking for trouble.

The other camels, who were watching, appeared to confer. It was as if they were saying, 'If they don't get the polite message when we tell them to get off, expressed with a good-mannered nose rise, teach them a lesson.'

Gently I patted her neck, clutching my saddle with its small sense of security.

That was the moment of disengagement.

The act of falling is never an elegant spectacle. Galileo showed that gravity accelerates all objects at the same rate.

He also postulated that air resistance means lighter objects may fall more slowly in an atmosphere. Heavier ones, on the other hand, travel fast.

Afterwards, I brushed myself down and limped to the shade of the palm trees, only too glad of a sip of brown water. I took painkillers and got back in the saddle, after which I had difficulty walking unaided.

As Suleyman offered me dates, I tried to read his thoughtful, caring expression. It was all about trust, balance, rhythm and confidence, he said earnestly, and, above all, submission. On no account would a camel ever submit to you unless you submitted first.

'This,' he added calmly, 'can take decades.'

✷

Hardly any shade covered the dust of the yard. Just one or two patches remained under a spreading acacia, which goats had commandeered for their siesta, their fat udders too heavy to lift their skinny legs.

We sat on the ground recovering. Sand blew in through the open door of the shed, piling up in miniature dune crests. Where was the healing plant, bark or root infusion when it was needed this time?

The look on Samir's face reminded me of his father's, hovering uncertainly somewhere between kind and patronising. He rattled off words in Tamahaq like the two times table, then, regarding my frown, reverted to French. 'May God cure you,' he said.

'I'm not ill, Samir. It's just a bad back, that's all. It's not surprising.'

'Let me make it better?'

'I'll be fine,' I said.

'You should read the Qur'an, it will help you,' he said. Off the top of his head, he quoted a verse said to have powers of healing. 'Really, you should try reading it one day. It would be an education.'

I did not reply. I was not sure how he would react to the news that this bruised foreigner had actually read the Holy Book already.

'There is nothing better than knowledge.' Samir had that distant look in his eyes. It was the one he had when he was dreaming about European universities and what they might teach him. 'You are my research.'

'And what will you do with your research?'

He thought for quite a while. 'Eventually,' he said, 'I will learn. Because there is nothing more truthful than God's knowledge.'

I wanted him to stop. If God's knowledge was telling me anything it was that I needed another painkiller.

Samir leaned back and rubbed the dust out of his eyes. I knew what he was thinking and he confirmed it.

'It's just that we are worried for you. We know what sort of unclean world you live in. We hear it on Al Jazeera.'

There was no talking him out of it. I was suffering from the influence of the West. It was like a disease, in his eyes, that he wanted to purge. At the same time, he was drawn to the benefits it could offer.

For now, it was my back that needed purging, and he and his father wasted no time in finding a solution for that: they prayed. Afterwards, having put their trust in Allah, they handed me over to the women.

The perfection of woman

Ewin en tamet

'Everything comes to you from your mother,' say Tuareg men, and it is not hard to see why. More than a century ago, before women had the vote in Britain, Tuareg women were arguably more liberated than in any Western nation.

While they remain faithful to the instruction of the Prophet, who advised Muslim women to act modestly and respectfully, at the same time they adhere to their own strong cultural traditions, which afford them powerful rights and incredible liberties. In love, young girls court at the *ahal* and have as many boyfriends as they like before marriage. Divorce is not unusual, and a wife will keep the couple's possessions.

It is women who teach Tifinagh, the written version of Tamahaq, to their children so they can write messages in the sand. Intelligent and independent, they are the designers, builders and owners of their homes over which they exercise rights. In rural communities their days are spent tending goats, tanning leather and weaving palm fibres, making rope and necklaces, cooking and carrying out chores. Noble Tuareg women are also accomplished poets and musicians.

No wonder I was in awe of meeting them. I had been waiting for this chance for days.

In a small, dark back room of the house, aunts and sisters sliced lemons. Large hoop earrings glinted about their ears. Tuareg women wear what wealth they have, like Qashqai nomads in southern Iran, like all nomads.

'*Assalaam alaykum.*' Out of fluttering ripples of cloth came a sure, soft voice. Dark eyes shone from pale, crêpe-paper skin draped around high cheekbones. A smile revealed a forest of higgledy-piggledy teeth.

'*W'aleikum salaam.*' I smiled back.

The woman was unveiled apart from a small headscarf. She was Amina, Samir's aunt.

'*Matulam?* How are you?' The young girl, oval-faced, with sea-green eyes, an arched nose and full lips, adjusted her neat braids of hair with hennaed hands. She was called Rhaicha. She was Samir's cousin.

'*Alcher, ghas. Matulamet?* Good, thank you. And you?'

'*Alcher.* Good.'

'*Ma dar tensed?* How did you sleep?'

'*Alcher, tannamert.* Well, thank you.'

'*Io.* Come,' said Amina.

I took off my shoes and stepped in.

There was little furniture in the room, just a table and an oven, and on the wonky adobe walls a few shelves, pots and pans, spoons and ladles. Translucent windows opening into the courtyard let in the cool light. Two young girls kneaded the *tagela*.

Another little girl wandered in, clutching a doll.

'What is her name?' I whispered.

'Doll,' she said.

'And she is *mehal*,' whispered Amina. It meant trouble.

'Like men,' smiled Rhaicha.

'Like all the men in our family,' said Amina, looking straight at the sea-green eyes that now sparkled.

Together we sat on the amber and russet carpet. Warm goat's milk was poured from a battered tin pot. I tried a few words in Tamahaq, sprinkling them with a smattering of French. Goodwill mopped up the missing language.

Amina had five living children and seven grandchildren. She had married her cousin, and when he had died she had remarried. She and her husband had lost many herds in the droughts and her sister had died young. She considered herself fortunate to live with her brother and daughters, rather than have moved away as so many women did to search for new oases.

I would have loved to know where her fortitude came from, and how her wisdom had unfolded within. What music had entranced her when she was young? What had inspired her? What were the landscapes of her youth, the long journeys she had travelled to achieve them? Why did she long to go further, to transcend this territory, and to what end?

Instead, she turned and asked me a question: 'Do you have medicine for your back?'

'I have painkillers,' I said. The goat's milk was creamy, different to camel milk, although said to help equally with fertility and purity, those things Islam asked of all women.

'And what about your other afflictions?' Amina glanced away.

'My other afflictions?' I wasn't aware I wore my broken heart on my sleeve and I certainly hadn't told anyone.

'I think you have not read and studied the Qur'an enough. For that reason you are *golama*.'

'*Golama*?' I echoed.

'It means orphan,' said Amina in French. She regarded me curiously. She took my hand.

'God determines all illness,' she said at last. 'In all creatures. He gives *baraka*, blessing, just as He takes it away.'

I nodded along with her. It was clear she did her bit to help Him. 'And do you heal camels as well?' I asked her. 'Like the *marabout*?'

'Men look after camels. It is the women who give out the real medicine in these parts,' she laughed.

She twinkled then, and pretty Rhaicha, who had been listening, twinkled too. We all did.

Among the mountains and plains of the Sahara, and at the fringes of the Sahel savannah, women cure other women in their villages and help with childbirth. In remote regions, where only donkeys and camels can travel, there are no Western drugs to aid labour.

Illness, according to Amina and all Tuareg medicine women, or *tinismegeln* as they are known, is a symptom of suffering rather than its cause. A disease is diagnosed by a person's appearance, their eyes, ears, mouth and skin, simply by touching the stomach.

But to have a healthy body and mind is only one aspect of the harmonious order between two different worlds in balance – the visible world of physicality and the invisible world of spirits. For the Tuareg, the two worlds combine to form reality, and the capacity of an individual to balance the two decides their physical health and wellbeing.

The head is thought to be where most spirits like to reside after they have entered a body, usually through the liver and stomach, whereas the liver is the seat of all those diseases associated with love, trauma and anger, felt as much in animals as in people. Invisible problems and scars left by bad experiences bear no symptoms except tears, and are the most deeply rooted, requiring the most skill to disperse. It is believed that love and loss reside in the soul.

Both are treated as physical illnesses. Date palm is used to treat emotional distress, for comfort and against sleeplessness, although the root, never the bark, can be used to treat toothache; thyme wood is for overall health and happiness; tamarisk for good humour.

Amina advised the stewed bark of the *alkhad* and a balm of *torha* root for my *alafaze*, a condition caused when one falls, usually off a camel, hot water for my back pain and a special ritual to rid me of my bad spirits.

'What is your country like?' she asked at last. 'Is it gold like ours?'

'To be honest, it is more grey,' I said. 'But gold and grey go very well together.'

We hugged, and as we did so I had the feeling that at the heart of this embrace we had reached a place that was neither shade. It bore a new colour, one of solidarity, and it lay at the intersection of our cultural borders.

※

Leaving men, camels and flies behind, we followed the narrow track that ran through the compound as the light scattered pink filaments across the horizon. Through the rough, varied terrain wound threads of tracks, born of sheep, donkeys and goatherds carving their own deliberate pathways, aided by the winds. A few shady figures stole in billowing robes across stone holdings. Snatches of camel dung caught in the air.

Beyond lay a low-strung, straw-roofed *zeriba* where an old woman, busy working leather, sat on rough matting. Old Lala, as she was known locally, was a wise woman. Shimmering swathes of material engulfed her tiny frame, weighed down by the fat, chunky necklaces and earrings that hung around her neck and from her ears. I heard she was almost a hundred years old.

Greetings were exchanged between the three women. Then Old Lala addressed me: '*Mattulawid d'asikel? Ulli-nnek, ma dulanet? Edunet-ennekm ma-d ulan asamid?* What is

your name? How old are you? What is the condition of
your goats? Your people? Are they cold?' She did not ask
about my back. She touched my stomach to discover its
condition, as was the custom.

The *tende* is a drum made from a mortar used by Tuareg
women to crush grain. The instrument is revered, even
more than a chief's *ettebel* drum, the symbol of his power
and his honour. Like the Qur'an, a drum must not touch
the ground. Old Lala's was her most treasured possession.

In the burnt sepia light the women tapped out an
ancient rhythm in a traditional rite, the *tende n goumaten*.
Trickles of music wafted like honey. Arms waved like tree
branches. As the beat grew faster, deep furrows gathered in
brows. Heads rolled back. Eyes closed and hearts opened
like flowers.

I am an orphan; I am a child burned by love,
That which has left with my soul is like milk with water,
Like the cushion of a camel saddle,
Like salted meat in the mouth,
Like water on a smooth rock,
Like the branches of a tent,
Like water in the well;
God who possesses me, like water, refresh me.

These are the words of the *tan daman*, translated from
old Tamahaq. It is the song of the soul, or *iman*, sung by
Tuareg women to a sacred drum pattern.

A *tende* song laid all knowledge at our disposal, said
Amina when they had finished singing to me. The best
songs were as deep as sand oceans. They reached into the
soul and came out through the eyes in tears.

I thought of the Aborigines who believe in song lines,

invisible links between people and the land, like maps, full of twists and unexpected turnings, entrancing the mind and imparting wisdom. Sometimes words contain the most healing. We just have to understand how to hear them.

Old Lala had it all worked out. It was not Fleabag that needed to see the *marabout*, she said. It was me.

✦

After a few more riding lessons my wonky vertebrae had rearranged themselves, although for my aching backside there was no respite. Some say that the camel was put upon earth by Allah the Merciful to help the desert people, but in my view it was put upon earth by Allah the Unmerciful to test the endurance of the infidel.

Fleabag's behaviour was erratic. Of her impulses, her hang-ups and her whims, her strengths and her weaknesses, she remained unaware. She seemed unhappy to be herself, or rather to express that which she didn't wish to be, or didn't want to carry.

Nor did her tongue sit easily in her mouth. It lolled about from one side to the other, its tip poking out. She sat ensconced, fed, watered and ready for she knew not what, a party girl dressed up with somewhere to go – only in all likelihood that meant nowhere.

Sometimes her tail swished, at others it hardly swung. One moment she seemed proud and stern. The next minute a stomp of irritation took up residence in her face, evident from the nose position.

At other times a sense of bonhomie descended, or a hurt, sullen look gave her the appearance of such vulnerability that it became impossible not to hug her. As soon as I was on her back, she would swing forwards and back again as violently as possible. I would give her an order, consulting her on any tricky patches, and she would obey, navigating the path as if she had heard the instruction and was responding to it. The next time I asked her, she would disobey, and when I showered her with praise she would invariably thank me with fly-filled snot. I still hated leaving her at the end of each day.

The blow was lessened as Samir and I always returned to smiles because I was covered in dung and limping. Often my presence drew a small crowd and I was assailed by youths who clamoured to offer me water. Shorn-headed children bore the expressions of their elders, wise and lost. I was touched by their generosity.

In the evenings the elders came together and ate simply, chatting and gossiping, while their womenfolk, Amina and Rhaicha among them, sat separately nearby, commenting on their decisions and over-ruling them.

At night I washed my clothes with dirty brown water and hung them up to dry. The high adobe walls rose around me, and through the tiny, high window the lambent sky cast a white glow across the courtyard. Under cover of my sleeping bag, I drifted fitfully, fretting about what seeing a *marabout* might entail, woken periodically by high winds that obliged me to chase after the thin door that flapped outwards into the yard like a disgruntled chicken.

Dawn at last rose, my nightmares floating upon a distant continent where oaks were nourished by rain. A symphony of goats bleated its shrill wake up call and I felt glad of my new friends, of varying shapes, sizes and colours. They were quite soothing for an aching back, a little like dung-scented hot water bottles.

A wonderful event
Day n-alas tazzarat fal tallit

Fleabag refused to budge. She stood still and gave a shimmy. Her head was up. She had a purposeful look.

She had learnt early that in the middle of the day, when it was hot and unbearable, a roar created a fuss and brought any human scurrying with the water bucket. A gentle tug of the rope to one side and a little foot pressure on the other on the neck sometimes did the trick, but I had to ask politely and use persuasion, for if I tugged too hard she would refuse. There was the inevitable performance while I tried to get her going again, and she left me in no doubt who was in the driving seat.

Samir was a few metres ahead on his favourite camel, Winaruz, barefoot, his sole resting on the neck. He looked like a Pasha, elegant, relaxed, as if on a throne. He wasn't trying to achieve anything; he was just being.

'Come on, girl!'

Samir chuckled. 'She's teasing.'

Fleabag swished her tail. Having been abandoned by the one who had first loved her, she turned to the other – he who had fed, nursed, trained and been there for her. She had learned all she knew from Samir. No wonder she yearned for him.

Perhaps it was the breeze that she wanted to smell, but for all her listening and tasting of the air, I could not understand what she was suggesting. She raised her head and stood alert. I tried squeezing, but it was no good. She swung round. She ignored the banana.

I tried again. Back. Forth. Back. Forth.

It was depressing that we weren't getting along. Where her dark moods came from was as much a mystery as her innate playfulness, which was at its most marked when I least expected it. She was remarkably observant. Where the ground was raw, stressed and complex she seemed to register its subtle changes and pause, as if to examine or comment on them.

Sometimes I allowed myself the fanciful notion that she was softening towards me, but several times she spat and I realised she was merely toying with me. There were periods of sulking as she ground smartly to a halt without warning. At those times, the most common look on her face was the one that said: 'This one is proving difficult to train.'

Now, as she came to her feet in her own good time, I felt there was hope.

Suddenly, like all women, whose prerogative it is to change their mind, she walked on. I patted her for that. We began at a slow amble with long, ungainly strides and the usual out-of-sync swing – hers or mine, who was to know?

Her gait was proud, nose reaching, sampling the air. The frayed rope knotted around her neck passed through her left nostril without apparent discomfort, and I remembered that first day when we had brought her to the palm grove, her poor nose ripped to shreds.

'What's wrong?' Samir had slowed, and we caught up. There was an air of exasperation in his tone.

'Nothing.'

'It's about the *marabout*, isn't it?'

Winaruz snorted. Fleabag snorted back.

'If you won't go for yourself, do it for the camel.' His voice trailed in the hot wind.

'It's not that I'm not keen to go,' I said.

'I know you don't believe in him.'

'I am open-minded…'

'I understand why you are scared.' He halted and wheeled around, Winaruz graceful and beautiful to watch.

'Of course I am not scared.'

'What is it then?'

I didn't answer. In truth there were a thousand reasons holding me back. Even a short journey into the desert posed risks and potentially horrific consequences. I didn't know how far we would need to travel or how long it would take. I didn't know if I believed in it. Of course, I couldn't air any of that. All the while, my inner voice was daring me to try.

'It will be fine. Trust in Allah. You will see.'

He glanced towards Fleabag.

Fleabag wasn't listening. Ears twitching, she trembled to the sounds drifting on the air, those furtive echoes, those lost memories in her own past.

A little way on, where the sand drifts were building, she paused again. Standing motionless, as if struck by a sudden thought, she threw a piercing gaze towards the mountains.

The curve of the earth places the horizon always at the same distance, a fraction under three miles, to be precise, but in the Sahara it seems impossibly remote.

I could just make out the soft drone of the wind and the tempo of my breath, the siren song of the desert. I strained my ears to it. Fleabag heard it too. She shook her head. Had she arrived at a decision? Did she have a plan? What thoughts were in her head this time about the awkward stranger weighing down her back? She appeared to understand my doubts and, no sooner than they had been pondered, swung her head to the side. 'I'm not sure who gave you the authority,' that noise said.

With a little encouragement, we edged forward.

'I'm not sure if she is ready,' I said.

'Of course she is,' Samir smiled back. 'It is not that she cannot. She just *won't*,' he cried. He trotted off, calling something else I didn't quite catch.

Fleabag understood perfectly. She lifted her head and strained her neck forward, then, with a new resolve, and a kind of bewilderment, took off.

We gathered speed before I could register what was happening. I turned my head to check on Samir and there he was, beside us, bobbing neatly upon Winaruz.

A wave of pride swelled up in my chest. Perhaps we should have called her Antigone, I thought, she who refused against all odds to understand the limits placed upon her by men.

My voice tried to steady her, but it felt more anxious than soothing. What was the strange new sensation rising up inside me, the wind on my face, the sun warm against my back? It had been so long coming, this shot of energy, this sudden lightness of being, that I hardly recognized it. I wondered if it might be fun.

Pulling on the rope made no difference. I hung on, out of amazement as much as fear, my instinct to cry out, and, as I did so, she answered. 'Roooarrrr!' she answered again, an overwhelming, resounding, 'Yes!'

We careered towards the palm trees, and suddenly we were together. Just a few days earlier it would hardly have seemed possible, but now Fleabag and I were submitting to each other.

Out of the corner of my eye, I caught sight of Samir, who was no longer watching us with his judgemental expression. Winaruz, who was still cantering, answered for his own part with a triumphant, stomach-splitting bellow.

We were four creatures on eight legs thundering across the desert in a moment of oneness.

It felt purely by accident that Fleabag began to slow again, and only then on account of the natural flattening off of the slope. Gradually we settled for a lumpy quickstep, or, as Samir christened it, the Saharan bounce, side to side and diagonally.

I pulled the rope and this time, to my surprise, she obeyed. She flicked round her neck and rubbed me. She swished her tail. She swung her haunches.

A new resolve flooded through me. I felt calm, strong, if a little pink and shiny. If Fleabag could conquer her fear of strangers, a small trek in the wide, open spaces of the desert might do her some good. It might even help with all her other hang-ups and issues. Even if the *marabout* proved to be a quack, to walk in a desert would be a challenge, and perhaps a solution. She had done so well, maybe I owed it to her.

An hour later the two camels were back in the palm grove, ahead of them the broken curves of mountains, the smell of faraway date palms in their nostrils. My veil had fallen, but I didn't care.

Fleabag and I had mastered our stop button.

The goat jumped
Tayat tegged

The room was packed and smoke-filled and the *eau de chèvre* had faded slightly, though a few droppings lay in a pile in the corner. Sweet tea and brown water were in limitless supply.

'So who is this *marabout, exactly*?' It seemed an innocent enough place to begin, but Suleyman bore a puzzled look.

With his pipe perched precariously between his lips, he lit another match, proclaiming that the Four Aces tobacco he had procured on the black market in Abangerit didn't taste the same as it used to in the old days.

'He is a *cheurfa* by birth, descended from the Prophet himself, *E alla, kay yer mer*, God bless him,' he said.

'And he is even a *tamadas*, a bonesetter,' added Samir, wide-eyed.

Palms around us were suddenly upturned in reverence.

'A bonesetter?' I said, slightly dreading to think what that entailed.

Turbans nodded and bobbed. Suleyman took an extra-large sip of brown water.

'And where is he, exactly, this bonesetter?'

'Oh, he is very close,' said Samir casually.

In the desert, which takes up a quarter of Africa, 'close' was a little vague.

'In kilometres?'

'A hundred… give or take.'

'Let us say, a hundred and fifty,' piped up Samir.

Suleyman nodded. A baby goat wandered in, looked

around with a lost expression, but its mother was nowhere to be seen.

'Right.' I was fanning with my hand. Flies buzzed about distractedly.

'Two hundred,' countered Samir.

'And could you not take her alone, Suleyman?' I asked.

'I'm too old.'

'You're not old,' obliged Samir.

'Well, you're not exactly young,' said Amina, who had been hovering in the doorway.

At this Suleyman looked even crosser.

'We three will take her,' he said. He lifted up his *chèche* in defiance.

I mentioned cost in passing. 'Allah's blessings are *free*,' he said, marginally lowering it again.

Amid a sea of shaking heads Samir slipped in, 'Almost.'

'How do you mean?'

'We offer a small contribution of a few dollars. Expenses only.'

'And what about our expenses?'

He looked deflated. 'Zero.'

'Really?'

'Almost,' added Suleyman.

'How do you mean?'

'Vegetables, water, flour…'

'…bribes,' added Samir quickly.

All the elders were sitting very quietly, the smartphones having long lost their draw.

'And would we drive?'

Suleyman shook his head at me. 'There are no roads.'

'None?'

'No.'

'We would have to go on foot,' interjected Samir.

'I am not sure I can make it,' I gulped.

'Of course you can.'

'It is too hot.'

'We will avoid the middle of the day.'

'It is too cold.'

'We will take blankets.'

'And what of the red tape?'

'The police will help,' said Suleyman.

'How can you be so sure?'

'We know everything in the desert.'

'Everything?'

'You must. She is *your* camel!'

'*Hader-ak Messiner*... Swear to God...' uttered the elders one by one as a series of nods swept around the room. It was obvious I was outnumbered.

Samir leaned over. '*Hader-ak Messiner*,' he said. 'I promise.'

There was that word again.

The little goat had settled and was being petted. It gave a further short, sharp bleat by way of consent.

And yet I couldn't help but be swayed by his earnest expression. He did not flinch as I asked him straight out about the terrorists operating in Algeria. Either he was brave or he was in league with them. Who exactly were Aqim? What precisely did they believe? Were they sympathetic towards Isil? Was al-Qaeda in the Islamic Maghreb? If so, where were their camps? Crucially, how would they react to a single Western woman travelling with nomads?

He did not answer these questions. The word 'kidnap' did not cross his lips. Nor did he shuffle restlessly as I had expected him to do, though his face did seem to grow a little paler.

'What if something goes wrong?' I said. I was playing chess in my head again, imagining the moves of others, playing them out.

'Think of it as an educational experience,' he replied. He liked that metaphor. He used it often. Of course, he said nothing of the infamous Saharan drug barons, the corrupt Algerian army officials, the Tuareg rebel leaders and the violent, greedy separatists operating in the region.

'We have a saying: trust in Allah and tether your camel. People must survive. They must eat. They must protect their families. We are peaceful people, but we must also be warriors,' said his father. He might have been more forthcoming, but his reticence was understandable. I was, after all, an outsider.

'Father is right when he says you must trust us,' Samir said. 'We have contacts.'

'And Mokhtar Belmokhtar? Is he a contact?'

Samir had that look on his face again, the one I was never quite sure about. It wasn't an unreasonable question. Khaled Abdou el Abbas went by many names, all equally intimidating, such as 'the one-eyed sheikh', 'Laaouar', 'the Godfather' or 'the uncatchable'. He was a former military commander of Aqim, and these days had his own spin-off group, Al Mourabitoun. He was also a ruthless, notorious kidnapper, smuggler, weapons dealer and certainly the most wanted jihadist in the Sahel.

In January 2013, Al Mourabitoun took 800 hostages at the Tiguentourine gas field near In Amenas. Thirty-nine people were killed, including three Americans. There had been reports of Belmokhtar's death, all of which proved inconclusive. By all accounts, he still played a major role in the spread of terror; having slipped under the radar, he had last been seen in south-east Libya.

The elders' lips were sealed. One or two had resumed studying their smartphones, which, by and large, were still not working.

'What I am really trying to establish is: what about the armed gangs in this region? And are we likely to come across them?'

'The area where we are walking has been secured, praise be to God,' said Samir.

At this point another goat wandered in and, without a sound, casually got to work on the other side of the carpet.

'*Ma petite*,' purred his father, ignoring it, 'do not fear. God, as our witness, will provide.'

'You are scared because you do not believe that you are strong enough. You have no faith in *yourself*, let alone Allah.' Samir's face had returned to its natural colour. Like the fixed, carved features of his father, his expression betrayed no noticeable tremors or clues as to the earthquakes that lay ahead of us. He knew he had touched a raw nerve. It was as if every single flake of insecurity I had ever felt and of which for so long I had wanted to rid myself had suddenly bubbled up. The desire to discover my limits, to face my fears head on, the urge to break all the rules in the book culminated in this one, single defining moment.

'OK,' I said. 'I'll do it.'

One or two people lifted their *chèches* above their noses. Sharp intakes of breath were taken.

Yattu stood up. He cleared his throat. 'Why would a foreign woman wish to travel alone in this region, only to discover there was nothing of interest beyond the horizon? Why would she want to meet faces that glowed with brown flesh?'

A mystified silence had descended. Looks were being exchanged. Gwazila began to pray.

'She is a Westerner, with a makeshift sense of life and death,' quipped Anamar.

Everyone nodded gravely.

They were right, of course. But I was determined. No one could have possibly talked me out of it. I had something to prove, to say, to express, to discover, not to anyone else – but to myself.

Amina, still in the doorway, nodded too. '*Yureh-as messiner tazadirt,*' she said. It meant God gives us patience.

I fished out a few dollars and spread them in front of me. They were for the *marabout,* to show willing. Immediately they were the focus of a room full of eyes.

'Take them,' someone said. 'If she dies, we'll be rich.'

The goat jumped. *Chèches* fell a little to reveal smiles so bright it felt they had drained the room of its non-existent electricity. From the kitchen there came loud clapping.

✻

The folds of paper unpeeled like a concertina across the floor and we gathered around. The elders began conferring and murmuring among themselves. Samir resumed his enigmatic expression.

At first sight the map looked murky. Bright and dark, the shades on the paper seemed to merge. Patches of ochre seeped into orange, beige into black, with just a smattering of what appeared to be inaccessible villages. Contours intended to distinguish the varying terrain blurred.

I had bought it in London. Looking at it now, there must have been a mix up. I wondered who had originally drawn it, concluding that it must have been done many generations ago, or the cartographer had been drunk at the time.

The names of mountains, oases, valleys and wells were

practically identical. Old and inaccurate, those place names that were marked appeared to have been spelt wrongly. Upon closer inspection, no wells were marked at all and the scale seemed to be guesswork. There were the usual suspiciously straight *pistes*, and a few villages that had long been in ruin, but most settlements were missing entirely.

A look of utmost gravity descended upon Suleyman's worn features. Waving his arms, he stood up.

'The map,' he announced proudly, 'is in my head.'

'Yes,' I said, wondering how I could get it out of there.

Pacing up and down, he began. Drawing from his memory, he sliced a canyon in half in the air and carved an *oued* on the floor. 'You are not to worry,' he said.

He expanded eloquently, regaling me with the breadth of his experience – how he had inherited that inimitable 'desert gene', by which only men of the desert can navigate the sands; how the skills of the nomad required the knowledge of the heavens, the land and its shadows; how he had walked the routes from Abangerit and Niger, from the Moulouya and In Guezzam, relying only on the *hassi*, the system of desert wells, the secret water sources known only to the Tuareg.

'Are you listening?' he said after a while, blowing little puffs of smoke into the hot air.

'Yes, father,' replied Samir.

I felt like a child too, and no less so for sitting cross-legged on the floor. No matter how hard I stared at the map, I still could not make out the route. Samir spelt it out.

We would begin on a vast, high plain in the area of Amrador. To the east were the cultivation centres of Tit and Outoul, to the south, the great Ahaggar, or Hoggar, Mountains. Wells would be our markers, our refuges small oases, *gueltas*, or rock pools and tiny settlements – Afousses,

Aoumecho, Azelli, Atabone, Arezaya.

Tenefek was our destination.

From there we would head back through more oases – Djerouiat, Edyour, Breri and Iferlil. There was not a road in sight, nor would there be. As the crow flies, the journey was about 100 kilometres – a snip.

A blast of hot air kicked up the flies and the elders began tucking into the dates. It was not the terrorists I should be afraid of, but the desert. As they delivered their wisdom in Tamahaq and as Samir translated it, I caught the gist and that was enough.

I was to think of the Sahara as a *grande dame*, they said. Cunning was required to outwit her or I would face death. If I treated her with respect, I might just get away with it. If not, with her co-conspirator, the wind, she would turn in a flash, obliterating all trace of me. She had claimed many souls, the cursed, the damned. Hidden riches were buried beneath her surface, carried by the great caravans of the past that had faltered. Now they lay entombed forever. Occasionally she would give back one of her trophies, but only those things you wished she had kept.

I would be at the mercy of her elements – hot sand winds that lasted for days, mists that never cleared. Salt lakes, whose marshy shorelines were lethal, could seize an unwary traveller, casting them into a deep, spongy abyss. Worse still were the treacherous pools of quicksand that lurked unseen on the surface. Even camels seeking springs or oases could be caught out, falling accidentally into an *oued* where they drowned.

If I survived all that, there were the scorpions, jackals, camel spiders with monstrous jaws, white orb-web spiders, tarantulas and horned vipers that would lurk by day beneath the surface of the desert, hunting by night for jerboas and lizards. Most deadly of all, the desert was haunted by Kel Essuf spirits and *djinn* who would taunt and torment me. Except for the good ones, of course, though they were in the minority.

A lengthy discussion ensued about which camels would be best suited for the trip and which to leave behind. Each would have to be at the top of their game, healthy and strong, not skinny and weak. We would have to think seriously about this matter.

'She's very independent,' muttered Samir at last, and his father shook his head thoughtfully. He knew all about independent women. They could be as awkward as camels and needed just as firm handling.

※

Later, I sat alone, head spinning, remembering those I had loved and lost, contemplating failure and fielding goats. A point had occurred at which the sheer strangeness of the place in which I had arrived had taken hold. I found myself far away, detached as though in exile, so alienated from reality that it felt as if there was no possibility of any home-coming anywhere, or any time.

I ran through what I knew.

We would go at a pace that was not too testing, walking rather than riding, since it was unwise when you were far from anywhere to be thrown off a camel. A daily coverage of approximately fifteen to twenty kilometres was snail's pace by nomad standards. For me it was a marathon.

We would rely on the constellations to guide us, those unknowable lights that helped every lost soul across the landscape of destiny. Only their tribe, the great Kel Rela, possessed this gift, like the migratory birds that effortlessly navigated the vast spaces, like the winds understood by their kin and his ancestors, a skill that was passed on from father to son, from grandfather to grandson.

When entering villages, we would need to follow the rituals of greeting, enquiring about health and family members, drinking tea and so on. After that, we could slip into the conversation what we really needed. Information regarding the purpose of our journey, father's name and mother's maiden name, and sometimes our passport details, would be required at all villages and checkpoints, just to make sure we were not troublemakers.

Timing was key. Soon it would be Ramadan, a time for fasting, praying, sleeping and doing nothing, a typical Arab pastime. And if we waited until after the holy month, we would hit the rutting season, when male camels become unpredictable. At that time, bulls would gallop great distances at the slightest whiff of a mating opportunity.

There could be wild camel herds along the way, and when females were nearby the males would show off, puffing up their mouth bladders so they ballooned out at the sides. Worse still, they could get themselves into trouble fighting wild bulls, competing for the attentions of the best females, who went all broody themselves. Interfering with the mating rituals could end badly.

As sunstroke was a very real possibility, it was crucial that the camels should not be overburdened or stretched too far, since they could have lapses, even dizzy spells. Suleyman thought it was a good idea that he was away long enough to give those camels left behind the space to miss him, but it should not be overly long, because then they might forget him altogether. That would be disastrous. Eventually, he decided two weeks was a good time to be absent, and that fitted in perfectly with our trip.

There would be a *small* amount of paperwork involved for the journey, which I duly interpreted as a *large* amount. Local authorities were strict and, although some approvals could be sought in advance, there would still be conditions... *'and understandings'*.

Of course, everything was subject to variables. We would try *things* first and test *things* out. If *things* looked good, we would go immediately. *Things* would depend upon Fleabag, and upon me, and those *things*, it seemed, were as unpredictable as the high winds that swept the great dunes and then pushed them without warning in the opposite direction. There were other *things* as well that would need to be arranged, about which both men were determined to remain silent.

As I glanced at my map this time, it showed another route: the one I should be taking to go home.

Among the stars
Ger itran

'*Quit! Quit!*'

Suleyman was tugging the nose rope while the bull thrashed violently to one side and strained against it, trying to free himself.

'This one we call Putin. He's a brute.'

Putin stood proud again, head high, settling. I hoped we were not taking him.

'*Shhhhhhh!*' Another bull lay down.

'And this one? Go on, guess?'

I shook my head as the short, stocky bull sat sternly, ignoring us completely.

'This one is Assad. Likes stamping on innocent victims.'

Assad let out a foul-mouthed string of abuse.

'And what about that one over there?' I pointed to a reserved, aloof-looking camel chewing on *jisrif*.

'*Inshallah*, we don't have a Western name for that one.'

The camel, a medium-sized beast, gurgled, then went on chewing, seemingly relieved on both scores.

I knew Suleyman was teasing. It was a humour that belied his deep malaise at a global situation he felt was entrenched and unjust. His nicknames for his camels seemed to echo the old calls to battle with the so-called imperialists that Arab imams have been repeating for decades throughout Middle Eastern countries.

'Are all of them named after politicians?' I asked.

He stroked his chin, eyes sparkling. 'This one is Arnie. He will terminate you if you do not behave.'

There were three dozen dromedaries sitting around that day. Suleyman insisted on introducing me to all of them. I was sure he had adopted the Western names on my behalf. Usually the Tuareg chose names that linked the animal's appearance with the land: 'Sings in the Spring Drought' or 'Dark as a Rain Cloud', who was even more prized. In his native Tamahaq they mostly began with the letter 't' −Tifawt, light, Tilelli, freedom, Tiwul, heart, Tumert, happiness, Titrit, star and Tamment, honey.

The most fearsome of the herd was an old bull called Usem, whose name meant 'lightning'. He had a terrible temper. He would fire green pellets at you if you came too close, but if he liked you, he would carry you to the ends of the Sahara. Once, Suleyman had been offered ten camels in an exchange, but he had refused.

'I owe my life to Usem,' he said.

I glanced over nervously and the camel gave a snort. 'What about them?' I said, pointing in another direction.

Still petting Usem, Suleyman told their stories. Tafalkayt and Tuftent, respectively 'the beautiful' and 'most beautiful', were a pair of matronly old ladies. It was they who strove to keep order when all the young calves tried to be naughty − and when not arguing among themselves over who was the most beautiful. I was sad to hear that they were staying behind. I would have loved to have more female company.

Winaruz, who Samir always rode, was a somewhat sprightly little Tibesti breed, whose name meant 'hope'. He seemed a typical young buck, keen to show off at every opportunity, especially with the females. Suleyman had watched his birth, and since that day had taught the camel to obey his voice. Winaruz understood the secret language of neck and heel and learned quickly, never biting or kicking, even during the rutting season when most males became unruly, shrugging off their loads and hitting out at their masters.

Agizul was a particularly large *mehari*, his hump a mountain of twisted gristle, whose name meant 'brave'. He had huge thighs that rubbed together and jiggled as he strode. He really was a most magnificent beast, regarding himself as infinitely superior to any human, an attitude that, according to Suleyman, he tried constantly to instil in the rest of the herd, but which was slightly undermined by an intermittent incontinence problem.

Eventually Suleyman decided: Usem for his strength and Agizul for his courage, Winaruz because he was nimble, and Tlatig, meaning 'has value', picked up for a snip in Libya, who was priceless when it came to negotiating uphill stretches – not that there would be many of those where we were going.

Lastly, of course, there was Fleabag, temperamental, skittish, disobedient, naughty, lovable Fleabag, the whole purpose of the journey or, ostensibly, the whole purpose of the journey.

She was sitting down, alone looking miffed. She hated her name. She had outgrown it.

Friendship

Imidiwa

Within the shady cocoon of the palm grove, we were wrapped in our own private camel bubble. It was too easy to be deluded into thinking that the threats surrounding us were mirages, so cunningly did the haze of the horizon mask them. No policeman approached to challenge me, and no army official ventured near to ask the purpose of my visit or to see my passport. I was in no doubt of the reality. Beneath the leaves that provided coverage from the sun, the spotlight of my foreignness shone ever brighter.

By way of preparation for the trip I received something of a crash course in camel handling, which – by some fluke of good fortune – turned out not to be literal. Soon I could recognize each of the camels individually.

They were all unique. Winaruz's patchy facial fur gave his chin the appearance of a bum-fluff beard, whereas Usem's fur was so shaggy it brought to mind images of Grünewald's *The Mocking of Christ*. Usem was enormous. Fleabag, by comparison, looked dainty.

Their singing voices also varied. Usem and Agizul offered the deepest, second-bass notes, whereas Tlatig carried the second tenor line, escalating to first tenor when agitated. Winaruz was the most versatile, shifting from bass to countertenor if excited. Fleabag liked coloratura.

Suleyman proved to be a master cameleer. He was also a skilled counsellor and camel anger management was his forte. Most camels had long fuses when it came to dealing with their human companions, although the goalposts often moved. A disgruntled animal could lash out forwards, backwards or to the sides. Any one of these kicks could put you in hospital for a month – and even sever your spine so you would never walk again.

At times, he would be surrounded in a scrum, the necks and feet of the herd crowding so dangerously that it looked as if they might trample him. But he would always reappear, tapping the nose of one or another of them, while the camels acted superior.

Samir was also an impressive teacher, demonstrating the importance of hump condition, how to read the language of camel song and neck while moving, and how to interpret head position. He was also a hard taskmaster. A camel that took all the water would be reprimanded. If they sang and bared their teeth in greed or jealousy, they would receive a lecture, the tone of his voice giving them no doubt as to where they stood. On appreciating this, they would lower their hump in shame.

Saddling was a match as much of wills as of cunning. It was necessary to approach from the rear and grab the tail. If not the tail, you could grab the ear and pull the camel's head down, at which point it would complain bitterly. Usem, in particular, hated the procedure and swelled out his muscly neck and gurgled menacingly. Guaranteed to squirt bile at your arms and hands, the others were quick to follow his example.

Once the saddle was in place, a rope noose needed to be secured around the lower jaw. Samir was emphatic. It was necessary to tether a camel, he said, because however fit or ill, all dromedaries were possessed of an inherent form of nomadism. It was in their nature to be restless, and they became even more restless when they allowed people to ride them.

Hobbling was an art. After the jaw rope was in position, another rope had to be taken over the head and tightened, while untying the head rope from a loop that was threaded through the right nostril.

Next, it would be wound twice around a foreleg before the two ends were twisted together, leaving enough spare rope to bind the other foreleg. A large knot was finally tied at one end through a loop in the other.

A ring through the nose was essential. The neck of a camel is so strong that you would have to have superhuman strength to control one with just the halter rope. Unlike with a horse, you could never insert a bit, since camels chew cud like cows and oxen.

A camel cannot drink with the rope looped around its tongue, but if you do not do this, it might bolt, and it was hard, even for Suleyman, the greatest of all camel handlers, to catch a camel with no rope and that was not hobbled. Most importantly, when you hobbled a camel, he said, you should always stand behind it, as it was less likely to kick your head in. I forgot many things I was told, but I always remembered that one.

And you should never, ever try winding a camel up, especially if it is called Putin.

I cry when I remember
Tãn-d-aktey ad ahâlla

Beyond the carved, dry skeletons of the village, the land rose and stretched. Dust devils danced across the ground like skittish ballerinas. Scrub bushes watched.

The pathway obeyed the willfulness of the drifts, which were their own masters. We had long passed the large rubbish plot where the air was cankerous, and we had made it through the heaps of abandoned, scrapped cars that lay like skulls.

'See how slow I am,' muttered Amina. The wind carried her words across the sands.

'You are faster than me,' I gasped.

The women were used to walking on sand, even without their rubber sandals, but I could feel the intense heat on my soles as they dug into the softness, lifting bright little cloudbursts.

'It's not far.' Amina smiled her wry, worn smile.

'How far is that?'

'As far as it takes,' Rhaicha answered, scurrying on ahead, hardly noticing the effort of moving, as if she was paddling on clockwork legs.

It was impossible not to be captivated by the block of nothingness that surrounded us, of beige, with red, yellow and milky white brushed in. The eye roamed out across a natural hollow, unbroken by vegetation or roads. It was as if the world was at an end here, as if every day drew its last breath.

Glancing back, it was possible to see how the settlements

lay gathered together as if they knew they were out of place. Any human intervention was out of place, an interruption to the status quo in a landscape drama of epic proportions in which humans were, at the most, casual observers.

And yet, we were not quite alone. Sometimes a sheep appeared from nowhere, then ran off, and on the horizon a few black specks were floating, receding ever more slowly up slopes and into depressions. The Ahaggar was full of hardy individuals who thought nothing of walking for miles to fetch water or firewood. Such disappearances were common, apparently without destination, the vanishing points uncharted.

The two women carried on chatting. There was a sense of apprehension, at the same time of concealment. What was their secret?

'You like Samir.' This from Rhaicha.

'Yes, I do,' I said. 'As a friend.' I knew the subject had been one of the items of gossip chewed over by them. It at least explained why they thought I was there, learning to ride a camel.

'Of course, a friend.'

'Yes, a friend.'

Amina smiled again and we all laughed, but I detected something else in Rhaicha, a sadness, or a resignation, as if perhaps she had her sights set on Samir.

'Really, there is nothing going on,' I said.

'Are you rich?' asked Rhaicha, after we had managed a few more steps. She had posed the question somewhat rhetorically.

I reflected for a moment. 'Most of us do not think of ourselves as wealthy where I come from,' I said.

Rhaicha turned. 'That is what all rich people say. It is what you tell yourselves to make yourselves feel better.'

I was forced to concede she had a point. In the West we like to think of ourselves as advanced. Our riches are measured in status and success. I wondered how the Tuareg saw wealth. For them, were riches really on the inside – honour, *ashaaq*, or in Tamahaq *ellelu*, courage, freedom – those that they maintained they valued above all else?

'Land is wealth,' said Amina. 'And the desert places.'

I wondered what she meant by this exactly, but she did not elaborate. The wind skimmed over our cheeks, across the barren plain where we stood huddled as one, as if tidied together by it, her words winding their way into the gaps between associations.

'And what if those places deny us access?' I asked.

'Then we must hurry after them,' she said. She was standing so close I could smell her henna.

That was the moment I thought once again of the risks in undertaking the walk to visit the *marabout*, and in which simultaneously lay the kernel of my resolution.

The three of us paused and reflected. Then, as if glimpsing an echo of a border, we turned towards the palms on the horizon, nodded and pressed on. A random point had been reached between us, a strange new place, that of convergence.

We continued over the landscape of sand rivers, with their currents of yellow ochre sand, towards the clump of vegetation that signalled an oasis. The formations of sky were mirrored in the land, in the humps of dunes and the sprays of desert grass.

Some way on, I looked up and saw bright saddles clustered like anemones. The figure of a man waved back. Beside him stood a tall and unmistakably fine dromedary.

﹡

It is said in these parts that a tree weeps when giving up its frankincense. The resin, once likened to the scent of heaven, is evident only when its bark is wounded, whether scored deliberately, damaged by livestock or struck by lightning. The cut oozes a syrupy kind of latex that over time becomes a resin, hardening as it ages into tiny amber droplets.

Our destination appeared to be a small impression in the land. A lone tree stood like an island in the dry dust surrounding it. Only now did I understand that our trip had been a pilgrimage rather than an excursion. It was an opportunity to seek protection.

The frankincense tree, according to the Tuareg, is especially holy – as holy as the great Tuba of Paradise. Even the ground in which it grows is considered sacred. Around the base of this one lay the remains of offerings, small shrines of water bottles so that the tree spirits would not die of thirst. The Tuareg believed it was a place of *al hima*, where, according to tradition, spirits live: the *ibedni*, the guardians of emptiness.

I sat on the ground, hugging my knees, watching as my new friends made their ablutions and offered dates. Part of me thought they were crazy to kneel to a tree, although Samir put my scepticism down to ignorance – and perhaps the possibility that a living tree had a consciousness, that it could listen to prayer and even respond to it, wasn't so strange. After all, trees have been worshipped almost universally throughout history.

Regarding it now, it felt like a miracle that the tree managed to survive at all. Like all desert plants, it lived, as the desert people said, with its head in fire, its feet in water. The dwarfed, twisted trunk stretched skywards, its gnarled branches, leaning to one side as if in mourning, filled with twittering birds. The leaves waved provocatively, pointing towards the plain where there was not the slightest sign of life. There was a sense of being drawn in, a gravitational field; its aim, emptiness. The *lubaan* was 'Allah's tree', said Samir. It wore its branches like crowns.

The leaves also make great fodder, as I discovered when a particularly bedraggled and smelly camel popped her head around the trunk and, without so much as a gurgle, began eating.

'*Miteuse!*' Samir shooed her away, upon which she hung her head dejectedly. I walked over to comfort her.

'We do not cut it too deep so as not to harm the tree.' Suleyman was concentrating hard, drawing his knife and scoring the trunk with the sharp blade.

He handed me the small teardrop and, as I took it from him, he handed me a memory, another jewel. Suddenly, I was watching Gobi nomads press water from saxaul bark. I had been thirteen years old at the time.

'If you offend the tree, it will bring you bad luck, and if you hurt it, you will go mad,' said Suleyman, bowing. 'We reach up to the top, so it reduces the pain.'

'Why cut it at all?' I asked.

'It will bring us *baraka*,' he said.

He set to work with the incense straight away. With reverence, he took out the small clay pot or *ten*, grinding the resin, mashing it up with some olive oil and beating it into a pulp. Then he put it aside in order for it to be given blessing by the sun.

Fleabag seemed to crave sunshine. Under the dappled light she stood basking in it, before ambling slowly back again. Winaruz, glancing up, bleated at her, and this set off a chorus of mutual bleating.

Samir gathered stray sticks for the fire. As the smoke swirled up, he sprinkled some of the frankincense over the flames. 'Ah...' he sighed and the women nodded deliriously.

At that moment, not twelve feet away, the long neck of Winaruz suddenly came through a gopher hole at the foot of a rock. The soft fur was thick about his ears and he seemed a little frisky. With a forward tilt of his body, he launched himself at the ground and went down choppily. His mouth was open and I imagined he was smiling.

'Are you sure he is not coming into season?' I wondered.

'It must be the *baraka*,' said Suleyman.

The fire was looking good. Soon, a few more pointy tongues lapped the air and, as more twigs were heaped on, a column of sweet-scented smoke twisted up and the flames emerged triumphant.

'So are you ready for the *marabout*, then?' Suleyman gazed towards the horizon.

'Yes?' Samir prompted. Still, he did not look at me, out of respect.

'Perhaps,' I said. Underneath I was not prepared at all. I felt inadequate, isolated, out of my depth, at the same time, complacent, exhilarated and, above all, resigned.

'You Western women are trouble,' Samir said.

'We Western women have a voice,' I protested, and the two women laughed.

Just for now, we had everything we needed: *tagela* to fill our stomachs, sweet fire-scented smoke, benign tree spirits on our side, and presently Fleabag, the nicest gift of all, sniffing the air like a lady at a *parfumerie*.

In the brilliance of light I closed my eyes and saw not

red this time, but pink. Little love hearts fluttered in my dilating pupils. I was overcome by fumes. I was intoxicated. I could not help but adore her long, thick lashes, her gungy eyes, her silky soft ears, her blubbery, pouting lips and rotten teeth. I rather liked the fact that her memory was faultless, particularly when it came to human weaknesses – above all, mine.

I even forgave her for the ringworm.

Hearts together, tents apart

Zannimahazat nawan tasinsinamagagam

'Where's the other tent, Samir?'

We were standing on the sand, around us a battalion of bags, bundles and boxes extending towards the horizon.

'Well, we are good friends...'

'Yes,' I said. 'Just good friends.'

'If we know that, there is no problem.'

'What are you trying to say?'

'I checked the equipment and there is good news and bad.'

'Go on.'

'We have found strong materials, solid poles, not rusty, very cheap.'

'And the bad news?'

'There is only one tent.'

'One tent?'

'Yes.'

'I see.'

'Sorry.'

'I thought you said you respected me.'

'I do.'

'Then why is there only one tent?'

'It's very roomy. Huge. Family tent. Enough space for twenty or thirty people.'

'It's a good thing I brought enough money to buy my own tent, isn't it?'

Against a cerulean sky, the nomad's gaze clouded over. Half an hour later two locally made tents appeared: not of wood and hessian, as I had expected, but of canvas and rope, with supporting poles and large steel pegs. But we had to talk. In a land without perimeters, we needed our own boundaries.

❆

That afternoon, father, son and I sat beneath a spreading acacia and divided up our duties for the forthcoming journey. Or rather, Suleyman announced he would look after camels and navigation, Samir said he would cook and look after the water supplies, and then, worryingly, with Samir nodding vigorously, Suleyman explained my role.

'It is clear…' He paused. 'I will guide us, Samir will feed us and you will…' – he fluttered his hand – '…be in charge of everything else.'

'Excuse me?' I said. I didn't elaborate.

Battle commenced over goat's cheese and bread. Samir came up with a list of dos, mainly what to say when – for example, it was essential to say *Bismillah* before entering rainfall, showering or eating, when completing a prayer and before putting on new clothes. Discretion and respect would be applied at all times by all parties.

Then we began on the don'ts.

To begin with the laws, or *gerro* in Tamahaq, as the men referred to them, appeared reasonable. I had no problem with number 1: one should not, under any circumstances, pour milk on the soil, because the earth was impure and it would undermine *baraka*.

Number 2 seemed just as harmless. When washing a milk bowl, the water must be poured on a stone. And number 3 was in all our interests. *Imujagh*, dignity, was to be guarded at all times. Boasting, coveting and jealousy resulted in illness and an attack of bad spirits. Words can reach the soul and be equivalent to killing a person, just as compliments can provoke jealousy and desire.

Nor did I object to number 7: all female camels travelling with us had to be milked daily, otherwise evil entered the milk and it would have to be boiled. Fleabag was the only female and she would have to have a baby before this became relevant.

Suleyman was welcome to the job of trimming the camels' toenails, checking their urine colour and monitoring their hormone levels. And that a camel should never, ever eat the leaves of the *difl*, or oleander, seemed understandable, considering that it was poisonous.

In return, I requested a few small understandings of my own. Number 1 was agreed with no disputes: separate tents. Whatever the terrain or weather conditions, however exhausted we were, there would be two – one for the men and one for me – pitched at a minimum distance of twenty metres from each other. Suleyman piped up cheerfully with his own contribution. He didn't want a tent, he said. He would sleep in the open beneath the stars. Samir could have a tent to himself.

Number 8 relating to physical modesty was mutually agreed. This included ankles and forearms, because in the desert showing those things would be tantamount to flashing. To this effect, we would be taking no almonds or peanuts, since they were high-risk foods bound to light a man's fire. My own fire, of course, was dead, obliterated by loss and by heartbreak.

The no-alcohol rule was potentially contentious. Samir's conviction was that alcohol would lead to immodest thoughts and, Allah knows, the mind was the weakness in men and the root of evil. And so we added a caveat, reserving the right to drink alcohol in emergencies and for medicinal purposes only. Suleyman waved his hand dismissively. He would prefer to drink the milk of a lactating she-jackal.

Number 6, that no one would be forced to eat anything they did not wish to eat, was received with good grace, despite hints Suleyman kept dropping with regard to catching things and shooting them, particularly those with scales and multiple legs, which, in his view, formed a rich source of protein.

There were restrictions about rations, supplies and, of course, water. Two cups a day was my ration for 'hygiene', apart from drinking water. That would be difficult. At home I was used to having a bath. The men would not require any, because, according to the Qur'an, they would be relying upon dirt to clean themselves. Upon negotiation, I managed to stretch the amount slightly, but with one final caveat. Law number 10 was my own, and I kept it under wraps: no matter how dehydrated, I was never, under any circumstances, to drink my own pee.

The avoidance of such topics as religion and politics came naturally. No matter what any of us thought of East–West relations, the ongoing occupation of Syria and Palestine, we would respect our religious differences.

The same respect applied to financial matters. I had already provided an advance, to cover all sundry expenses, and was happy to resolve any outstanding fees at the end. However, I made sure they inserted the word 'reasonable' for good measure. That caused another raised eyebrow.

Subsequently, Samir and I added a few laws between ourselves. There was number 11: no flattery; telling a girl how nicely she smelt in relation to camels was another slippery slope. And number 13: no dancing was a question of tradition. A Tuareg man would never dance. Dancing was not done. It was undignified. It was too physical.

We worked our way down the long list until the final commandment, no physical contact, and the deal breaker: no one was permitted to sneak into my tent. I was aware of the freedoms between young Tuareg men and women and of their elders who would turn a blind eye. But I was British. I had standards.

Samir looked at me and as I glanced back at him, I felt as unknowable and alien to him as the great seas of water across the Atlantic where he hoped to swim one day. Somehow, despite all the odds, and against my better judgement, we had a plan, although it was a sketchy one with a raft of stipulations and get-out clauses.

The camels had their own set of laws, of course, although they alone were privy to what they were.

※

Stress takes on its own momentum. In times of anxiety we are as children peeking through a hole in a fence, not catching the view in its entirety. Ignorance all too often misconstrued as naïvity is in reality wilful denial.

Inevitably, there was even more to the trip than I had at first understood. Only now did the *other* stories emerge – those of travellers getting lost, or running out of water who would die of thirst. They all ended up the same – buried by sand or eaten by jackals. People knew exactly what happened because the victims wrote it down. There is time to think in the desert when you are dying.

Passing a sign beside the track that led south, I felt strangely consoled that we were not travelling by road. The weather-beaten words, in French and in English, spelt out for the benefit of European motorists the dangers of crossing the desert and advised them to take precautions. Few appear to have heeded its warnings, and even in the heyday of tourism in the area, when the traffic wasn't masked and gun-bearing, there were often tragedies.

Reading a book about the Sahara did not help matters. It was a small academic tome and, as it fell open, a light brown scorpion stared out, claws snatching.

Scorpions can reach 5 to 8 cms in length and, despite their reputation, their sting is no more dangerous than the common bumblebee.

The exception to this rule is the Saharan fat-tailed scorpion (androctonus australis), *which is generally around 10 cms and is the most venomous in the world. Its sting causes paralysis, convulsions, heart attack or respiratory failure. These scorpions are common across the deserts of north Africa.*

I turned over the page.

Thirst is felt when the body has lost about half a per cent of its weight from dehydration. With a two per cent drop the stomach will no longer take the amount of fluid needed. You feel tired, flushed and irritable. Beyond five per cent the saliva glands pack up. There is dizziness, blurred speaking, difficulty in breathing and the skin turns blue. A ten per cent loss is the point of no return. After three days without fluid the skin splits from dehydration. A fever sets in, the saliva dries and the tongue swells until you feel like choking before your throat closes, resulting in gagging and disorientation. Walking becomes impossible. That is the turning point, when your liver is failing and the blood, now thick, cannot circulate. You begin seeing

*things – a distant oasis, a deadly beast – but by then it is
already too late, your suffering only cut short because you
know you are about to pass out and, when you do, death
is inevitable. Your body will be discovered many years from
now, burnt to a crisp or, worse, a skeleton, all flesh
devoured by vultures.*

It didn't bode well.

Of course, I did not attempt to call my mother, or any
of my family. I was trying to protect them. Wondering if
meditation could form a shield against anxiety, I sat
beneath an acacia, around me the absence of life, the earth
scorched as if by a gigantic blowlamp, the emptiness in my
wake. There I adopted the deathlike passivity of an animal
wishing to remain unnoticed by its predators, motionless.

The men did not see my fear or, if they did, they
ignored it. They spent so much time with their camels that
they didn't even notice that I smelt like one. Amina and
Rhaicha understood. Tucked away, in a quiet corner of the
compound, lay their leaving gift.

A shelter of twigs had been woven into a dome, over
which coarse blankets were secured. Inside, lay two
buckets, towels and a slab of black soap. A fire had been
built between rocks, its flames heating a pot of water.

There I sat cross-legged, scrubbing, apart from camel
sheds and goat rooms. The dirt lifted from my skin in sheets
and a gritty river of dust and sand flowed out of my hair.
Some time later I opened the blanket, stepped into the
cool dusk and let the cool air wrap me in silence. Beyond
the compound the plain seemed unending, the sun now a
gold disc behind the land. Reckless folly or extreme
adventure, in reality I could not grasp what I was about to
do. But for Fleabag's sake, I was ready to try.

Of the light
Tufta

At first light of dawn the loading began, accompanied by frowns, invocations and muttered curses. I thought nomads would travel light. I had been told that a man of the desert would take just a dozen or so objects at most, but Samir had stacked up a ton of stuff, including an amulet to guard against the Evil Eye, and his cartons of cigarettes.

What Samir and Suleyman were leaving behind, I was making up for with a pile of essentials that left my extra-large rucksack bulging at the seams. My fire steel was my most important piece of kit, consisting of a metal rod and a flat piece like a blunt razor.

As always when travelling to high-risk destinations, I was also taking a few select items of solar-powered emergency equipment recommended by the SAS in Afghanistan: an Inmarsat Mini-M satellite phone (I had been tipped off that it was forbidden, but I was taking it anyway); a miniflare rocket and an EPIRB, an Emergency Position Indicating Radio of the kind operated by ocean yachtsmen. This was my kind of safety.

I also had an industrial supply of antibiotics and other medicines, plus a wide range of travel fans, lotions, creams and an insect repellent guaranteed to ward off any living creature that came within twenty paces. I had thermals for the freezing nights, water purification tablets for stinking well water, rehydration powders, snakebite and scorpion kits and a high-tech sleeping bag to keep me warm at Antarctic temperatures.

Crucial items I would carry in a bag at the front of the saddle – my money, papers, digital compass and some noxious black paste that Suleyman said was an essential for sore feet. My luxury items consisted of a volume of Tennyson's *In Memoriam* – in honour of Edward Wilson, who had carried one with him on an expedition to the South Pole – and my lucky stone, so round and smooth that it reminded me of a dinosaur egg I had once picked up in the Nemegt. It was a touchstone, used for assaying metals and gold. Well, you never did know.

On top of all this, there were spare ropes, straps, hobbles and halters for the camels, cooking and eating supplies, pots, pans and utensils, as well as a kerosene lamp and a stove consisting of a gas bottle with a cooking attachment.

To one side of the pile stood a small teapot, six sticky glasses, plus a selection of water canisters, some filled, some empty – at Suleyman's insistence – and, of course, one neatly disguised bottle. 'Our forebears walked days with just a goatskin of water. Look at us now – we need rivers to last hours,' he remarked.

For bedding there were three thin mattresses and a half-dozen camel-hair blankets of varying sizes and coarseness, designed from ancient patterns, the dyes from berries and the wool from family animals. Two crates of vegetables, boxes of tea and three cones of sugar, two small hessian sacks of rice and semolina, and another two of oranges, dates and lemons would see us through.

The camels had their own supplies, including oats, dates and salt. Camels could go for long periods without moisture, even as long as six or seven months, but they needed to eat daily and would starve if they rejected the unfamiliar vegetation. The good health of our camels was vital, for upon them all our lives depended.

More alarming was the arsenal of guns and knives that Suleyman was packing. The centrepiece was a sabre that Samir unearthed with particular pride, but when I asked about it, all he would say, as he stroked it tenderly, was 'Allah favours the servant who is prepared for any eventuality.' There was too much else to worry about to keep pressing him about it.

A lengthy discussion took place over which pot should go in which bag, which box or crate should be carried by which animal, which rug should protect which rump. It is important not to overburden a camel. A half-ton cargo is normal capacity, but it has to be balanced perfectly, the canisters of water hung especially carefully. Any imbalance means the saddle rubs, which can cause a wound, and any soreness leads to the camel growing irritable. That, in turn, can result in disobedience, and even in lameness.

The saddles consisted of a wooden frame with two cloth-covered extensions connected by two arcs of metal. Over these two large baskets were tied together with rope, into which were placed the supplies. Next came the bedding and, finally, the cargo was secured firmly with straps that wound around the camel's stomach and hump, both vertically and horizontally.

Suleyman laid rugs which acted as cushions over the camels' backs. 'This one doubles as a prayer mat,' he said, breathing in the strong smell of camel dung.

A raucous chorus of protracted grumbling and dirty looks ensued. The girths were made fast and the holding ropes put on. Tlatig turned in circles to avoid the girths being attached. He had learned that a well-timed shifting manoeuvre from one side to the other would dislodge the stuff he didn't want to carry and enable him to saunter off. Fleabag tolerated the process a little better than I had anticipated. I stood beside her and she smeared me with her gluey snot and bilious spittle. It was not a pleasant experience, but it could have been worse. She might have vomited.

An age was spent fiddling with equipment until, at last, the saddles were on, the packs distributed evenly and life, for a moment, was in balance.

Suleyman tied the camels, passing the rope from the one in front to the halter of the one behind, ensuring it passed through the girth as it went, the nose line attached to the saddle in front to keep each camel from hanging back.

Villagers gathered, dressed in black out of respect for the shadows that awaited us. Everyone wanted to bear witness. We were to pass beyond the limits of their horizon, as far as the mountain guardians would allow.

'Samir will look after you. It is something that has to be done,' said Rhaicha, and her shoulders bunched up.

'It is.' Amina nodded. She would think of us every day. She handed me a paper bag of perfumed frankincense. 'We have prayed to Allah for your safety, and to his sprits of protection to look after you.'

This was the place we parted, a clumsy embrace, copied on their part from what they had seen in the movies, and on mine from my travels. We were at the beginning of another road – although there was no way of telling where it would lead us.

'*Islem key alla! E kay islem yalla! E alla kay islemen!* May God protect you!' The women waved and rubbed their eyes, filled with copious tears, I suspected, of pity.

At last, like experienced weightlifters, the camels were up. Winaruz resisted to the last, baring his teeth and swinging his neck around to try to see who was to blame for his burden.

We led into the sun, I consumed by fear of this unknown territory and my inability to deal with it, the two nomads in front of me striding confidently. None of us knew if we would actually make it, or, to be precise, whether I would.

Noon

Terut

+ ÷ ○ ÷ +

I feel the sun

Tigrau-hi tafuk

'Breathe'. The word comes from the Latin *spirare,* meaning both spirit and inspire. In the desert, inspiring feels a more accurate description than breathing. The air is so clean that it has a crystalline quality. I felt buoyed up by a sense of weightlessness, as if decompressing after deep-sea diving, as if swimming to the surface and gulping.

The desert lay like one of the planet's limbs, pulsating, throbbing, blanching. Rocks and stones lay scattered like fallen vertebrae, eroded, as if searching for something irrevocably shattered. Where there was sand it was fine, swept smooth by the winds, sometimes with minuscule footprints hinting of moonlit hunting dramas.

It was easy to see why the Tuareg called this place the Tassili-n-Ajjer, the plateau of rivers. Not just sand formed its heart, but a landscape of extraordinary diversity, where sand and vegetation mingled with dry riverbeds, rock pools and stony areas over a massive 115,000 square kilometres.

Ahead, its horizon felt unreachable, the distant peaks stark and impermeable, like the wall of stone that separated the two sides of my life – before, when there was hope, and after, when it had gone. The thin line of the *piste* was oblique and meandering, winding, perhaps, towards another, new place, where regrets would become dust.

Father and son seemed to be in their element. The two men talked – about the weather, its whims and idiosyncrasies, about rain clouds that were dream-makers, about trees that could kill you, and those that could keep you alive – and it struck me now that they were a perfect foil for each other.

For Samir, the desert held a hypnotic majesty. It was a place of oleander blossom, acacia and palms spreading their shade in the sun, of expanses vast and wild that held a mystical beauty, of all creatures and all things magical. To his father, these were lands where the soul and body were tested, where inner strength was crafted and insight gained.

Samir noticed the patterns of the sky and land, the ever-changing winds. Suleyman warned that the hot ground burnt holes in the soles of your sandals. Samir believed in love. Suleyman felt sorry for those poor souls who felt love, the type found in the West. For him, love was just a disease of passion in which the senses and emotions gave way to madness.

All the while, the camels listened, heads held high, swaying their necks in agreement, or snorting as if in protest. Fleabag resisted her nose line, as if uncomfortable in middle position. Walking beside Samir seemed to soothe and calm her, and often I caught her nuzzling at him.

Occasionally we passed strangers, old prophets in long robes, a bride being fetched by camel, as was the custom. They led their lives apart, kept themselves to themselves. They cultivated their faith because it never let them down. They were polite to strangers, wherever they were from.

Children ran along the errant dust tracks, a small boy collecting water, a child shepherdess. They knew the art of shoe repair, about snakes, spiders and scorpions, the foibles of the winds and the scarcity of rainfall. There were no computer games for them.

Where does she sleep? Where do you sleep? Most importantly: can she cook? They addressed Samir, turning their eyes towards me. Why are you here? Where are you from? Where are you going? those eyes enquired before they averted them again.

'*Et teqqamed selhir*. Stay healthy,' I said, at a loss how to answer them in English, let alone Tamahaq.

'*I kkes yalla imiksenen-nek!* God let your enemies disappear!' called Suleyman after them.

'*Ayr emir iyen*. Until the next time,' they waved, as if there would be one.

We marched until the light began to fail, squeezing a bit more out of ourselves. Late afternoon, among the powdery rubble, a smooth patch of ground was enough to pitch camp and couch our tired camels, who carped and wriggled. Large bushes with prickly foliage cleansed of their winter dust, or an isolated tree provided wind shelter.

I gave Fleabag a stroke and she gurgled, regarding me through her long lashes as if to say, 'Agh! So you are still here. What do you want, exactly?'

'I'm not really sure,' I told her, and she pouted, as if to say the discussion was over.

The tents didn't take long to put up. Samir began a fire, first making a small pile of wood fibres. He didn't use a flint, just rubbed a green stick sharpened at the end to a point with another, longer, dry stick. When the flames leapt over his fingers, Suleyman threw on some wormwood, *teheregle*, to dispel bad spirits.

Supper was stew, or *duwaz*, eaten from a shared pot, and *tagela* with oranges and cardamom biscuits. We leant back against sun-warmed rocks that would burn your skin if you touched them in the daytime. Now, as the temperature fell, they were like hard electric blankets.

After we had eaten, Samir 'cleaned' the dishes by pouring sand on them and swishing it around with his finger.

Despite the exemption from prayer that Islam grants to

all travellers, Suleyman slid out his prayer mat, performed his ablutions and recited his prayers. I had the feeling that no matter what might have happened, he would still have praised God and thanked Him, and that his son would have joined in unquestioningly.

In the dying day, the camels played in the dust. The high peaks looked unworldly in the distance, sparkling from the radiance melting over them. Suleyman told stories about the deeds of his forebears, those navigators of the great routes whose invisible paths traced the past like small tributaries.

We sat listening to the silence for a while, although for the two men it was not silence because they could hear the sounds of the wind and the animals.

As night's cold gathered us in its arms, Suleyman spoke of the practice of fire watching, a kind of willing the heat to enter the body practised by nomads on long desert journeys. It reminded me of gTum-mo, a spiritual heat created by breathing exercises performed while focusing on fire I had learnt when I was fourteen years old in the Kuen Lun Mountains in China. Monks would drape wet cloths around themselves in freezing temperatures and dry them out using their own body heat. Suleyman found this amusing – and he had never heard of China.

Darkness fell and we retired. I undressed inside my sleeping bag, relieved to have survived the first twelve miles unscathed. The torch made circles on the canvas sides of the tent, a pale ring outside a darker one like a kaleido-scope with a dot in the middle. I switched off the light, remembering an old love. Romance was dead and it could never be resurrected, because it had been entombed for ever in the greatest gravel pit in history.

The great desert
Teneret chegret

I had lain, a sarcophagus in my tent, waking with the wan light of a new day pale as silk on the canvas above me, wondering where I was. I had missed the dawn. Both men had been up for hours.

'Why didn't you wake me?' elicited startled expressions.

Breakfast consisted of an orange, dates and a boiled egg. I watched Samir poke a hole in the bottom of the shell. 'Why do you do that?' I asked.

'To keep the devil from stealing the souls of children.'

Suleyman seemed fascinated by my toothbrush. Why did I always foam up my mouth like a mad dog? Why not use a small twig to pick out the bits, as he did? He opened my compact mirror with a dull sense of recognition and when I plastered on sun cream it baffled him.

'Why is your skin so white?' he asked me.

'It just is.'

'Our ancestors used to say it's because white people eat the flesh of small children.'

'And do you believe that?'

He picked at his teeth. 'I don't discount anything the ancestors say.'

We packed away the tents and utensils. I gripped my hands above my head and did a couple of stretches. He gave me another of his curious looks.

'But brown skin's from the devil,' added Samir, spitting on the cooking pot and rubbing it with his finger. He glanced at his father.

I wondered what Rhaicha, Amina and the other Tuareg women would have said. In the West women spend so much time and effort trying to be thin and brown. Here, they craved the opposite.

'It doesn't matter what colour your skin is,' I said.

New words tasted like strange fruits – mine with their nasals and funny vowels, theirs more pungent with their throaty gutturals. We were surrounded by *asrir,* empty land, and *amadal* and *hidban,* gravel and rock. Sandy land they called *rag,* but if it contained gravel it was *mham.* Each type of dune had a different name. Those without vegetation were *alakwas* or *uruq;* but if one had the tiniest scrap of vegetation lying on or around it, it was *tehedit. Azekrih,* meaning forest, seemed to refer to any land that had a bush on it.

Predictably, there were hundreds of words to describe sand. Moving sand was known as *iluk.* Flat, smooth sand where we could couch the camels was *edeien,* but if it contained rocks, it was termed *aselres.* And *erg* did not mean sea, as I had believed, but vein or belt.

Grasses were referred to as *zayyat,* herbs *tabaidot* and bushy shrubs *rinkidan.* Other plants that were known by many different names (*listrif, sabay* and *atil*) all looked identical to me. There was also a raft of weather words, including hundreds of wind names, such as the *shirgi,* which blew sand at 90 miles per hour at 120°F. A drought was *shidda* and a heat haze was *aghmam.* I enjoyed learning all of them, but it was the swear words I remembered best.

Samir lined the camels up and, with a steely command, his father whooshed them all down. Blankets and saddles were loaded first, then the girths and finally the nose lines, these taken from their tails and secured to the saddles. The loads were checked and rechecked, and given a final once over for good luck, before at last Samir asked the camels to stand. As they pushed themselves up, they bared their teeth and made a wailing sound like a chorus of children stuck in the back of a car wondering when they would arrive at the journey's end.

It was the first hour of walking that I loved the best, when the air was still cool and the camels were at their brightest. Usem led, his great thighs wobbling as he went. Behind him, Fleabag sniffed, unnerved by the air's unfamiliarity, grunting when she found a new plant or leaf. She seemed excited by the scents and the feeling of movement that the wind gave her. I patted her, but she still chided me for forgetting my manners.

Around mid-morning, we sought out the shade and found an acacia. The sun beat down from a cloudless sky, its light hitting the earth like blows from an open palm beating on a closed door, demanding to be let in.

I switched on my army of battery fans and Samir handed out biscuits. You have only to walk for a while in a dry country to appreciate the beauty of water. Now, as I swirled it in my cup, it seemed like nectar.

Then we began methodically across the plain again. Sometimes the track ate its way through high sand drifts. At others the way lay open, strewn with rocks and, upon occasion, ancient Saharan cypress trees that had stood in the same spot for thousands of years .

When the chatter fell silent, there was nothing to interrupt the wind's sighing but the whirring of insects and periodically the strange cry of a bird.

Walking there now, I saw with my own eyes why the Sahara is known as *Sahra al Kubra*, the Great Desert. It is called great for a reason: for its mystery, for its power – like the sun – to take life or to give it. It is a blazing abyss, the planet in the raw, with more than 3,600 hours of sunlight a year and a summer temperature that can soar as high as 117°F in its broad, flat expanses. It extends across 3.6 million square miles, from the Red Sea in the east to the Atlantic in the west, up to the Mediterranean in the north and south to the savannah of the Sahel.

It is also immense. The Algerian part extends south of the Atlas Mountains for 1,500 kilometres towards the Niger and Mali frontiers. It is a region of great diversity. Huge areas of sand dunes known as *areg* occupy about a quarter of the territory, including the Grand Erg Oriental, with its great dunes. Much of the west is covered by *humud*, rocky plains, and in the south-east it is dominated by the mountains and their highlands, sandstone plateaux, cut into deep gorges by ancient dry rivers, or *oueds*. A desert of pebbles stretches as far as Mali.

The desert can never be imitated in a photograph, or summed up in a souvenir. Every aspect of its complexity defies capture.

Colour is electrifying. In a universe of yellows, the smallest contrasting bright shades stand out. Details appear magnified, more intense – the beige of camels brighter against the duck-egg blue of the sky, the black of a fly deeper against the mauve of a stone. From out of the sun's glare, the figure of an insect takes shape, a sand beetle perhaps, a solitary player in the vast spotlight, all of us players in this drama of desolation.

Sounds, too, are made more audible by their rarity, piercing the silence like torn silk. Sometimes the silence faintly hums like the press of a pause button and then a fresh sound blooms like a flower. A tin can clatters across the dust as if someone playing percussion in an orchestra has suddenly rattled the castanets.

Here, where nothing rusts and there is no mould to rot the seat leather, there are distant reminders, scattered vestiges of another way of life. Half-buried old cars lie blackened by the sun, just sand and wind blasting at the paintwork and reducing it to a dull metallic sheen. Every make, type and nationality of motor vehicle has fallen victim, from Minis and Citroëns to Ladas and Mercedes. Many have acquired moisture, and from those cacti sprout. In others, small animals have made their homes.

Time ticks at its own pace. A sundial would be more useful than a watch. At noon, the sun is merciless, the sky's glare a white fire that melts rhythm and space. A haze covers the earth, which gives the impression of travelling through light itself, as if wading through quicksilver.

In the late afternoon the sun's glare begins to wane, trickling upon the land like liquid caramel. There is an ethereal quality about this hour. An eerie silence descends, a betwixt and between-ness, as in a lull before battle.

Without any warning, the light suddenly vanishes, as if someone has switched off the sky. The power of this darkness is absolute. It orders the sun to leave. Its trillion firefly stars stand to attention. It enfolds and engulfs like a tyrant. As the temperature falls, frost veils still, glistening creatures. In bushes it hangs on leaves like spun sugar.

At that time I was reminded of how vulnerable I was, comforted by those creatures of the sky that looked down like light maps – Aquila, whose wings raised him over the mountains, and, dazzling like a diamond, Venus; Polaris, 'the star that does not move', born, it was said, of the sun, abandoned by his father, and who sought sanctuary with his mother, the moon; Indosa, the star that pulls the night across the sky, that we know in the West as Sirius, a light in the darkness for all those seeking refuge; and the *shat ihedd*, or the daughters of the night, the wise ladies who watch over us and guide us to safety.

Just before dawn is the quietest hour, when the day is readying itself to be born. Shadows creep from the rocks like dark branches, and the wind's cry becomes pleading, the wailings urgent, stirring the fine grit and lifting it in small gusts, wiping away the tales of the night written in the sand and cleansing the footprints of the creatures that had entered into battle there, now returned to their secret refuges. At last, calming to a breeze, the air whistles an umworldy song, whispering through the dips and crevices of the land in lullaby rhythms.

The first rays push up from the plateau, shifting the blues that play in the sky before sunrise. With the rising sun, tumbleweed flits aimlessly through the camp in feathery bundles, buffeting the half-withered shrubs like lost souls. There is an honesty about this time, a purity.

The luminous globe edges above the horizon and the light crosses the land, illuminating small details – a red ant sitting on a shimmery, mother-of-pearl pebble, a prickle of green on orange sand.

As the men performed their *rakas*, I wondered if God would answer their prayers when He had ignored mine.

The sun does not take breaks

Tarfuk tebbedei

In the midst of an electronically shrinking planet, deserts are expanding rapidly. The future looks hotter, drier and brighter. The Sahara is not even the world's largest desert, but it covers approximately eight per cent of the earth's land area, ample space to fit the entire United States of America with a few thousand square miles left over.

In the West, we crave the sun. To us it seems hardly surprising that the ancient Greeks worshipped Helios, the Zoroastrians its fire, Ahura Mazda. We worship it too. In the Middle East there is too much of it. The uninhabited settlements are built the Islamic way, just as the Prophet Mohammad decreed, without windows looking out as if, out there, beyond the walls, the only vision is tragedy. The blazing inferno that ripens crops and brings life feels like an assassin as much as a friend.

I was about to experience its full-on intensity.

Day three began rather murkily, as often happens after insomnia-fuelled nights, when we fall into a deep sleep and wake before dawn with a start, bleary and disoriented. I crawled out of my tent just as the stars were fading and a glimmer was spreading across the cobalt.

As the sky brightened, shapes slowly came into focus, their round, blurred edges hardening. I recognised these shapes. They were my clothes.

Trousers, scarves and shirts lay strewn across the ground like confetti. The sleeve of my brand new cashmere sweater was smouldering over what remained of the fire, and a pair of shorts dangled precariously from a tamarisk branch. Beside my empty parachute bag a cloud of flies feasted on some baklava.

The camels had disappeared.

'Fleabag!' I cried at the top of my voice. 'Fleabaaaaag!' It made no difference – although it did have the advantage of waking a distinctly groggy Samir.

'It doesn't help, shouting out names,' he said sleepily, pulling on his rubber sandals. 'Camels are not like your cowardly politicians.'

'How do you mean?' I grabbed my shorts and clutched them behind my back.

'Everyone knows your politicians are like your dogs.

I didn't find it funny. The thought of becoming embroiled in yet another political discussion so early in the day felt unbearable. I decided to stay silent. In Westminster they might have called it pragmatism.

In the bowels of his tent, Suleyman was stirring. So much for sleeping under the stars. But as he emerged, *chèche* loosely wrapped, still doing up his trousers, he was certainly in touch with nature.

'First desert lesson,' he said drowsily. 'Take it easy.'

This seemed a little rich considering we were in the middle of the desert, clothes half-missing, with no proper map and no back-up truck, facing a day that promised to be hotter than Hades without any means of transportation, not to mention the bandits and terrorists.

But Suleyman didn't seem bothered at all. He glanced around. 'Jackals,' he shrugged. 'The usual.'

Stretching again, he started off into the distance, from time to time casually casting an eye over the dark droppings sprinkled liberally across the dust and humming softly like a bumble bee. Behind him, Samir, equally unconcerned, took off at a similarly slow pace armed with a bundle of sticky green foliage, the irresistible bait to camel taste buds.

'Are you sure we're going in the right direction? They could be anywhere,' I called after him, and he swung around, stroking his chin as if the action would draw out some ancient piece of wisdom.

'Camels are like women – predictable,' he grinned.

That old chestnut, I thought to myself. He was just like his father. He was winding me up.

I wrapped the loose tail of the fabric around my head, covered my face up to my eyes, blinking away the showers of sand blown up by the vagrant wind.

Tracking camels is a devilish process. In theory there are toe marks and droppings to follow, but to me the marks appeared as faint splodges that ran around and over each other in ever-decreasing circles. Every single pattern on the ground looked like a camel print.

I examined the horizon and saw beige. Dunes looked like standing camels. Swaying branches were camel tails. Rocks were sitting camels. In the sky, fluffy hump-shaped, camel-hued clouds floated.

Up ahead, Suleyman had already read the toe prints as if they were words written in the pages of a book. I realised I should never have doubted him. From babyhood Tuareg boys and girls know how to recognise the footprints of each camel in a group.

Suleyman, a seasoned professional, could tell the sex, when it had last been watered. The depth of the track indicated whether a camel had a rider. If the prints showed the impression of loose skin, the nomad knew it had come from the sands. If smooth, it had come from gravel, which made the pads hard.

Veils around our cheeks, Samir and I followed behind him along a ridge that seemed to go in a circle, then, at last, to behind a low rock cluster. We snuck up in silence and peered down.

There they were, all five of them, nibbling at some shrubs without a care in the world. They caught our scent, looked back with that disdainful look camels adopt, and sauntered off, splitting up in different directions.

Samir clambered down towards them. He crept quietly towards Usem, the ringleader.

But Usem and Agizul, the two large bulls were close allies. So adept were they at avoiding retrieval, I could swear they were in league, conferring with their deep voices so as to make it as difficult as possible to catch them. Winaruz, the young bull, was learning from his elders.

When Samir reached Usem, he patted his flank. Usem dropped his head, but as Samir made a grab for his ear, he was forced to let go again. The big bull was playing hard to get – and he was setting a fine example.

Winaruz advanced, perhaps driven by curiosity. Samir managed to slip a rope around his leg, then made another attempt to grab Usem's ear. But almost immediately he was forced to let go again. Winaruz turned away and Samir was left suspended between the two animals, one arm bent backwards, while Agizul and Tlatig screamed hysterically.

Twenty minutes later, back in camp, Suleyman clattered around, unearthing kitchen utensils and shovelling tea into a tin pot. He remained philosophical. When it came to camels, he whispered, you had to have the tactics of a chameleon stalking an insect.

'We are going to do fourteen or fifteen kilometres today,' announced Samir confidently. 'Conditions are excellent.' He sniffed, tested his lungs and coughed. 'Good, clean desert air,' he trilled, adding an enormous lump of sugar. 'Perfect for Fleabag.' He added yet another lump.

'Wouldn't it be better to let her lead?' I gasped, as the wind blew sand into my face.

Suleyman looked horrified. He rubbed his forehead and turned to Samir. 'Foreign women. Tricky as camels.'

I glanced at Fleabag, who issued a no-comment snort, adopting the look of someone about to visit the dentist, while the other camels adopted their standard 'I've-seen-it-all-before' expressions.

'Agh,' muttered Suleyman, turning again to Samir as if his point had been made.

Samir shrugged his shoulders.

Achy and shattered, an hour or so later we had made a truce with our little *amagur*, as we now called them. They still complained bitterly as they stood up. Then, as if to gain maximum sympathy, Winaruz resisted, baring his teeth and roaring, swinging his neck around as if taking a good look at who was to blame for his unnecessary burden. At last, they conferred again, as if to say, 'They might have won the battle, but this is *war*.'

We moved off towards a vast empty landscape, the mountains like the edge of a saw along the horizon – two nomads, five camels like giant tortoises with their homes on their backs and a bewildered stranger.

※ ※ ※

The sun climbed higher, the shadows grew shorter. The light turned up the heat dial. I could hear the whisper of the wind and smell the charred brown-sugar smell of the baking desert sand. The air I breathed through a thin veil could have issued from the mouth of a kiln. I thought we were going to be walking during the cooler hours. The only so-called cooler hours were freezing.

Sweating profusely, I placed one weary foot after the other, the burnt sand penetrating the soles of my shoes and scorching my feet. Rocks tinted silver by the sun took on the shape of an aeroplane. I imagined that it was probably a vulture.

The interpretation of the desert in Western art seemed preposterous in the face of the reality. I recalled Vincent Wallace's opera *The Desert Flower*, and Puccini's *Manon Lescaut* – where Manon dies of thirst and her lover, des Grieux, falls across her body, unconscious and with grief – and could think only of how they romanticized the truth. The reality was ugly – a matter of sweat, sore feet and aching muscles.

Less than half a kilometre on, Fleabag whined pitifully. I kissed and stroked her. I sneaked her cinnamon biscuits. 'What is it, princess?' I whispered in her ear. 'Do you want to go back, like I do?'

At this she let out a call that sounded a little like a cow on heat and proceeded to wee over her back legs enough liquid to make a stream. She turned up her nose. She weed again, this time a river.

I tried speaking in Arabic. She lifted her nose. She let out her special bellow, the radio version, which sounded like vomiting, without the repeats. As her humped backing singers joined in, I longed to turn down the volume.

Fleabag took offence. She spat.

We hiked wearily on to sit out the midday furnace in Afousses, and, as we rested our limbs, the camels cooled themselves by lying down and bathing in dust, reminding us once again in their dissonant a cappella that they had not forgotten their morning battle.

Stinking already, I washed in half a cup of water and let Samir take over. This made Fleabag very happy. A look of suffering common to all tired, lovesick camels came over her as he swirled around, robe flowing, crossing the sands towards her like a black-sailed yacht at sea. Then she began her plaintive *koo-wee* throat noises, as if to say, 'I don't need to visit the *marabout*. I already have my *baraka*. It is you.'

I left them alone with what I hoped was good grace, to enjoy their *anaiwak* time together.

I'm in the fire

Ennehreyer temsi

'You have no memory, that is why you cannot recite the Qur'an,' snapped Suleyman, wiping his dripping nose on his tatty sleeve.

Samir leapt to his feet. '*Alhin!* Evil ghost!'

Suleyman leapt to his. '*Amenuhug!* Selfish man!'

'*Segi!* Go away!'

'*Tegi! Mouss!* You go away!'

Suleyman strode furiously off into the wilderness, spitting. '*Iqqed-kai yalla dar Temsi...* God is going to fry you in hell...'

Samir stomped crossly towards his tent in the opposite direction. '*Tuer-kai tilrant ta teggaret eyhiod...* The misery of the donkey will come to you...'

Timidly, I called out goodnight into the ether, crawled wearily into my tent and closed the flaps, assuming it was that typical male leader-of-the-pack instinct that surfaces in the presence of a lone member of the opposite sex.

Lying in my lumpy sleeping bag, wriggling to make a body-sized dent in the hard mattress of the desert floor, I felt glad day four was over. Not for the first time had Samir repeated verses from the Qur'an that he knew off by heart, giving himself marks out of ten, all of which were high. His father had awarded him paltry ones and twos.

It was not just the Qur'an that divided them. Where to set down camp proved a continuing subject of debate. Suleyman insisted that, according to desert lore, we should never pitch our tents in a dried-out riverbed in case of a flash flood, while Samir argued that the spots Suleyman chose were too stony or exposed, insisting we set up near the fire to discourage mosquitoes. Already there was a raft of missing objects, equipment mislaid and essentials forgotten. Neither of them mentioned the jackals.

In the morning they draped blankets around their shoulders and ate breakfast in silence. In the evening they squabbled in whispers. Suleyman sang to the camels, Samir stuffed rags in his ears in response, and afterwards they argued about whose turn it was to do the dishes. There were disputes about the route, the well locations, plants, the camels and the cooking. Minor arguments between the two flared into raised fists on more than one occasion, until finally they united against the greatest foe of all – woman.

Already, the laws were in pieces. Suleyman had broken first. He just couldn't be bothered when it came to the toilet arrangements, returning to camp with his trousers not done up properly.

Samir, on the other hand, was possessed of that youthful male habit of being unable to stop messing around. Often I caught him staring at a picture he kept in his pocket, which he would surreptitiously take out when he thought no one was looking and which he seemed determined to hide from me, snatching it back immediately if I asked about it. It was hard to see why he was embarrassed. The woman wasn't even naked. There was a diaphanous cloth draped over the pertinent crotch area, and even that was concealed by a well-worn crease.

He maintained that the picture reminded him of Paradise – the skin pale as a *houri's*, dark eyes wide and innocent as a gazelle's. Once he would have thought such a picture unacceptable, but having met me, he had been forced to modernize his opinions.

The camels did things at their own pace, where and when they felt like it. Usem was the ringleader. You could push him so far, but he would always draw the line, pausing at frequent intervals, showing his disapproval by bellowing in a bout of triumphant peeing, while Agizul protested by dribbling incontinently. The two largest bulls had the process of evasion totally worked out and were masters at avoiding retrieval.

Fleabag learned from them quickly, enjoying playing hard to get, particularly with Samir, while I hung around like a gooseberry. She stalled frequently, but issuing any discipline only proved counterproductive, inviting even stranger noises.

Her vocabulary was expanding rapidly. Low, gutteral groans were powerful reminders of her past and required sympathy. Willowy peals were to alert me to *djinn* lurking in the thorn bushes. High vibrato to show excitement was reserved for wide, open pistes. Then she could really let rip. I feared now that in helping her I had spoiled her.

If I had been anticipating a revelation or a release, I had to accept that nothing particularly transformational was happening. I was the same inadequate soul, empty of things, comforts and people. Bruce Chatwin once wrote that a dervish wandered the earth because the act of walking dissolved the attachments of this world. His aim was to become a dead man walking, his feet rooted, his spirit in heaven. I am not sure where my spirit was at this stage, but I certainly felt dead.

In reality, we were all exhausted. Suleyman was having breathing difficulties. Samir's legs were aching and my entire body was packing up. The copious consumption of dates was disagreeing with my system and I frequently had to head off, clutching small shovel, loo paper and a box of matches, and hike for England to catch back up with the group. Blisters were appearing on my feet, I dreamed strange lucid dreams that left me feeling thirsty and confused, and I had developed an unhealthy obsession with jackals. With a fair wind I reckoned I would last another week. The others gave me less, which was unfortunate, because we were in such a remote spot that it would take twice that to get out of there.

As Suleyman put it, 'Allah loves us. That's why he gives us problems.'

The way I put it, 'If He loved us a little bit more, He'd give us a few less.'

Tensions abated amid the daily welter of detail and frustrations, and arguments were adjusted into terms such as 'debates', 'challenges' and 'discussions'. Suleyman made tea of the *tegar*, a particularly tough wood, for our souls. The two men prayed to Allah for deliverance and we pressed on, our spirits buoyed up by the prospect of a *baraka*, which now, more than ever, was sorely needed.

One branch does not make a goat pen

Azal iyan war iggit afarag

'Moving' and 'on' are two small, apparently insignificant words, but when you put them together they can seem daunting. 'You must move on.' When someone says this to us after a break-up, usually accompanied by alcohol, it feels like a reflex. We nod knowingly.

'Yes, I know,' we say, and take another sip, for courage. The advice is always well-meant, although some might say it is a banal cliché, issued to those of us in pain by those who have our interests at heart, but who can no longer bear witnessing that pain.

For the first time in years, I was looking forward to moving on that fifth day. I could pack up my tent in a matter of minutes by now. My troubled past had faded. It was concealed by a smog, like all the other dangers.

The haze that hung over the ground was not of water droplets, but of dust particles. It lifted in some patches. It covered my skin with a dry film. It seeped into my flesh. It clouded my judgement.

How we delude ourselves with our ideals, our visions of veiled Tuareg as brave warriors mounted on horse- and camelback, magnificent in their indigo robes and *tagelmust*, feet shod in leather sandals. Not only the desert had been stripped of its veneer.

The rose-tinted spectacles lay trampled into splinters, their lenses cracked by bickering and sloppy standards. Reciting poetry and telling tales of fearless warriors and heroic deeds just didn't work any more.

And yet, huddled in the cold dawn air, it felt simultaneously as if there was an intimacy in conflict. Respect involves distance.

Suleyman and Samir had said their morning prayers regardless. As they cast cursory looks in my direction, I wondered if they had been praying for my soul again.

We hunched in our blankets, sipping tea and eating *makroud* biscuits, and the light became watery green across the horizon. The lifting sun brought with it a new sense of determination. Both nomads vowed upon the Qur'an that the arguments were behind us. In future, we would work together as a team.

Father and son listened keenly as I recounted Alexandre Dumas's story of three men who rode large horses and defended innocent women. They identified with it. And when I told them how Athos, Porthos and Aramis became faithful friends with d'Artagnan and how they kept each other going, they said it was *ummah*, or brotherhood.

'Do you have good friends, Samir?' I asked.

He thought hard for a while, 'Everyone wants a good friend, but no one wants to be one. What about you?'

'I think friendship is very important,' I said, thinking of the telephone that had not rung as I was losing my home.

At that moment, Fleabag turned her head.

George Eliot must have been deluded when she said, 'Animals are such agreeable friends. They ask no questions, they pass no criticisms.'

'All for one…' Suleyman tasted the words. 'This writer, Dumas, he was a Muslim?'

'Quite possibly,' I replied, and he seemed pleased, but it was only when I mentioned his penchant for exotic beards and advanced swordplay that the idea seemed to lift them. We had to work together as a team, they said, because all nomads knew only too well, one branch did not make a goat pen. Without fuss or fighting we packed the camels. Samir looked over the ground to make sure we had left nothing behind and kicked out the fire. There he stood, like a young Hermes, lost in his own world, seeking to prove himself to his father, like a pupil with his mentor, with the due respect that underpinned all disagreements.

The next sound I heard was Suleyman peeing, too close by, behind a rock that was too small to hide him.

We began on again across the plateau, swaying galleons on a desert sea, buoyed up by forced optimism and blisters. Heads alert, our five dromedaries seemed to understand everything. They were experiencing their own solidarity. I even imagined they were enjoying what Suleyman politely described as our lively exchanges.

Walking across the smooth streams of sand often felt more like treading water. Sometimes the *piste* ate its way through three-metre-high drifts of sand. At other points the plain lay open to view, strewn with rock clusters. Mountain ranges broke the skyline in all directions: the Immidir and Tedefest to the east, and Ahmet to the west, measuring their existence in millennia.

Closer up, other, smaller mountains poked out among the drifts. I thought I was seeing camels, but I was not. Each cairn stood on its own, like an upturned pudding, an enclosure for the protection of kid goats, strategically placed along well-worn camel tracks, although the men knew them as sanctuaries for the *djinn*.

It wasn't the *djinn* or what lay at the end of the road that scared me as much as the road itself. That and the noxious, papery fumes that rose from the columns of the industrial plants that wrinkled and prickled my skin as I thought of them. No one discussed those, of course. They ignored the canker of commercial reality and talked only of majesty. They blanked out those things from which they wished to remain blind. It was much easier to skim over them, to pretend. Underneath, nothing had changed. I was just as blinkered as ever.

Samir dropped back sometimes to walk behind me, his advice subtle but kind, his eyes always one step ahead. When I glanced over my shoulder, he was already looking at me. He was unaware of his charm. Sometimes he formed his young face into the wrinkled countenance of his father and it was difficult to tell them apart, so subtly they mirrored each other in stature and gesture.

They continued to bicker, of course, their voices as shrill as the jackals that stalked our nights and whose calls as Samir liked to point out, were not as rasping as his father's singing.

When I asked questions, about the route or what they thought about what was happening in the world, the two men simply closed ranks.

Shakespeare invented the word 'moving', and now I wondered if he knew what he was letting us in for. Perhaps, I started to think, we were not so much 'moving on' as 'moving through'. Moving on implies a direct, straight route, one-dimensional. In our case it was like zigzagging down a ski slalom.

If Rhaicha and Amina had been with us, I was sure it would have been different. Women are complex, but they tend to be the healers of society, whatever their culture.

Samir expressed his thoughts in enigmatic utterances: 'Westerners absorb the shortcomings of their leaders' and, by way of a slight variation, 'Westerners cannot be held responsible, because they are blind.'

Indeed, these sentences were the only ones he uttered,

as if he intended them to remain hanging in the air. His father, mulberry eyes set above high cheekbones, slightly open mouth, uttered neither approval nor reproach.

'You mean we have a collective guilt?' I offered the words half-jokingly. I didn't want to believe he was serious. I imagined he was just testing me.

'I think you have to bear responsibility for what has happened in the world.' As he said this, lost in thought, Samir's gaze came to rest upon a point on the horizon.

'Perhaps,' I said. That was all. Then, in the thinly veiled guise of musketeer solidarity, we moved on.

❋ ❋ ❋

We had been under way for an hour when we came across our first checkpoint, manned by a brawny officer in a sweaty uniform that accentuated his bulk. Spotting an opportunity for advancement, he promised to put in a good word for us with his superior to ensure the smooth running of the rest of our journey. 'It is a pleasure, *mes amis*,' he said, waving us through.

The sizeable wodge of dollars merited no showing of paperwork. Not one of the officers questioned or stopped us along the narrow track that twisted through the compound, past the metal gate and the windowless solitary confinement cell within. Only the wavering shadows loitered as disconcertingly as the prickly desert grasses.

But best behaviour was obligatory with the authorities. Cigarettes were always stubbed out and an air of gravitas adopted. Further down the track more men approached, apparently concerned for my safety. As usual, Samir did the talking. Once they had determined that I was neither a spy nor a terrorist, their curiosity was satisfied and we were all waved through, the inevitable conclusion being drawn – that the only danger I posed was to myself.

Could the benevolent hand of fate be smiling on us after all? I wondered.

Inevitably it was not. The next checkpoint had not been informed about our journey. Fortunately, Suleyman put in a good word with the security chief. My passport was stamped and we were on our way again. This was due in the main to good luck. Apparently it had rained several weeks earlier, so they had decided to relax their usual formalities.

Fingers carved into the hard, sharp sand, once again the two men prayed, and then again, and now at last they gave special thanks for making them members of the blessed desert people rather than yodelling Arab dogs.

During meditation the dissolving circles of light felt dimmer than before. In my mind's eye I felt compelled towards that strange yet familiar place which was my past. I sought sanctuary in this place. Macbeth understood it. He called it *mortals' chiefest enemy.*

So often we are driven to seek the tightrope across the chasm without truly sensing it. It was easy to feel seduced by the notion of blessing and *baraka,* into thinking we were greater than fate, above chance, but this was a more dangerous highwire than I could have ever imagined, and, not for the first time, a delusion.

Snake!

Taschilt!

'How many camels do you have in your country?'

'Not one.'

The little boy running alongside our caravan delivered his sentences in different languages. He didn't want to beg or sell anything. He was just being friendly. He looked disappointed at my answer.

'Does it rain there?'

'Always.'

'Do you go to school?'

'I used to.'

'What did you learn?'

'A little. And you?'

'Everything.'

He ran off and was soon a fleck among the other flecks, his robe a tiny wing on an endless breeze that vanished over the line of the earth in every direction.

Knowledge is the most dangerous journey. It is like a tree. It is the root of all matter.

'*Ilm*,' nodded Samir. He was staring at me without blinking.

Studying him now, as he paced deliberately alongside Usem, I wondered if I might be falling for him. He appeared so confident and in control that I was lulled into a false feeling of safety.

Under a thin *etafi* tree we settled down for our break. He doodled in Tifinagh. I could see his hands moving with the pen, the slope of his back, the angle of his jaw. He wouldn't say what he was writing. I didn't ask.

Looking at him sideways I felt my interest was visual. What power he held over me was held through the eyes. Only some of this had to do with sex. I had a great affection for him, but it was no more than that. My fractured heart was not ready. Samir was not ready either. Suleyman had lavished upon his eldest care and attention, but where women were concerned he had a great deal to learn.

We had walked into my past and in my memory I held another hand. On that occasion we had strolled with apple blossom arching overhead, the sound of cool water from the edge of a lake burbling in our ears. We had stood in the light falling through the leaves and watched the black swan swimming. We had reached up and touched growing fruits in amazement, sitting below mossy branches. I had opened my book and read out a line.

'Fig trees need no male to bear fruit.'

There is a fig tree in London's St James's Park.

Suleyman was regarding me oddly. Men's faces change with time. They mellow, ripen, they ache.

We were in a twisting *mijbid* in a cracked *oued*. The camels were meandering as quietly as cows coming in for milking. In pole position was Usem. He held his nose in the air, his taut neck poised. Behind him Fleabag's oatmeal faded against taupe, almost a shadow.

Without warning, Winaruz, larger than life, shot out from behind her like a squid, feet thundering. His head was low, neck elongated. Usem screamed. The two camels were at an angle to each other. Winaruz's gut howled. Their necks locked and they whirled and lashed.

The argument had to be settled. Suleyman took his rope. Kicking, wheeling, somehow Usem was soothed. Then, as unexpectedly as it had started, with neither camel hurt, they stopped fighting. There was Fleabag, panting, walking meekly, Usem, tall, proud, victorious, and Winaruz, head bowed and flustered. It wasn't clear what had spooked him, but half an hour later they were friends again, without a bellow or a gurgle.

'Are you sure it's not the rutting season, Samir?'

He shook his head. His face had turned pink. He knew I was just playing with him.

It was mid-morning when he began dropping behind again. Always so sprightly on his feet, he missed his step and stumbled, and I heard him groan.

'Samir? Are you all right?'

He took a few more wobbly steps and half-turned. I hurried over to help him, leaned towards him and his drawn, pinched face looked back. I was convinced he had heatstroke; I knew the signs well by now. As I reached him, he tore away his *chèche* and threw up over a doum bush.

His father caught up. Falling to his knees, Suleyman spoke gently, all arguments and differences drowned and forgotten. In the shade, against a cool, north-facing rock, he opened his goatskin and gave his son water.

Dry and burning as it was, there was not a drop of sweat on Samir's brow. He mumbled something about a blurred place where everything had doubled up, at which his father mumbled back that he had been there on many occasions, in his youth and drinking contraband whisky.

Samir grinned. This looked hopeful.

'*A bu siha,*' he winced. 'Poisonous.'

He ratcheted up his robe and we stared in horror at the bite marks on his leg. There were two dark holes welling with blood.

'Are you going to suck it out?'

Suleyman shot me one of his withering looks. 'You have been watching too many movies.'

'Will he be all right?'

'Inshallah.' The old nomad scanned the sky as if he would find the answer in the endless sheet of turquoise. With open palms, he uttered a prayer from the Qur'an. My satellite phone was dead. His was dead. We were, in his view, in the hands of God. We would observe His will. In Suleyman's eyes everything was certain.

'*Inshallah.*' My voice echoed in the dust.

❋ ❋ ❋

As we talked it through, the task seemed so logical and straightforward.

Number 1: while Suleyman cared for Samir and watched the camels, I would form an advance party.

Number 2: I would inform the authorities of our predicament and they would telephone for assistance.

What could possibly go wrong?

Clutching a compass and a rifle, I headed off. It was hot and hard underfoot. Rocks loomed in shattered blocks with spiky splinters at their bases and soft sand in a lethal combination. Beyond, a cracked riverbed suggested there might once have been rain there. Behind me, a thin line of smoke threaded upwards from the campfire and a white tent that sparkled beneath the great white dome of the sky. Flies landed on my sleeves. I strode. Grit swirled into my eyes. I ran.

I have no idea how long it took me to reach the long, high ridge they called Hell. The hour was measured by the sun's heat and the dryness of my throat. For some time I sat on the sand facing Mecca, nursing my rubbery ankles. Already my water bottle was empty. I remembered law number 10. No, I said to myself. I am not drinking that.

Then I remembered my mission. All that mattered now was getting Samir to a doctor straight away.

Out of breath, hot-cheeked, I was about halfway down the ridge when I noticed that not only had my original footprints disappeared, there were also fresh tracks coming up the slope towards me. I wondered what creature could have made them. At last, concluding that they must have been my own footprints, I felt ridiculous.

About a mile or so off, the thin greyish splodge of the checkpoint we had just come from was visible. Stumbling along the curves of spurs, the going felt smoother, although the checkpoint was less clear from this angle.

The compass wavered uncertainly. I didn't know how it could have happened, but I must have walked in a circle. Only five minutes ago I had been so confident.

A falcon turned above me. It swung low, its curled yellow talons reaching for the rock. Settling its slender body, the long, barred tail and blunt-ended wings, as it landed before me, I saw it was a wren. Bird and woman regarded each other, heads cocked as if to ask one another if we were the only females in this godforsaken place.

Moments later, the other bird flew off, spinning in thin spirals. She knew freedom. She had nothing to prove.

Starting off again, I avoided the row of shrubs with their dark red berries, as if blood-filled like the flies that circled them. The sand underfoot was deep, the loss of balance inevitable. A heat haze, the *aghmam,* was obscuring the checkpoint. There were impressions as I went down – the stench of carrion mingled with wild jasmine, a giant ant, the metallic glare of the sun.

Two hundred yards on, the path opened out, curving left and then right. My chest swelled with optimism.

The soldier, clean-shaven, with dull eyes that must have

seen everything and nothing, didn't seem to notice my pee-smelling face, or at least he said nothing. He wasn't unsympathetic when I explained, but the bribe we had given earlier had had little impact. Instead, it was the Saudi falconers who were passing at the same time, intrigued by the unexpected appearance of a lone Western woman babbling disjointed Arabic, who proved to be my saviours.

They were hunting desert hawks in four-wheel-drive vehicles, their white robes clean as freshly laundered bed sheets, the cotton bands of their headdresses belying their foreignness just as markedly as my own. I explained the emergency and they telephoned for a rescue vehicle. They sped off, angels without wings, into a seamless vacuum.

Perhaps Allah was a benevolent God after all.

The soldier walked back with me, and his dismissive, condescending expression, my protracted journey by foot covered in minutes by taking the direct path.

He exchanged a few words with Suleyman and left, without asking how our small party came to be crossing the region. Word travelled fast in the desert. That bribe had signalled our arrival.

It was dusk by the time the truck drew up and we were driven out into the void. By then it was not just Samir who needed medication – we all did. I remember little about the journey. There was sand streaming the bonnet, smoke panting from the engine and patches dancing like disoriented birds in the dim light of the headlamps.

Samir, sweating, head heavy against my shoulder, was unconscious; Suleyman remained cool-headed. 'Don't give up now,' I remember him saying. 'We'll be in Djanet by suppertime.'

There was the crackle of rubber on dust, then nothing.

The flies are on the wall

Iltay ess ayalla

The moon teaches us that things are almost never as we assume them to be. Although outwardly moonlight appears blue and silvery, it is neither. It just seems that way because of the sensitivity of the eye and its tendency towards the blue end of the colour spectrum at low illumination levels. Its glow consists mostly of sunlight, starlight and earthlight.

When I woke I had no idea where I was. The twilight was whimsical, deceptive. I could not see anything clearly. I did not know Djanet.

It took a while for my eyes to become accustomed to the shadows, but the darkness soon dissolved. Objects and buildings began to glisten.

Around us lay a maze of streets. A few pathways led back to the main road. Others twisted off into dead ends. Rumour had it that this was to fox the *djinn* that wandered at night, preying upon the innocents. I wondered who else might be lurking there. The monsters in my mind were real, not spirits.

The white truck that delivered us glistened in the half-light. It was open at the back, and the camels sat quietly, heads and necks sticking up like flowers. Even as the brakes screeched, there was no sound from them, as if instead of being sedated, they too were in shock.

The driver climbed out first. I couldn't see his face, so I couldn't read it. Just his heavy, awkward frame and thick musk aftershave stood out. A deal was struck, oaths sworn upon the Qur'an. Only then did Samir open his eyes.

Somehow we managed to get him out. He could still walk. Before us, the oblique mass of a building felt more like an office than a house. It didn't seem like a hotel and I didn't think it was one.

Suleyman called from the doorway. 'Ahmed?'

A gruff male voice answered. '*Ma kainsh. Shkoon?* He's out. Who's there?'

The door opened slowly and a diminutive, wiry man peered out uneasily. After the usual greetings, Suleyman explained our predicament.

'Ahmed is not here,' replied the man, warming the palms of his hands. He was sorry to hear Samir was unwell. He couldn't help mentioning that he kept a few coffins ready in the basement.

Suleyman bowed. He left us then, a spirit vanishing into the darkness to join the other dark spirits that lurked there. He didn't say where he was going and I didn't ask. Nor did he mention Ahmed again, whoever he was.

The small man, who was called Mahmoud, spoke French without 'vh' or 'z'. He was, he said, from Mali. He apologized for the insects, as if he was addressing them personally. 'They grow very large here,' he said, slyly closing the door behind us.

Taking timid steps, we climbed the steep concrete staircase, following him to the first floor and into a murky corridor where, moving along to room number twelve, we paused. The dry, hollow smell grew more acrid. A mattress grew out of the gloom.

Samir stepped in. 'I just need time to rest,' he said, and stumbled to the narrow bed.

It was with the greatest reluctance that I left him.

Room number seventeen seemed an equally dubious destination. '*Merci,*' I said, and Mahmoud scuttled off.

Ineptly, I wrestled with my clothes, placed my sleeping bag on the bed and lay down. Sleep came erratically, my thoughts juggling unease, doubt and fear. Occasionally, the headlights of a passing vehicle lit the window, flashing first on one wall, then moving on to the next, where the light illuminated the cracked plaster and shone on the backs of resting cockroaches. The flowery-patterned duvet beneath me crinkled its static in my fingers.

Sounds carried on the midnight air: the low, angry buzz of a mosquito, voices drifting from the doorway, the falsetto of mopeds a familiar serenade, their rhythm like the words of the *shahada*, slow and steady. It was meant to bring God as close, as the Qur'an says, 'as the vein in your neck', but he felt more distant now than ever.

When I woke, the room, so icy at night, was an oven. My legs were numb and moving them made the muscles flinch. I struggled to sitting position, reached for the little pot in my pocket and rubbed the foul-smelling black paste Suleyman had given me into my charred, blistered soles. He was right. It did help.

Further along the corridor dawn had broken long ago. A square of golden light fell through the open door to room twelve. The tall, gaunt man sat away from the bed where a pale outline lay, dark circles under his closed eyes. Samir was still sleeping.

Suleyman stood up unsteadily, rubbing his eyes, still somehow managing a civil 'Good morning'. The doctor had come very late and had administered an antidote. He suspected Samir had been bitten by a sand viper.

'How is he?' I glanced at the limp form lying immobile on the bed.

'He is very lucky. It's a dry bite.'

'Will he be all right?'

'*Yuren-as Messiner tazidirt.* God gives us patience.'

The air conditioning began exhaling a damp, muggy waft while emitting a loud rattle. Samir did not flinch. He lay half-sleeping, stirring occasionally to sip a little water. Sometimes, his fingers moved slightly, but his eyelids remained shut, his body in the bed so shallow that the mound was as slight as an old grave. Once, raising himself on his elbows, he looked anxiously around and murmured that the light was too strong.

There was little we could do apart from sit with him. His father visited often, leaving at intervals to check on the camels, who had been installed in a nearby *palmerie*.

Suleyman treated his son according to Tuareg tradition, with sap of the *alkhad*, a plant with small gourds like tiny melons, and with the crushed roots of the *moringa*. In addition, he gave Samir what he called tonics to abate the *tenede*, the poison.

There was little point in challenging him. As he mixed, pounded and blended, no doubt crossed my mind as it had done previously. I trusted that he knew what he was doing. He reminded me of a master bartender I knew in Arosa in the Swiss Alps where, as a student, I once worked as a cocktail waitress.

I consoled myself with sterilised water that tasted of bleach. I watched the speckles of dust float in the light shafts. I whispered words, 'Help him. Please. No camel or *marabout* is worth Samir's life.'

Samir seemed to recognize my voice as he dropped back into the wells of fevered sleep. He muttered in his dreams about a beautiful *oued* where some goats wandered, although they were not goats, but strange fluorescent dogs with turbans. The dogs became monsters. They reminded him of his grandmother.

For some reason, Suleyman didn't think there was anything unusual about that image.

I wondered what exactly was in the concoction he had given his son. The thought occurred that Samir might have been drunk. His father denied it, of course. He stood in the light of the window, gazing into the distance as if imagining his freedom. As he coughed painfully from time to time, I worried he was smoking too much.

A deep sadness welled up inside me. The green seeped from the distant palms and the orange sun died. I decided to leave them.

☾ ☾ ☾

There comes a stage in all developing situations where time and energy dovetail perfectly. A critical point occurs at which a conscious decision must be made. We drink a glass of wine, and taking a glass of water becomes crucial to avert a hangover. We begin a relationship, and unless a conscious effort is made, somehow things seem to dwindle. A crunch point becomes inevitable.

People get engaged at their critical point, or married, or have a baby. Some critical points are – literally – critical. Other journeys simply end.

There was no way I could contemplate tomorrow or the next day, or even the day after that. Today was enough. Our journey was drawing to its close. I felt responsible for what had happened and, if I could, I wanted to help. Uselessly, powerlessly, I fretted about all the camels. No matter how adequately Suleyman had it covered, now I had only made it worse for Fleabag. I could hear her raucous, scrambled cry in my head. I could touch her insecurity. But at least she was not alone and she was safe.

With my mooncrater feet and lightbulb nose, I searched for distractions. Further investigation inside the building unearthed a sombre world beyond the familiar route to my room. A labyrinth of corridors lay in which to lose bearings, the only light penetrating the interior a dim blue haze filtering through the courtyard windows and the faint glow of a gas lamp.

A few steps revealed a well-trodden staircase leading to another dingy passage, but the route was blocked by a uniformed man slumped in the corridor. An empty vodka bottle rolled beside him and a scent of nail varnish remover lingered on the air.

On now, after another turn in the opposite direction, towards an open door, where from all directions flapped shouting voices, and where a half-dressed toddler was crawling. I was just about to turn back when there was a tap on my shoulder. The woman who begged me to sit down must have been no more than twenty.

Sitting on the bed in her room, she spoke of her life, her fat fingers flying around swatting flies, her lipstick mouth apart from her real one. I had seen that look many times. It was the look of disillusionment. It carried no desire, not even authority, just a world-weariness; but there were also touches of exuberance – the kohl-rimmed eyes, the bright-red nail polish, the bold patterns of her skirts, even the way her curves of flesh gathered in soft folds around her midriff, a stark contrast to the cacophony of running engines and motorbike horns.

She earned her living by servicing the soldiers. She looked after them and they looked after her. In return she was given accommodation. It was a profitable business, and there was no other way she could take care of her young son and elderly grandmother.

'Do you seek love?' she asked after a while. Her face looked tired, her thick lips blotted of their lipstick, her dark skin covered with a patina of grease. It was the face of experience. She knew men all right – how to please them and how to manage their expectations. She controlled her heart, if not theirs, and for this she was much wiser than I.

'No, but I would like to understand it better,' I said. It was as good an answer as I could muster. I recalled my own failed love, with its stifled hopes and trampled dreams.

What is it, anyway, this romantic notion of love that we cling on to, that allows us to believe against all odds that we will find true happiness?

It might be argued that love in the West is a sugary-sweet bubble of everything perfect that we are certain as adults we will never be able to attain. Valentine's Day notions do not represent real love, that which is moulded and crafted in the furnace of sacrifice, compromise and acceptance. And they are a world apart from a continent where the scourge of Aids is no less prevalent for the lack of hygiene.

Despite the rich tradition of erotic Arabic literature, promiscuity is generally regarded as a grave abuse of Allah's intentions under Islam. Satan is depicted in the Qur'an as 'the insidious tempter who whispers in the hearts of men'. In reality, the fine line between rampant polygamy and unbridled promiscuity is rather less defined.

Prostitution is banned throughout most of the Muslim world. It stems from way back, before even the advent of Islam, when it was more obvious and widespread. Despite Muhammad's condemnation of it, there is not a single Muslim town of any importance without a brothel.

'Love is easy.' The young woman was taking long drags on her Marlboro.

'Do you actually mean love?' I said. I was overcome by a sense of futility. It was hard not to wonder how she, of all women, could still believe in it.

'You question me because I am Muslim.' She scanned my face, searching there for a disapproval I imagined she had seen in others.

'I mean, you live surrounded by Muslims,' I said. 'It must be complicated.'

She nodded. Lowering her head, she added, 'I have to feed my boy.'

In the speckled light cascading through the doorway she reached out and lifted her son effortlessly, as though he were an air-cushion child, made of desert wind. He was her bubble of happiness, a gift from the Allah who ignored prayers. Arms outstretched, she held him up, high as a balloon, finally lowering him and bouncing him on her knee, and then the teardrop that had been welling in the inner corner of her eye suddenly broke and made its dirty furrow down the side of her nose.

I left, a few dollars lighter and seemingly no nearer to reaching any objective or helpful conclusion, winding my way back through the confused maze of this guesthouse, or, as Samir had called it, this deviant place for sex and for drinking.

It was said there was no love here; but there was a heart, and perhaps that was enough *baraka* for the time being.

I wasted time

Aghshadagh el waq

Samir was sitting up. His eyes were closing. Suddenly they flashed open again. 'Were you worried I might die?' he said.

'I thought you said you were invincible?'

'You came into my bedroom.'

'I was fully dressed!'

However ill he was, I still wasn't going to conform to his stereotype of a Western woman. It would only succeed in reinforcing his prejudices.

Bread had arrived with a murky pond in which a few sad lumps of something indeterminable were lurking, and a gristle-laden dish called *lahm ihalou*, with meat chunks which were red-raw.

I handed him the small glass of camel milk brought up earlier by Mahmoud and he took it, staring into the distance, lost for a second. The serious look hadn't quite gone from his eyes. He was still weak. I noticed now a little fat had been taken from his cheeks, and his throat was stretched and gaunt. I could imagine how he might look when he was older.

Suleyman stood in the light, gazing out of the window with a look of relief that I had not seen on him other than in the company of his camels. He also looked exhausted.

'He will be all right now?' I asked.

The old nomad nodded slowly, as if pondering the question. 'He is strong,' he replied.

'What exactly did you give him?'

He shook his head. His *ten* was not beside him. He seemed lost for words.

'Suleyman?'

He put his *chèche* to his lips. Reaching down, he picked up the bottle from under the bed and handed it to me.

We had packed the bottle labelled alcohol for medicinal purposes and emergencies and I was glad I had not broken into it as I had been tempted to do on a couple of occasions after a hard day's walking. It did look a little like wine, but it certainly was not. It had the air of caustic soda. It tasted worse.

'Let's go and find the camels tomorrow?' Samir's mouth began to broaden as he said the words.

'Yes, tomorrow,' I said.

'And after that: the *marabout*!'

He beamed a grin so wide so that even the little dent in one of his diamond-white lower molars was laid bare. At that moment I felt a tide of tenderness towards him. It must have been the camel milk.

✳ ✳ ✳

Founded by the Tuareg in the Middle Ages and the nominal authority of the Ottomans who left a few fading architectural jewels, Djanet rests on the edge of Tassili Taghit, a high sandstone plateau with rock formations that have the air of Norman castles, and cave paintings that date back to Neolithic times, before the area turned to desert.

In the old days, thousands came to study the paintings and to watch the famous sunsets over the dunes of Ajjer. Today, only a few visitors come. The town is a sleepy oasis, an island in the expanses surrounding it. Even here, in what in the loosest possible terms may be described as civilization, dust permeates all matter. It seeps everywhere. Always it is in a state of flux. It fills and covers the streets where the ground appears scuffed and degraded. Things are either fashioned by it or take on its hue, its smell. Buildings melt into it. Bugs emerge covered in it. Faces are powdered with it. Heat, poverty, thirst and conflict are infused with it. It lurks in hopes and dreams.

People here are not possessed by possessions. Nothing is wasted. Every object is passed on, reused, recycled: a car seat becomes a sofa, an old garment is made into a bag, a chair half-eaten by beetles becomes firewood; a length of rope is coiled and saved, something precious. Hence, there is no trace of rubbish. Everything feels constructed from sand and history, built out of rebellion and resistance to the authorities. Everything lies in the shadow of something.

It is a place of reflections. Over the doors are Qur'anic verses and mirrors, so that you feel as if you are being watched from behind. The formation of the sky is echoed upon the land, in the humps of dunes and mountains, in the curves and cracks of the mosque, in the wrinkles upon faces.

Two days had passed since our crisis. Fleabag and the camels were still resting. Samir was still recovering. I was the one who was feeling restless.

My room was an entomologist's fantasy world, with its squadrons of fat flies, fleas, beetles, ants, spiders and mosquitoes. The squatting toilet was no longer a problem to negotiate, and the difference between Land-Rover and Toyota horns was rapidly becoming my *Mastermind* special subject. With my eyes shut, I could even distinguish petrol from diesel, single-cylinders from two-strokes, mopeds from motorbikes.

But I still didn't know Djanet. Now, as I worked my

way along the street, the hot wind blew sand. Light came down in brilliant sheets, splitting the distant mountains in half, a great strip cracking down on one side of the range, gliding gently over the crags and ridges. Close up, it wobbled over rooftops like jelly.

The rhythm of the street was syncopated, its key dissonant. Men smoking pipes in the shade of doorways noticed as I stepped behind the thin screen of donkeys. Unpolished by Western capitalism and imperialism, their averted gazes told of priorities they were not willing to confide. What did they feel? Who would they tell of my presence? It was impossible to tell.

An elderly man walked by pushing an elderly lady in a wheelbarrow. He glanced back. She glanced back. What were they thinking? Was I a curiosity, or could I become something more valuable?

I felt the wetness of sweat on my skin. I heard the whack of my fortissimo heartbeat.

The resentments people outside Europe feel for us are complex. It is not simply about race or tribe, sovereignty or land rights, or land grabs, although it is all of those things too. Their grievances are as deep and winding as tree roots. They take advantage of our goods, our smartphones and missile-guided weapons systems, but feel deep down in their own hidden boxes that they have been sold a pup.

At the market, lines of people offered small bundles of vegetables, like ancient sibyls who had climbed out of history overcome by the burden of their poverty. Among them the ill or the disabled wove, hobbling on crutches or pushing themselves along on smalltrolleys.

They looked at me imploringly, as if they wanted to leave, as if they wanted me to take them. They longed for better healthcare, security, employment, but to get there required crossing the desert – a journey across a living, burning hell, with only their wits as bargaining chips. They had no money, but they clung to their dignity and their humanity, riches that could never be traded.

Outside the small and empty-looking shops I became aware of the transfixed gazes of veiled Arab women, as if they wanted to press me into their hordes of children, as if they knew something I didn't. One tried to sell me family snapshots. Memories here are cheap, just a dollar apiece. Soon you yourself disappear and become only a memory.

Above the oasis, fading into the rock lay older adobe houses with small windows like black eyes and, at last, a kiosk that doubled up as a *téléboutique*.

My mother was out. The answering machine clicked in with a chirpy message indicating that everything was well with the world, and I poured my heart into the vacuum that didn't know how far my message had travelled to fill it. There was no point in calling Amina to tell her about Samir. She didn't have a telephone.

I bought bread, biscuits and camel milk, and carried them gingerly in a thin plastic bag. I hoped the milk would help Samir. He seemed to like it.

A staple in desert countries for centuries, camel milk is enjoying a reputation as a superfood in the West. It is believed to contain qualities that can help in the treatment of diabetes, cholesterol, irritable bowel syndrome, Crohn's disease and hepatitis, asthma, even autism. As well as being delicious to taste, it holds ten times more iron and three times more vitamin C than cow's milk, as well as having powerful immune-system components, high levels of insulin and unsaturated fatty acids.

It is also a laxative.

Let's unite
Ad nenmenak

'Thank you,' Samir looked better today. His cheeks had a bit of colour. The medicinal alcohol concoction must have done the trick, and it worked wonders as a fly deterrent.

'For getting you into trouble?' I said, still feeling bad.

'You went for help.' His gaze darkened from within and became more insistent, as if wishing in this instant to be understood.

'It was nothing.'

By now I knew which tiles were loose on the stairs. I had ordered a taxi very early and we had descended them expertly together.

'Where is your father?' I asked, and Samir shrugged.

'He's not coming. He has business to attend to.' He had been leaning against the wall and changed his position so as not to put pressure on his right leg.

'Camel business?' I offered him a mint.

'Desert business,' he quipped.

'What sort of desert business?'

He shook his head.

'It's nothing to do with what I said about Syria?'

'No.'

'Or what is happening with Palestine?'

'Afghanistan?'

I ventured the names of the countrie tentatively, and then he ventured his own, familiar words with his usual confidence.

He had that look on his face again, the one he brought

out for promises, but this time there was another, darker ambiguity there, a secret that he was holding from me. It worried me. That snake bite was like a warning.

Then again, it was quite possible that I was just being paranoid. It seemed a pity to disturb the peace when there was so much to be grateful for.

By now we were sitting down, perched upon the cool, shiny white-tiled floor, absentmindedly glancing around like Vladimir and Estragon. Suddenly, Mahmoud appeared from nowhere and, in a very British way, offered us tea. He was a strange Pozzo. He had an improved sense of time.

'What is this place? It doesn't really feel like a hotel.' I had directed the question at Samir, but it was Mahmoud who obliged me with an answer.

'It's the gendarme's residence.' Mahmoud whispered it as if it was confidential information, and scampered off.

We had been sitting for such an eternity that it felt as though even the flies had retired for their siesta. My legs were beginning to go to sleep. My mints were finished. It was a bit like being at a cricket match.

Taxis are a law unto themselves in the desert. When and if a taxi appears depends on the heat and whether a driver is actually prepared to make the trip. The money they earn is always secondary.

Mahmoud hobbled back, a tea service trembling in his shaky hands. He set it down on the floor beside us and handed out the glasses. For a split second, the dates on the little side plate became English strawberries.

'Will you be staying long?' he asked. 'One more day, a week? Indefinitely perhaps?' He looked hopeful.

I held the glass in my fingertips and was about to tell him that, in all honesty, I didn't have a clue, when the door was flung open, the wind gusted and dust blew over us. I stood up and spotted the same elderly man I had seen the day before squeak past with his wheelbarrow, only this time it was empty.

'*Ahlan!* Welcome!' A young man with a hooked nose and a curious stare appeared as if against all odds Godot himself had materialized. 'I am sorry I am late, but I had business to attend to,' he announced

I am not quite sure why, but I assumed that whatever the business was, it was illegal.

We settled the bill with Mahmoud and climbed into an old camper van, three up in the front seat. The engine roared like a freight train as the genie turned the key, and we trundled towards the horizon with the hot air flowing over us in waves.

The concerns I felt at being driven off by a complete stranger in an unknown vehicle faded marginally as we got chatting. He was called Sidik and he came from Niger.

'At least you are not French,' he said, brushing the air as if to brush those colonialists out of the country.

He was a youngish man, short and stocky, with a kind face and thinning hair. He wore a black tracksuit zippered tight around his neck. Ahmed – whoever he was – was a friend of his too, although he hadn't seen him lately either.

I asked him if the French were so bad.

'They are daredevils,' he said. 'They want to prove they can conquer the unconquerable.'

He turned to me, taking his shrewd eyes off the track for what seemed an inordinately long time, and I warmed to him, the alert eyes, the lemony-brown teeth of his smile, his confidence. He rather impressed me with his show-off swerving around the sand drifts. It had a flair that seemed to hint at a taste for adventure.

Indignantly, Samir folded his arms.

Sidik's response was perhaps unsurprising. Any mention of the French provokes an intense reaction in the Sahara. Algerians maintain that the French conquered the desert in the early twentieth century, then tried to understand it afterwards. They say that the French had serious intentions for the desert. They drew lines through it for the purpose of colonial administration.

The Tuareg find this ridiculous, because, as everyone knows, there are no straight lines in the desert.

Sidik was still trying to work out where I was from. He was glad I wasn't Scandinavian either, or, in his eyes, those profiteers who drove down in wrecks they called cars to sell on to the Malians and Nigerians. As far as he was concerned, they were just like those motorcycle riders for whom the desert represented the pinnacle of adventure. They didn't look cool at all in their cycling shorts.

'With your looks,' he said, 'you could be Australian.'

I think he intended it as a compliment – and I took it as one.

We moved away from the thorny issue of Europeans and on to the subject of commerce, taxi-driving being merely something of a hobby in his life, on the basis that there was hardly any call for taxis nowadays because of the decline in tourism. He described himself as a trader in 'rare commodities'. I asked him to explain. Modestly, he called himself someone who sold things. For example, he had some orange juice, if I was interested.

'Niger is very poor, but you can find everything in Algeria,' he said. He looked very pleased with himself.

I asked him if he found business difficult, with the long distances, lack of roads and telecommunications, and non-convertible currencies.

He grinned and said, 'We are all Muslims.'

I smiled back, and Samir cast me a weary look that had nothing to do with his health.

Thinking of the difficulties of desert-driving, I asked Sidik if he ever considered riding camels instead.

He said no. He was not a dreamer. Cameleers still got lost. People took short cuts and died, or their camels ran off, leaving them stranded.

He didn't have to tell me that.

Samir hummed a slightly flat note.

The white heat of day had faded to green. Tall fronds cast dapples of light and shade. Melons nestled in irrigated rows beside snowy almond blossoms and mulberry trees. In the fertile earth, oranges, mulberries and figs lay tangled in lover's knots.

I stepped down from the camper van, stretched my shoulders and bought some of Sidik's orange juice. As he turned to go, I asked him whether the risk of extreme Islam had complicated his work.

Suddenly discombobulated, he said, 'Oh, you're aware of that then.'

Samir still didn't utter a word. The camel milk had worked and he had to go off to the loo.

Sidik disappeared in a cloud of dust. I waved and turned, catching on the air the sweet, familiar stench of camels. So where was the welcoming roar? It was in the distance, about three hundred yards away.

As Samir caught up, I was struck by his sense of purpose. A look of relief came on his thin face, and a brightness.

Some way off a head popped up, furry ears pricked. A grunt of 'Where exactly do you think you've been?' preceded predictable pleas of neglect and protestation. There was no mistaking which particular camel they were coming from.

Then all the camels raised their heads. Soon the tails were going too. Usem began his bass solo. Winaruz made it a duet, while Agizul and Tlatig formed the backing group, their gutteral vibrato joined in perfect synchronicity.

They reminded me of a choir I had once been in at university.

Dates were offered as olive branches, although actual olive twigs might have been just as well received.

Fleabag, the star soprano, took a whole handful. Her scissor jaws sliced and she swallowed. Nuzzling Samir, she wheezed fondly, lowering her head towards him. There. At last she couched.

He knew the benefits of bribery.

Hesitantly, I extended my hand in an effort to make my own peace with her and, as usual, she flicked away her head. But then, as if reconsidering her position, she turned it back again, brushed me gently and swished her tail. With soft bleatings, she frothed a little.

'I think she missed you.'

'No, it is you she missed, Samir.'

'You are mistaken. Just look at her.'

I reached across to put my arms around her neck and planted a little kiss on her. She didn't pull away, and Samir rolled with laughter.

There were three of us in this marriage.

My friends, what have you got to say?
Imidiwan, ma tenam?

Day nine had begun later than usual. I had had a lie-in, Suleyman had returned from 'desert business' and Samir was up and about, messing with his mobile. It still wouldn't work, however much he banged it on the table.

We were sitting in a large smoky room, full of potted cacti. Male representatives of families had come to bond and smoke Nassim cigarettes. They brought livestock with them and bales of cloth from their handcarts. Here they were corralled together, the flip-flopped, the beady-eyed, the disenchanted, the wily. Perching on the child-size plastic chairs, with their mahogany complexions, noble noses and crumpled turbans, they ate deep-fried snacks, drank fake pop and haggled down the price of their coffee.

The first item to arrive was a blubbery kind of stew. Suleyman tucked in. Cheeks bulging, he opted for a polite, 'And how are you today, *ma petite*? Did you sleep well? You can speak freely.'

I thought of my bed, of how, on closer inspection, I had discovered the mattress was resting on a broken slat, the duvet was stuffed with an assortment of old rags and the unwashed nylon cover had a magnetic attraction for flies who appeared to mistake its decorative flowers for real ones. Sleep had not been an option.

'Fine, thank you,' I said, and felt my resolve waver. 'And how are you?'

Samir, who was looking exhausted and still nursing his wound, smiled bravely. 'I'm fine too.'

'Good. We are all fine.' His father glanced up from his gloop and emitted a painful, deep, chest-rattling cough.

Around us an atmosphere of curiosity was bubbling. Hard faces rose from strange draughts and card games to gaze at our unusual threesome.

'Actually, I was wondering if it might be the perfect time to... well, stop.' The sentence faded into uncertainty.

'It would be a pity to do that,' said Samir, gnawing determinedly.

With a sinking feeling, I stared at my own plate as if it was an enemy to be defeated. A heap of congealed rice stared back, at the summit of which perched a small, threatening-looking meatball, grey as the winter sky in Hertfordshire.

I had reached the sandstone flatlands of Tassili Taghit, but also an internal plateau. In the alien vocabulary I understood as few meanings as the legal goods being traded across the borders of the Sahara.

It was frustrating not to have been able to speak to my mother. Somehow, with the aid of two unlikely guides, a camel and some Saudi falconers, I had managed to cover almost forty kilometres of desert. I had had the spirits of solitude knocked out of me by a holy woman and I had made friends with a camel. Was this not the time to give thanks and say goodbye to my friends?

Without much success, I was still searching for the correct phrase when Suleyman pushed his empty plate aside and said, 'Of course, quitting is out of the question.'

'Actually, I was thinking the opposite. This is the perfect time to *go home*.'

He waved away my protestations, along with their incorrect inflexions and bad grammar and a fly. Someone called out a greeting. Suleyman did not respond.

Another unidentifiable dish arrived. Samir peered at it warily and then, as I feared he might, began to tackle it.

'I am homesick.' I glanced around. It was tempting to whine. I was a coward.

'You are woman.' Suleyman made it an explanation.

'You are Tuareg. You respect woman.' I folded my arms.

'You are foreign woman.'

'To me, you are foreign man.'

'This is your home for now.'

What exactly did he mean by that? He didn't know the meaning of the word home. His predisposition was to wander, like his camels.

'We need you. You need us.' Samir had put the phone down on the table.

'He means it is an expensive trip,' said his father, before adding almost in the same breath, 'but good value.'

Immediately I became indignant. 'You mean you need my money to complete it.'

'Yes.' Allah shone in his diverted eyes and became an impatient, exasperating look.

The atmosphere had become awkward and it certainly had something to do with my being a woman, and a foreign one at that, but there were other factors at play, and from my point of view money was not among them.

Perhaps I was being unfair. Individuality is all too often mistaken for arrogance. When alone for long periods it can feel like we are in prison, trapped among our own subjective associations, thought processes and inflexible judgements. It is perhaps inevitable that we react over-hastily in the heat of the moment.

Samir shrugged, as if we were planning a short stroll in the park. 'I would very much like you to continue walking with us,' he said.

'The camel needs you.' His father picked up the phone and began dialling. Somehow he had made it work.

'I won't try anything on,' whispered his son, when he was sure Suleyman was not listening.

This was strange, considering everyone else seemed to be. Looking at Samir closely, it occurred to me that he'd lost something, some mirage I used to think was part of him. He had come to realize that even I, a foreign woman, was human. Or was this simply a performance? Perhaps men should never be told anything about themselves. It only makes them uncomfortable.

'I do not feel safe any more.'

'You can trust us.'

He hadn't changed. I presumed he would be promising to protect me next.

'I will protect you.'

Suleyman put down the phone. 'Don't worry, Ahmed will arrange everything,' he cooed, and picked up the charred remains of a camel tail.

'Who is Ahmed exactly, anyway?'

My gut contracted. I didn't know where all these feelings were coming from. I felt conflicted. Torn between the sensible option – to give up – and yet in my heart longing to trust. I was also suffering from fourteen blisters.

He thought for a moment. 'The fourth musketeer.' He grinned back, chewing. 'And he cooks. Locusts, toasted over the fire, with honey.'

Just as I was about to ask another question he put up his hand to silence me. 'That is it,' he said. 'We will speak of it no more.'

I was still picking at my plate as we turned to the subject of terrorism that up until now we had all been so neatly side-stepping.

The security situation was worsening. A surge of operatives from Isis was causing problems and the area was becoming more isolated. Kabylie was forbidden to Westerners, especially around Boumerdes, Tizi Ouzou and Bouira. The Atakor was out of bounds for the same reason. Rumour had it that terrorists roamed the peaks armed with AK-47s and Kalashnikovs, raiding what little traffic dared to venture there. Was the rumour true?

'There are terrorists,' Samir confessed as if he was one. 'Before terrorists there were bandits and robbers. There are always bad people. It is life.'

'But it is worse now,' I persisted. It was well known that terrorists had links with Tuareg separatists.

His jaw tightened. He counted on his long, slender fingers. 'Corrupt politicians, drug barons, army officials,' he said, and paused before, 'our own Tuareg rebel leaders and arms traders.' Then he said, 'Trust in Allah.' Then, after a long pause, he added, 'Besides, you will be safer with us than making your own way back.'

He was right about that.

Over bread and almonds – those things I had come to cherish as safe foods – Suleyman continued to ignore my objections, adopted his competent face and offered his wisdom.

While good fortune had played a large role in the first stage of our journey, he explained, fate had ironed out the mistakes. There were the insufficiencies of the supplies and the inadequacies of the saddles, but we had, in retrospect, been ill-prepared. Where planning had failed us in the past, the second stretch of the journey would require skill and endurance. This next bit was about stamina.

I wondered what he thought the last bit had needed. It had almost killed me.

As far as I could gather, we had two choices. There was the secure route that involved the usual confrontations with corrupt officials, or the illegal one littered with landmines but which came without the hassle. It wasn't a good choice. Both men seemed quite certain of the direction we should be heading in and, as they were in agreement and I didn't know the terrain, it was impossible to argue.

Suleyman summed it up eloquently: 'We thought it important for you to experience the charming, obliging side of the system, rather than the torture, the corruption and the mysterious disappearances.'

There was something so calm, so reassuring about his low, gravelly voice, and his manner felt so strong that I was momentarily lulled into a delusionary state of well-being. Faith allowed him to go on when the way was unclear and the wells ahead might be dry. Rational thought and logical calculation found no place amid his certainty.

He also spoke of *khamast*, an ancient understanding or contract between the different classes and tribes of Tuareg in the region that in the past entitled the landowner to four-fifths of the harvest. Officially abandoned some years ago because it gave rise to many disputes over land rights, in reality the *khamast* has somehow endured – just like the other ancient, unwritten allegiances.

The *khamast*, without doubt, would save our lives.

If Suleyman believed alienation and subordination had been the destiny of his people, still he could not be quite sure of it. Fate remained to him as mysterious as the sun. For him, life and death were Allah's law. Whereas, where I was concerned, it was more a question of Murphy's.

We retired soon after in a spirit of reconciliation. Somehow we had managed to overcome ourselves, while disentangling the web of adventures we spun in our imaginations, each of us over-egging and underestimating our limitations. We had worked past our critical point.

One by one, the people around us disappeared, silent witnesses to our presence. Those who walked off into the desert grew colourless and became one-dimensional, flimsy paper cut-outs of themselves, eventually vanishing into the wall of dust haze like flat templates. And now they looked as if they had been sculpted out of the sand itself, sinking back into the oblique realm of shade. No more than pale flurries in the wind, they slipped into oblivion. Ahead of them lay only the afterlife, so luminous it was perhaps the one thing to have survived the effect of the sun, the destroyer of all flesh.

It felt as if we were destined to follow them.

And so we began our preparations once again. I still had little notion of what the desert could throw at us, but I was less afraid this time. Ahmed was nowhere to be seen. Like the Kel Essuf and the other spirits of solitude, he had an influence that extended beyond his physical presence.

My heart is dry
Ulh-in ashas

It was getting on for *asr*, the time when your shadow is said to be twice your height and the faithful slip through the heat of the day to prayer. The air was diesel-scented.

Behind us, in the honeyed daylight, a building stood apart from the muddle of other buildings. Sand-encrusted, wind-battered, its high walls, worn like a velveteen rabbit, leaned apologetically, as if to excuse the crumbling plaster. It was the *gendarmerie*, a ramshackle chunk of whitewashed concrete stained orange by dust, and we were on our way to pay our respects.

On the moving ground, the wind left alternating textures, frosted glass reflections and silky slopes. I looked up to see two masked men climbing from an old banger, haggling, arguing, pulling on ropes to test their cargo, as if worried the police might stop them. I was more worried that the masked men would stop us.

As we hurried along, soldiers stared with hard eyes as if they were hiding something. Perhaps it was a truth I kept hidden from myself, a fear that crept with the sand.

A hunched man carried a tiny cat. An old lady picked her way through the drifts, skirts lifted. A car radio blared Bollywood dance music. A woman washed her child's feet in the dribble coming from a street tap. A row of courgettes sizzled in oil on a car bonnet.

I watched two young boys with shaven heads leading a baby camel, before the tableau turned to liquid black as they vanished in the glare. Where everything is other, it is perfectly possible for the surreal to appear normal. The desert is a master conjuror.

What else did it have up its sleeve?

The white-bearded man praying at the roadside muttered the *fatiha* faultlessly, reciting *surah* after *surah* into his open palms. His command of the verses seemed perfect. In a pause between *saqias*, he slowed and halted his recitation. He regarded me with scepticism.

'What religion are you, *Masih?*' he asked as we passed by. It meant a follower of the *Masih* or Messiah.

He knew I was a foreigner, but it would have been an insult to say it to my face, and at least he didn't call me a *kafir* or *kufar*, with its echoes of hellfire and apostasy.

'We are going to see the *marabout.*' Samir said it as if we were going to meet royalty.

'*Marabouts* are *shirk.*' He waved an arm through the air as if at a bothersome mosquito and walked away, muttering something as he went. I didn't quite catch it. Perhaps he was trying to tell me something about the rutting season. Perhaps it was a warning of something more sinister.

※ ※ ※

The black door opened. I took a deep breath.

The warren of dark rooms within was silent and apparently empty except for the metal desks. A few sticks of ancient furniture riddled with woodworm lay about. Insects were multiplying in every corner.

Here, where secrecy was at its peak, hatred would have been easier. With hatred you know where you stand. Hatred is black, metallic, hard, unwavering.

In the gloom I saw a light off to the side, but it was not a candle; it was the beam reflected back off the officer's glasses from the sunlight outside. He didn't need to look at the form. He knew it by heart. It was me he was watching.

Reluctantly, I had learned the way things were done here. As was expected of me, I didn't meet his gaze. I bowed my head automatically. I played my usual role, a largely non-speaking one.

It took more than an hour to fill in the many dusty sheets of foolscap.

He eyed me oddly, like a novelty. A lone Western woman was a very rare species, rarer still that I attempted to communicate in his language, a reason for even greater suspicion. Perhaps he thought I was smuggling dates.

Next he studied Samir, curled his moustache and sucked on a cigarette, wafting out blue ghosts of smoke that highlighted the cobwebs clinging to the motionless sails of the metal fan. He gave Suleyman a quick once-over.

What were our professions, addresses and telephone numbers? Where were our life insurance certificates? How much did we earn? How much property and livestock did we possess? Where were we intending to go, for how long and via which route? What would we do when we reached our destination?

'What is the tribe of your grandmother?'

'The tribe of my grandmother?'

'You have to answer every question.'

'Of course I do.'

'*Vous êtes française?*'

I considered this seriously. I wondered if Huguenot counted.

'Come on. Who are you really?' He looked me in the eye. His left brow lifted.

He was a short man with red eyes and a round beer belly, whose office was stifling, with a fan that didn't work and a high window through which drifted the smell of urine. He lit another cigarette, puffing on it imperiously, randomly selecting from an assortment of ashtrays, all of which were full.

I handed him my passport.

He opened it, glanced at it cursorily and handed it back. The low quality of our dates did nothing to impress him either.

At least he could be assured I wasn't smuggling them after all. I ducked my head. I scribbled my heart out and wondered who read all these forms.

'*Ah, oui, bien sûr, une anglaise,*' he said.

He pulled a face and, as I tucked my passport back into my bag, I thought a few dollar bills would have been a better gift.

'Where is the letter?' He asked it as if his job was a curse and we were responsible for it.

'What letter?'

'The one from your government.'

'No one said we needed one,' countered Samir.

'We have laws,' said the officer.

Not more laws, I thought to myself.

Suleyman coughed. 'No one told us about any laws.'

I surrender, said my eyes, while my mouth was trying to find the right words. I dug into my bag, rummaged around and fished out some dollars.

This served merely to irritate him. He grabbed his packet of cigarettes. He shook his head.

'It is not enough,' he muttered, lighting up.

'It is enough,' insisted Samir.

'It is more than enough,' added a defiant Suleyman in his patrician voice, and the official threw up his hands to show that the situation wasn't actually in them.

'If it were up to me…' he said in a more conciliatory tone. 'But I must report to the chief police officer. He is answerable to the governor. The governor reports to the regional governor, and he reports to the prime minister.'

'The prime minister,' Suleyman repeated and folded his arms. 'Ahmed is a good friend of mine and we are staying at his house.'

The officer blew a smoke ring. It was like moving a bishop. 'Come back next week,' he said, 'and we'll sort out the paperwork.'

'We are on a tight schedule,' protested Suleyman, lips trembling with anger.

'There's nothing I can do,' snapped the officer, his face a crescendo of pink.

Samir and Suleyman pushed back their chairs. As they walked outside together, I felt a swell of pride worthy of Athos.

I soon came back to earth with a bump. As I turned to follow them, the officer began whispering into my ear, pouring condensation into the lobe: 'I think you are a spy. If you are, I will let you go. You don't have to tell your friends, I promise.'

Now I felt trapped. What could I say? If I said yes, I had sided with him against them. If I said no, I had spoiled it for all of us. I felt myself turning hot then cold. He was ogling me.

'I don't know,' I said.

Striding back into the room, Samir tried one last gambit. He leaned over and snatched the cluster of notes.

Now it was the officer's lips that trembled. He waved his arms. 'Given the exceptional circumstances, I might be willing to allow my generosity of spirit to override my personal misgivings,' he said, eyeing the money. 'I can let you know' – a long pause – 'tomorrow.'

Negotiations that had begun with furrowed brows concluded with amiable handshakes, and I was surprised to see my two companions sporting grins and with a fresh spring in their sandals.

'It was, I would say, a positive encounter,' said Samir.

'A positive encounter,' added his father. 'I am glad you thought to bring the dates.'

'Positive?' I grimaced. 'What if he says no tomorrow? He thinks I'm a spy.'

Suleyman gave a hoot of contemptuous laughter. 'You didn't fall for that!'

With my tail–between–my–legs head, I couldn't think properly. I felt doubly mortified, once by the officer, once by Suleyman, but inwardly I did not recant. Who were the judge and jury here? Whose story did I tell? My own? Or theirs? Everyone has their secrets. Suleyman continued with his. Was he on my side? Sometimes he seemed to be. Sometimes he was not. It was impossible to tell.

What I did know was that societies each have their mechanisms. The officer had demonstrated his authority by delaying us for a day. The adequate number of dollars, still an unknown to me, had changed hands, and we would head off once more across the sand like the ants marching across our makeshift camp, oblivious to any rug or piece of clothing that stood in their way.

How can we ever understand what it is like to belong to another culture? In the East, how is it ever possible to judge what it is like in the West, and vice versa? We are controlled by what we are told, by stereotype and by reputation. The news forces us to guess at the contents of those boxes unknown to us, but we can never really open them. We fear the unopened ones. We keep them sealed in case they leak wounds.

❊ ❊ ❊

After the meeting nothing happened all week. Samir was still recuperating. His father tended the camels. I ate alone, watching the desert. I nursed my blisters.

A sore had appeared on Winaruz's back from one of the wooden frames that kept rubbing on him, but there was no *tischgar* root to soothe it. Fleabag's ringworm had returned, as had her ticks. Usem had pulled a leg muscle and Tlatig had a sore foot. Suleyman took it in his stride. He administered turmeric mixed with engine oil – to all of us.

At this point, I believed that if I walked far enough, at some stage there would be a destination of sorts, another critical point, from where a new, brave, positive place could be reached born of achievement, somewhere that would contain wisdom and clarity. Now, as I look back, I think of it differently. I see only unanswered questions.

In the dusty yard of Ahmed's residence, cross-legged, I sat a world apart, trying to fill in the blank spaces and blotting them out again. Memories drifted in my conscious mind like newspaper cuttings, faded and bleached around the edges. I put them behind me. Perhaps the past is the most distant place after all, that horizon where we can lose ourselves forever.

By now I had become the most unlikely expert on the workings of an Islamic *marabout* imaginable. I knew the detailed whys and wherefores, all the various methods and even the names. I still didn't have the vaguest clue what one looked like. It was tempting to think of him as an archetype, all tattered rags, toothy smiles and benign welcoming gestures. But I was aware this was naive.

Shrouded in the uneasy veneer of my innocence, I felt blinded not just by sunlight, but by a continuing sense of foreboding of what any holy man actually signified. I suspected he existed as a metaphor, a smart code name for an unspeakable destiny.

Defiantly, I wrapped the veil around my head and went shopping again. Many extra provisions were needed. To Samir's relief, I avoided purchasing any more camel milk.

Usually Tuareg travel with a minimum of water, but we now had three five-litre plastic containers, one for each of us, filled and wrapped in dampened camel hair to keep them cool. There were three crates of vegetables and rice, and four sacks of flour; plus two battered tin troughs for watering the camels and a plastic bucket to act as my bath.

The men thought it might be too much groundwork. 'Some people say making preparations is unnecessary because it shows a lack of trust in Allah for our sustenance and safety. This is wrong. We must choose what we think is the right course for ourselves – *and* trust in Allah.'

Was this a paradox? Perhaps it was not. Some people also say the Tuareg have always protected knowledge above all else – in their traditions and in their cunning, in wisdom passed through the generations and by experience. It was hard not to imagine what this signified for me.

On our second visit to the *gendarmerie,* a different official with overblown courtesy refused the cash gift offered to him and stamped our papers immediately. 'I shouldn't have to do this job, you know. And the pay's terrible,' he grumbled.

'Such is life,' said Suleyman, hand on heart.

'If you are going to see the *marabout,*' said the officer, ignoring me, 'he is not in Tenefek. He is in Mertoutek. You must go there instead.'

He disappeared for lunch without handing over the stamped document.

'Do not worry,' said Samir. 'Allah's decisions are always perfect. It is his *ilm*.'

It was an unsurprising line. In Samir's eyes, Allah in His infinite mercy provides us with all knowledge. And He has given us common sense and reasoning so that we can prepare for future events and address our needs ourselves. Man can have nothing but what he strives for.

Secretly, I thought to myself, sometimes we strive for something and still don't get it. Critical point or no critical point, it is not meant to be.

It was Saturday before we came face to face with yet another police officer. By this time, there was a long line of people waiting for papers and the officer issued us passes without a word. I had an idea who was being paid for what and by whom, but I could not be sure. What I did know was that we would now not be journeying to Tenefek as we had planned. Samir, meanwhile, had to arrange yet another pick-up truck, because we needed to begin from an entirely new place. There was no point in my asking if Ahmed would arrive, or what exactly he had to do with my receiving the necessary paperwork.

Two days later, as the sun touched the land and began its daily odyssey above the horizon, we set out on our own. Samir called ahead to check security. 'Will it be safe?' I asked hesitantly.

'*Tawakalma 'alla Mulana*,' he said. 'We rely on our Lord.'

What would I take with me this time? The name of another small village scribbled unintelligibly on a tatty piece of paper, and an address for a healer who I assumed was a ghost, since, as I now understood, most *marabouts* had died long ago.

AFTERNOON

Tadäggat

+ · V · E X · +

My soul is thirsty

Afudan man saswatahi

It is often said that when we travel we become a different version of ourselves. The quotidian grind of bills, texts and telephones recedes into the distance. Instead, the zoom lens of our attention focuses on a chance to savour spontaneity. We dwell solely in the moment, emptied of the baggage of our normal lives. The act of observation is liberating, while the object of our observation remains weighed down. This state is in itself a form of meditation.

Striding across the Sahara with two nomads and five laden camels felt almost familiar this time, the boxes of forgotten belongings as remote as the stars. After a few days' rest, my feet had healed and the radio of my thoughts had tuned to a new wavelength. Before I had been lethargic. Now I was the reverse. I crackled with adrenaline. I popped with energy. I bristled.

My inner luggage remained. Beside me the shadow of Fleabag wavered. She seemed conciliatory, her gait content. It not she who was weighed down by the burden of her inadequacy.

On this occasion we were heading south and the track was dwindling into the depths of another wilderness, this one south-westerly, through the largely unknown tracts of land in the shadow of the Atakor, and through a succession of oases — Aheggar, Edjele, Iniadjg, Allioum. We still had sixty kilometres ahead of us.

For hours we walked that first day, rejoicing in the sight of a white bloom on a thorn bush, the drum of the camels' footfall marking time across the sand. Wells came and wells went. A dry riverbed faded to dust.

It was no wonder there weren't any reliable maps for this region. There was hardly anything to register, as if the scenery had packed its bags and left. Land and sky met so symmetrically that they had a blurring effect and could have exchanged places, the world turned upside down. A scattering of trees lay dotted on the horizon, their wispy branches coaxed by the wind into tormented shapes. A few twigs poked out from the ground like punk hairstyles, but that was all.

Occasional disturbances provided a distraction – an elderly shepherd and his goats, children gazing with star-struck faces at the camels, and then, all of a sudden, the horizon opened up again.

In our world of pips, hums, pings and ringtones, silence has become so rare that it is intimidating. Omnipresent white noise accompanies every moment of our lives: the rush of cars, police sirens like wailing babies, helicopters that rattle the windows in their frames as they hover over cities, more now than ever before. In silence we hear the beat of our own heart, the throb of blood passing through our brains, the inner voice that guides us.

In the desert, silence is literally golden.

Only small sounds were constant – the creaking of the camel loads, the whistling of the wind, Samir mumbling something about the *marabout* and *baraka* like pirate's treasure. The constant repetition of one foot after the other had a mesmerising effect. Suspension of thought occurred naturally. Locked in inertia, objective and reality appeared to merge.

In the West we often understand concentration as a restriction of movement, whereas in the East all movement of the mind ceases, allowing it to become one with an object of observation.

This I was at last experiencing. I was unplugged from the plugged-in universe of invisible bonds. I could imagine that the key to knowledge was not speed of movement, but the absence of it, and this brought to mind the meditative experiences of seers and mystics at all times and in all places, from Hildegard of Bingen to Jakob Böhme and Emanuel Swedenborg. Where there was consciousness of an object, there came with it a suspension of all movement. This was that elusive *svarupa sunyam iva*. *Svarupa* means the essence of a thing. *Sunyam* means vid. *Iva*, as if.

'Essence as if a void.' Only now did I begin to grasp this. It was as if I myself had been emptied.

The camels plodded on regardless. They were experiencing what all camels do when travelling with humans who have no idea where they are going but are too proud to admit it.

I knew more things about Samir now than I once did. I knew about his ambition, his melancholy, his vanity, his stoicism, the corners of emptiness in him that needed to be filled. He did not recite poetry any more. If I raised the subject of the *marabout*, I was ignored. Men, I had learned, must not be alarmed by too many words, spoken too fast. In particular, Tuareg men reacted by reverting to Tamahaq. Nor would he hear mention of violence or of Isis. He said those things were too disturbing for him and he wanted only to forget them. He said there were many ways to die, and some were more pleasant than others.

He still carried the picture in his pocket. He took it out often and gazed at it. I wondered if he had a woman hidden away. Who knows what he was bending to his own use, or to counterpoint me, all the while protecting me from himself. He knew me better as well. He knew my imperviousness. It was like a wall, but he could not resist banging into it. Wherever he tried, he could not break it down. The wall was everywhere. It was the border that did not exist. It was the very line of the horizon.

His wise father pretended he hadn't noticed. Suleyman seemed thinner now, more haunted. The cheekbones of his long face were more angular, his eyes more hollow. There I was, in those mirror eyes, in duplicate and monochrome, like an atom or a particle. He sensed my mistrust.

'Do you want to talk about it?' he asked.

'There is nothing to say.'

'Trust me then,' he said.

We loaded and pushed on, our steps mechanical like second hands circling a clock over the flat no-man's-land, our veils shutting out the light and our thoughts.

Further on ahead, the sometimes barely passable *piste*, edged by boulders, led us to an archipelago of drifts dotted with cacti. There we diverted ourselves with barbed, spiny vistas, wandering like lost strays. Homeless tramps leading our wayward camels, we travelled across the thorny borders of our own histories, disturbing their fault lines, averting our eyes to the eruptions that lay ahead.

Above drifting clouds a whizzing plane cut the sky with a cotton wool trail. When I saw the flash, I did not trust my eyes. It quivered above the quicksilver flats of early-morning, dipping, as if it was landing.

'What's that?' I said. I traipsed along, sweating and shooing off flies. My sunblock was melting.

'Where?' Samir steadied himself. He held on to Usem's saddlebag.

'There,' I said, squinting up and pointing.

'It is a bird.'

'Are you sure?' A low roll rumbled in the distant sky, a bear growl.

He shook his head, fumbled with one of the saddle straps, adjusted it and walked on. Usem didn't notice.

'It isn't a bird,' I said.

Samir grunted. 'You are seeing things,' he said. 'It's your eyes. Planes fly at night over the desert.' He pulled up his veil, his own wall of defence against anything he did not wish to discuss, and changed the subject. He was avoiding confrontation. He had recovered from the poison only a few days before and he was weak.

Insistently, I pointed again the silvery flash in the sky and the hole where the plane had been. 'What's it doing landing here, in the middle of nowhere?'

'Nothing for you to worry about,' muttered Suleyman.

'Four miles to paradise,' said Samir.

Hopefully, he didn't mean literally.

I was sure I had seen a plane descend and land about five or six miles from us. There was no airport or airstrip. It could have been my imagination, but the way both men were so against discussing the matter convinced me of it.

It would be later that day that I discovered I had been wrong, but not entirely. Dramas here are always sleepers. Where everything occurs in the midst of nothingness, all events are rare and therefore extraordinary. It might just as well have been a beetle scuttling over the land. Each gathers rumour. No sooner have they been realised than they become part of the folklore.

We paused for our siesta as a sun-infused haze blanked out the mountains and all their secrets. Thoughts of jet planes ceased their purchase in my heat-addled head. Fleabag was quiet, so quiet that I wondered if there might be something wrong. Her irritated skin was still causing her distress. She persisted, her long neck reaching towards her back to scratch her itchy hump. Winaruz sat beside her, still, disconcerted, set free from the rhythmic pound of his soft feet and snorting occasionally as if to sympathize. His back had healed well. Nearby, the elder statesmen, who had also recovered, bore phlegmatic expressions. Tlatig nibbled oats. Usem chewed cud. Agizul dribbled a little.

Suleyman went off to collect some *ebiki* grasses for his asthma and we settled down to sleep like vampires through the midday heat. Samir was reading the Qur'an.

The sky was brilliant blue, the air hot and still. I was picking prickly pear flowers, handing them to Fleabag who found them delicious. There it was again, that same angry grumble I had heard earlier. This time two separate notes could be discerned, one higher-pitched. I looked up to see a jet thundering overhead like a colossus in descent, under-carriage open, wheels unpacked, in undeniable clarity.

As the aircraft let rip its ear-splitting roar, Fleabag's head turned. She bucked. Fortunately Samir had her neck rope. The force of the engine certainly shook the sand off her back. She was strong against the rope, but he held her.

This time the thunder was at ground level. I jumped back, avoiding being hit by inches. It was Agizul. He took off, flew across the half-submerged tent at top speed and pulled up 200 yards away, settling near an *agar* tree.

Seconds later I was sitting down, sheltering in Fleabag's wide shadow. The plane had gone. Gritty figs carpeted the sand where prickly-pear flowers glinted like diamonds.

Suleyman, having quietened Usem and the others, was on his way to retrieve Agizul. He headed towards the tree. He shouted something back, his voice an echo on the wind. Samir, who had somehow managed to calm the other camels, lifted his head and sighed. He knew he had been rumbled. But even as the figure of his father grew pocket-sized upon the flat, he remained silent and aloof.

Agizul was still flustered upon his return, his long head a little lower than usual, blubbery lips a little paler. Suleyman hauled him back and hobbled him tightly. Still chewing, he couched beside the others.

But it was Samir who calmed him down and who, on closer inspection, discovered his swollen, crimson lip. It was not only the aeroplane noise had bothered him. He was slavering green spittle.

A poultice of *tajart* leaves had to be applied to cleanse the infection. Suleyman had gathered the ingredients and pounded a paste from leaves. Afterwards he suggested more turmeric which, he said, was very soothing, and would be equally effective for our eyes, because obviously they were deceiving us.

He wasn't fooling anyone. I decided to tackle him there and then. 'What are they doing landing a plane here, in the middle of the desert?' I asked. 'There's no airport, is there?'

To his credit, he just came out with it. 'It's the drugs operation,' he said.

I wasn't surprised. It is common knowledge in the West that as far back as 2004 South American drugs cartels started transporting hundreds of tons of cocaine annually to remote airstrips along former caravan routes. Hashish is sent in from the Rif Mountains in Morocco and opium from Afghanistan. The drugs are then forwarded on in an intricate network to 'poison' the West. The money in turn is used to buy guns and make bombs – the same weapons of violence that are used by terrorists all over the world.

There was nothing to do but slog on.

Underneath

Daw

Imagine what it must be like to see your home swallowed up by nature, to be uprooted like a tree and displaced. Hardly noticeable at first, sand can drift for years and even decades in one direction, and then suddenly it moves in another. The dunes move in and hold sway, cascading in sheets and leaving only ghosts. A shovel is essential, although it is a bit like using a Beretta 3032 pistol when a Type 93 surface-to-air missile is required.

It is traumatic to be so at the whim of the elements, but perhaps it is karma – nature settling its score with man, who, with all his violations of the planet, is waging war. It is the only way the earth can respond.

The experts use terms to explain the movement of sand. Saltation, for example, from the Latin *saltus*, leap, is often used to describe the shifting of particles, a word applied to avalanches as much as to sand drifts. At low velocities the force exerted upon the particles allows what is known as a reputation or a creep. In deserts and rivers it is a continual process. Suspension of particles occurs when a static electric field is caused by friction. Sand is lifted into the air, and more and more particles begin shifting. This is just one of the ways in which the land is moving, as if the desert itself is defying capture.

The sand was deep and soft underfoot. My footsteps had a slow, drawing quality. Alternately they were light and energized before being dragged down. Everything ebbed and flowed as if it were moving, swerving, then static.

There were no marked routes. We looked west over a hundred miles of sand, east and south across the vast Amrador plateau that ran towards the great Atakor. In that direction, marbled crags meant interminable rough terrain, with its unseen oases, gorges and *oueds*. The tops of the mountains were shrouded in mist, the veil that protected their anonymity.

A few jagged rocks sharpened their nails in the furnace of the sun, a silver eye piercing the sky. Slowly they became forms, upside-down triangles, concretions of blocks and isolated cones that followed each other like notes in the melody of the land.

The smidgen of greenery felt like a glimpse of Eden. I imagined what it must be like for a man cast adrift in a rudderless boat who sees land across the choppy seas, rubbing his eyes and looking again. Someone had stuck another pin in a blank pinboard land, and this one shiny, pale-grey point was a checkpoint.

The barrier came close. A guard materialised, smoking heavily, in a uniform that had adopted the colour of the dust that had settled on it. Samir handed over our papers and the guard looked suspiciously at them. Striking a defiant pose, he waved us on, as if disenfranchising himself from the real issues, or hoping for a tourist boom. The trickle of travellers can have brought in hardly any cash.

As oases went, it wasn't much to go on about. Two unkempt banana trees and a single palm made a curious threesome. A few solitary buildings, once houses, had been half-destroyed by the tide of sand and left to their fate. Now they stood like bones, overturned whale carcasses washed up on a beach.

'*Mort* Bouteflika.' Someone had scrawled this with a finger in the dust on an abandoned door. Inside, decaying under its gritty cover, were chairs and even plates and a cup drowning in the drifts. Jerboas had taken up residence, their tracks forming patterns in the sand. An unsavoury stench was coming from one of the rooms which had obviously been used as a lavatory, by man not beast. Fallen bananas floated like flotsam.

The sand had unearthed and moved things. Abandoned mattresses and other household items lay scattered about as if after an explosion. Brown sludge choked the well. Even the water was submerged. Not far off a car had been half-dug out, waiting to be stripped of its parts. Looting was commonplace. Traffic signs bore empty warnings against it, devoid of meaning because there were no drivers to pay attention to them.

But we were glad of the chance to rest. Samir selected a spot to pitch camp on account of it being 'leafy'. In reality it was a bare patch of land with about four or five spindly-looking twigs on it. Suleyman called it a *ghaba*, a forest. We unloaded the packs and the camels set about grazing, nibbling tips of *jisrif* before moving on to the next feather-leaved, sweet-scented branch, manna in the wilderness.

Being in this parched wilderness, it was clear why the Islamic conception of Paradise as an oasis of calm is so appealing. It epitomizes all that those living in the desert can aspire to. This dire oblivion of dust will disappear. A lush garden unparalleled upon this earthly plain will surround them. Gone were their threadbare, filthy robes and turbans; there they will be robed in silk and brocade, enjoy fruits and palm trees, and drink milk and honey and wine that will never make them drunk.

No wonder it has proved such an inspiration to so many. In the East Jalaluddin al-Suyuti wrote of a beautiful oasis filled with trees, with trunks of pearl and branches of topaz that reached the sky, and winged horses beneath, encrusted with pearls and hyacinths. It is said that even Dante was influenced by it when writing *The Divine Comedy*. I remembered my oak trees, leaves dripping with grey drizzle drops. How distant they felt. This inferno was more like his vision of hell.

We sat for a while to allow our muscles to recover or, as Samir said, to allow mine to recover.

'Ametous,' he said. '*Voilà.*'

'This is it?' I glanced about and he nodded.

Only now did his father finally speak. 'It wasn't like this last year,' he said.

'And the year before that?' I asked.

He tried hard to recall it, but the memory had gone, reabsorbed like dust into the depths of the shadowlands.

But he remembered Abdelaziz Bouteflika, the seventy-nine-year-old who had been President of Algeria for four successive terms since 1999.

'And do you also want him to die, Suleyman?' I said, thinking of the message on the door.

'He has dug his own grave,' he said, before, absorbed in reflection, he added, 'Actually, I met him once. He visited Tamanrasset. It was as if he was entering a foreign country. He does not like Algiers. He despises the Algerian people and he abandoned us. He blames Allah for everything.'

Suleyman hadn't named any camels after his native politicians. Now I knew why.

'Can you forgive him?' Considering Bouteflika has not been seen in public for two years and is alleged to be so ill that he can hardly speak, communicating with his ministers by letter, I hoped I would find compassion in his eyes.

'Everything ends,' he said, without looking at me.

I wished he hadn't said that.

We were some distance from the buildings because, as both men swore, the Kel Essuf spirits had moved into the village and had become its rightful inhabitants.

Hesitantly, I unearthed the carton of 'orange juice' I had purchased from Sidik in Djanet, mislabelled so that the faithful when taking a nip of whisky could pretend that no edicts have been broken. Drinking alcohol in any extreme temperature is a terrible idea. Combining it with water and an obscure Saharan desert root extract called *yadin* is folly.

Samir produced three sand-cleaned glasses and poured.

'Drink it,' he said. 'It is safe... as we are.'

I churned it around my cup.

'It's a little deserted here, isn't it?' I said, remembering the brown water and lamenting the time I had been so sniffy about it.

'Is it?' Suleyman took a gulp. He poured a second glass. 'This is *normal*.'

Samir, who was by now clambering up the palm trunk, his bare feet adeptly avoiding the segments of razor bark, dropped down a cluster of canary-yellow fruit.

'From the food of the date palm and the vine you can derive wholesome fruit and drink,' he called down.

He didn't say anything about Surah 5, verse 90, which holds that intoxicants are the lures of Satan. The Qur'an said nothing about the evil *yadin* root. He kept quiet about that as well. Nimbly, he shinned down again. I handed him a whisky. 'Medicinal purposes.'

'Medicinal purposes.' He downed it breathlessly.

Alcohol can be an effective distraction. On this occasion it worked. Even if it did look like rat pee.

'How far now?'

Suleyman didn't react; he just kept his eyes ahead. 'It's

not far, *inshallah.'*

'How far is that?'

'Off limits, *inshallah.'*

'You mean we are lost,' I spluttered.

The crude statement was met with mutual expressions of consternation. Men and camels were of one language in their communications – they used grunts.

There was a long pause and then Samir forced his lips into a smile. 'We really appreciate the contribution you are making to the camel,' he said finally.

Clearing his throat and with a cursory nod, Suleyman excused himself.

I was concerned for him. He was not in control of our journey, and now it was in danger of coming apart. Each passing problem dampened his spirit. In fact, it seemed to be making him ill.

Beneath swaying banana leaves we withdrew to our tents. I spread out my rug, clutching tightly the small paper sachet perfumed with frankincense that Amina had given me. I hoped she would keep that promise to pray for us.

Old roses drifted in my nostrils, with churches and sandalwood. Blue dragonflies darted in my eyes. But it was not just the drink. Underneath, I suspected that I was being misled, that it was all a lie. Because it was not only the sand – our route was drifting.

A far-off grumbling tore the silence again. It was Suleyman snoring.

Suffering and loss

Ghas kay tekassat

Heraclitus held that fire is the noble aspect of the human soul, but there are many other definitions of the light, heat and flames that constitute the force in our world that is fire. Strictly speaking, fire is the effect of combustion, a process in which fuel reacts with oxygen to release energy. For some it represents passion, the cauldron of our hearts, for others it epitomises danger. Whatever its significance, fire is almost always too hot to handle.

Like suffering, it is all too easy to burn our fingers.

I remember vividly 25 March. For four days we had ventured out each morning into the vast, indifferent plain studded with rocks that resembled Furies. The heat rose as we followed the track. Further and further it wound, up a barren escarpment, down along a low ridge, opening at last to a wide valley floor.

Samir walked slowly, as if his bite was still paining him. He was pensive that morning, even as I quizzed him. This was not the great desert he had wanted to show off to me. He did not want to see.

Ahead lay a city of tents. It lay cowed by the land, in the shadow of the mountains. The camp had no name and it was not marked on any maps. Officially, it did not exist, but Samir knew it well, as did his father. Everyone in the region did. Its perimeter was marked by woes, encircled by thirst, imprinted with hardship.

Many of its inhabitants were Izeggaren – red- or dark-skinned – of the Harratin, nomads who originally came

201

into central Sahara from the oases of Tidikelt. They had fled in 2012 when northern Mali and Niger were besieged. France sent troops to pacify the region, not that it stopped the violence. Attacks on Tuaregs were commonplace in their homeland, and they had nothing to go back to.

The closure of Niger's border with Nigeria after Boko Haram tried to set up a base there has had far-reaching consequences in the region. When the Tillia, Tazalite and Intekane refugee camps in north-eastern Niger reached bursting point, around 300,000 refugees from sub-Saharan countries became doubly displaced. Only 3,600 people were granted asylum in the West. For the vast majority, it was not the golden backdoor opportunity to enter Europe that they had dreamed of. It was a prison sentence.

More and more people fleeing the violence in Niger, Mali and Libya flooded northwards. Many didn't make it. In 2015, ninety-six migrants' bodies were found, among them women and children, who had died of thirst after their vehicles had broken down. They had been journeying from Arlit, ninety miles south of the Algerian border.

The people who live here survive in the face of their homesickness. They have never known such hardship. The great droughts left fertile regions arid. When the rain eventually fell it penetrated only lightly, resulting in flash floods that did little to solve the chronic water shortages. Water for washing is rationed to once a month. There is not enough food to feed the children and, thanks to the irony of medicines made available by charities, the population is growing.

As soon as it was in sight, someone called out.

'Ça va?'

Beside me, a young boy had appeared, pimpled and gangly, curly hair stuffed under a skullcap. He scanned the caravan. '*Française? Americaine?*'

Another boy stepped out from a rock and loped along beside us. '*Cigarette?*' he cried.

The first youth patted Usem. '*Haj*, give me your camels. Can I ride?' he asked. Suleyman waved him on.

News travels fast in the desert. A succession of youths appeared, selling tapes, henna, their own sandals even. They walked beside us.

'Good day to you, young man!' called out the curly-haired one.

'Young? I was born in 1949.' All the same, Suleyman sounded flattered.

'And where are you going?'

'To Mertoutek, *inshallah*,' said Samir.

'How long will it take?'

'A week.'

'And what track are you taking?'

'The road to peace. You?'

'The one to liberation,' said the boy.

Samir hobbled the camels and they chatted on.

An elder was hammering on a coconut with a stick. His home was where he sat. Suleyman addressed him and the two men began to talk. Only now did I see the compassion I had been seeking in his eyes in Ametous. It had crafted them into glitterballs.

But dignity was turning to dust in the heat of the desert camp, where tempers boiled with frustration.

'Come…' The young woman in the bright-ruby dress welcomed me over. She had a feather-light handshake.

Inside the tent the stench of sweating bodies was over-powering. There was no water for washing. A green plastic bag stood out like a warning; bright orange and violet T-shirts hung like flags; proud fathers hovered hawk-like.

Soup was on the go on a gas stove. Women were diluting fizzy drinks in neon colours. Others had left their washing.

Mothers dressed in black with kohl eyeliner cradled babies. Other children lay listlessly on mats, the girls with veils deftly draped, the boys with oversized tops over too-short trousers. Flies formed black rings at their mouth edges, although only the tiniest seemed disturbed by them.

Kafka once wrote of hunger as a metaphor, but this was true hunger, raw, ugly. Metaphor intellectualizes and, in so doing, distances indigence. Words cannot convey its reality.

Outside Suleyman was busy talking directions.

'The *marabout*?'

'God grant you *baraka*.'

'There is no *marabout*.'

'There is, God willing.'

The heat rose around us. There was nothing for miles, but no escaping the claustrophobic, airless despair inside the tent.

'Will you ever go back?' I asked the young woman in the red dress.

She answered me in French: 'We do not want to. It is too violent. We are outcasts in our own homes. Still, we have hope the world will remember us one day. We have to be positive for the sake of the children.'

The prettiest little girl began to cry as I got up to leave.

'Which people are yours?' the woman said, tracing her face with her pointed fingers. Her dark eyes met mine; even in the light I could not fathom their depths.

How far she had to travel before she came to her dreams. How she craved the foreignness that I was cloaked in. How I reeked of it, this so-called winning streak of the West that she longed to savour, of which she had heard so much; how little I had to offer in response. I travelled in a different dimension, that of transience. I had nothing to give her but my inadequacy.

'I'm not sure who my people are,' I told her.

We waved our farewells and became small dots among the other dots fading on the horizon, locked in the spiral of our own frustration.

This was not the only unofficial refugee camp. Many unnamed camps have mushroomed into virtual cities in the middle of nowhere. People from all sides of the Sahara trickle across the vast desert wilderness where borders and border controls are meaningless. They live in dilapidated tin shacks, shabby, discarded military tents and beneath scraps of fabric held up by sticks.

Like all illegal immigrants everywhere, they look for work and survive on almost nothing. Their children go hungry. There are no schools or hospitals for them.

I recalled once asking a baker in Kabul that typically empty English question, 'How are you keeping?' To which he had replied, 'Pain, loss, death. The usual.' How could anyone think straight about anything when all they could think about was persecution and penury?

Tribal feuds and conflict have caused many battles in Africa, but the greatest enemy of all is poverty.

❊   ❊   ❊

That evening I sat down on the sand and tried to make sense of it all. The camels sat broadside to the tree. They gathered together to keep their body temperature lower than the air temperature, lapping up every patch of shade. I could not go to them. My body was inert, empty.

Samir spoke of his dreams. Largely, they were snatches, patchwork images, scents and colours as if the pictures were fugitive pieces of a land he called home, but which he did not quite recall. I was a little jealous of the women in those dreams, and there was no country portrayed in them that I recognised.

The helplessness he had witnessed earlier at the camp had related to his own sense of displacement. The Tuareg have suffered nothing less than ethnic cleansing. Successive governments have marginalized and terrorized them. The establishment regard the Tuareg as high-handed and brand them slave-keepers. They deny them hospital treatment. Their children are excluded from schools.

Suleyman tamped down his pipe, lit the tobacco and stared broodingly into the distance. He spoke of his own dreams as memories. He told of the wild addax, the white antelope with long, twisted horns; the *mouflons,* or horned sheep, ancestors of our own domestic sheep; the wild oryx that once roamed the mountains – all hunted to the edge of extinction. He told of the wild onion sprigs he had collected for heat rash and the turmeric for my sunburn.

Asawad, or dream spirits, visited in his sleep. They determined good and brought evil.

After that he told of war. He told how new soldiers in new uniforms swept across the lands like locusts, stole their wells and forced his people to confront the enemy they feared most – that of thirst.

'In Algeria, we have been more fortunate,' Suleyman said. 'In Mali and Niger, Tuareg warriors were defiled. *Tagelmust* were stripped off our chiefs. Swords were stolen to cause as much humiliation as possible. We tried to find the answers in the Qur'an, but we could not see them.'

The way he told it, Western intervention has helped no one except, perhaps, stockholders in the international oil and mining companies that benefit from lucrative contracts from corrupt Western-backed governments. From time to time he consoled himself with the thought that his kinsmen remained the true masters of the desert, that place they would never be torn from.

Not far off, the camels sat, heads up, as if in sympathy. Having battled infections and pulled muscles, they were fighting their own war against the flies. Their ears buzzed with them, their half-closed eyes wept thick, black tears of them. Their tails swished and flicked at them.

Night drew in, the stars so low they might have been mistaken for beacons. Behind the camp, the mountains loomed like prison walls against a dull sky.

Suleyman puffed more smoke. 'The trouble is, we did not know borders back then,' he said. 'We had no need to follow maps. They took the desert and drew large black lines over it. All of a sudden, we had to have papers they called passports. I had to pay for a visa to visit my cousins in Arlit. If you had no money, you could not travel.'

'So how does everyone travel these days?'

'The old ways, the forbidden ones,' he said, by which I assumed he meant the illegal ones.

'Is it possible to turn back?'

Samir shook his head. 'We can never turn back time.'

'We are condemned to roam lands that belong to us, yet are lost to us. We have only our past,' said his father.

'Then we must find that *baraka* very soon,' I said. We raised our tea glasses as one.

Abandon your illusions

Ayyet temerit

Contrary to what we might think, mirages are not actually hallucinations as such, but genuine optical phenomena. In a mirage, as opposed to a dream or a daydream, light waves bend. How much depends on the time of day, the angle and our perception. A trompe l'oeil occurs that makes distant objects shimmer or ripple, or seem different to how they really are. Oases appear where there is sand. Stars twinkle. At that point the mind takes over and false hope becomes inevitable.

Dawn had faded and the white light reflected on the land was blinding. We were well on our way to Mertoutek. Sand flats rose on the horizon where more smudges bled fumes. Algeria is the fourth largest natural gas reserve in the world, and that is aside from the rich deposits of oil, phosphates, mercury, zinc and iron ore.

Samir strode along merrily, admiring the little flecks of cloud as they passed over the horizon. I was just admiring how much effort he must have made to snap back to his usual happy self, when out of the blue it came.

'Don't you love the beauty of Islam?' he said.

'It has beauty, but other religions have their own beauty,' I replied. 'Buddhism, Judaism, Christianity.'

He frowned. 'Yes, but Islam took the best bits from those religions.'

'Are you saying Islam stole from them?'

'Islam is not a thief!' His pace quickened. Then he paused, as if the idea had just come to him. 'It borrowed.'

'There is nothing new in that,' I said. 'There are many overlaps among the world's great faiths.'

'Islam is the best.'

'I'm not arguing with you, Samir.'

'You are always interrupting me.'

'You mean, I am offering my own opinions.'

'Islam completes the other religions,' he said, walking on, calling into the air without turning. 'Why would Allah have sent the Prophet Muhammad, peace be upon him, if Jesus had done his job properly?'

'Perhaps Allah meant it that way?'

'Meant? How do you mean? The one thing that Allah, praise be upon Him, the great one, the most merciful, meant to happen was the spread of Islam, because it completes what Jesus began. Islam fulfils all our needs, answers all of our questions, praise be to God, and in every way contains the Truth, praise be to Allah and may He be exalted. Don't you agree?'

'Samir, as you know, I respect Islam and Muslims.'

'Then it is only logical that you should convert. Why don't you do it?'

I sauntered along at a casual pace, still behind him. He did not seem cross; on the contrary, he chuckled.

'Petite fille!' he shouted in mock reproach, but as he glanced over his shoulder, there was laughter in his eyes.

Fleabag plodded along, chewing over what we had discussed. Wisely, she kept her opinion to herself.

So, shrewdly, did Suleyman.

I closed my eyes and, just for a moment, I could not see the sun. When I opened them again I realised I was locked in my own box just as Samir was in his. It brought to mind a painting by Salvador Dali of a line of elephants with long legs like camels. They are wandering across a desert, each carrying a pagoda-like house on its back. The procession appears ceremonial, and the people staring up at it from the sandy wasteland are diminutive, inspired by something they do not understand. We are all slaves to our religions.

It had been only four days since we left Djanet, but it felt much longer. The rotten smells of the camp lingered in our nostrils. Watching and listening to both men, I had felt a new respect for them, but this felt one-sided.

It was not just a matter of being addressed in a manner that felt patronizing. Samir's insistence on bringing up the subject of Islam was always likely to end in tears, and a warning that I would be unable to escape the 'burning winds and boiling waters of Gehenna', the place where Muslims believe all infidels end up. He wanted to save me. My conversion to Islam would create, in his mind, both a natural conclusion to our journey and award me all the *baraka* he felt I needed. He worked at me like the winds upon the rock.

For me, it was one desert too far.

Samir had retreated back into his cocoon. I felt him as a source of strength, but unquantifiable, shifting. At the same time, I continued to suspect there was something alarming about him. If only I could see anything clearly. All I could see was a dotted line whose fragments refused to be joined.

Further discussions about Islam did little to help matters. It would have been unfair to say he had not been a gentleman. He had never once come to my tent at night, or compared my scent with that of the camels, but it was obvious he wanted to break down my defences.

Suspicion grew in clumps like tufts of desert grass. I couldn't tell you anything about his friends, but I could tell his mood in the morning before he knew it himself. I knew what angered him, what made him sad and what kept him going. I could tell you that he exhibited a cautiousness that belied his outward confidence. It was not just about Islam that we bickered, but also about small things – usually the packs or the supplies.

Deep down, I wondered if he was uncertain, not about what he wanted to do or where he wanted to go, which was as far as possible, but about whether he could do it. I admired his lack of conformity, the courage of his bad manners. Throwing a pomegranate had an authenticity about it, and a practicality. After it had burst open, it could be eaten.

With Suleyman it was different. I knew of his beliefs and saw how they brought order to his life. I saw how they guided him. Still, I caught only glimpses of his past, fragments of his memory, most notably the futility of maps, the preciousness of camels, or the majesty of the elements.

Although an aristocratic Tuareg would always maintain reserve about his past, when he did reminisce he was cagey, choosing innocent subjects, such as when Samir was young and they played *melghas*, hide-and-seek, and *sellenduq*, when one person pretends to be a jackal and chases the other. This was sweet but irrelevant. Nowadays we were playing the *abanaban* – blind man's buff.

Thinking of his frequent comments about the West, I began to question Suleyman's loyalties. Each passing event was adding to his burden and testing his spirit. He hated it if I queried the route and talked down to me frequently. He gave me reproachful glances when I challenged him about the *marabout*. Tuareg society may well be mainly matrilineal and its women awarded freedom, but independent thought from a Western woman was not something he was accustomed to. No wonder he loved history. He hadn't moved on from it.

He often disappeared without explanation, as he tidied his weapons or polished his sabre. It was beginning to make me anxious, this wandering off alone into the drifts, as if he had something to hide. At least Samir met our problems head on.

The camels were an example of courage in adversity, or rather of our mutual strength based on shared weakness. That was except Agizul, who, having dribbled a little urine, would shift nervously and masticate. It did nothing to settle my nerves.

Fleabag provided respite. At least camels didn't question your map-reading skills. When in doubt, they headed for the juiciest thorn and stayed there until you had worked it out. They didn't always have to prove you were wrong, and if a camel wasn't happy, it told you. Plus, worst-case scenario, you could eat one.

I guessed it was that state at the heart of all marriages – that of mutual co-dependence. Here, in one of the greatest expanses in the world, we lacked space. I concluded the major problem was my intolerance. When we travel we learn things, despite ourselves, that we would prefer not to have learned at all.

❊ ❊ ❊

The valley of Iherir extends from a distant wilderness. It is a mystical landscape, of shade and shadow. Precambrian granites rise in giant structures that don't seem to belong to this earth. Nature's art has lain sculpted by the wind for 600 million years. Many formations stand narrower at the base than at the top, like rock monsters, or trees.

Some seem benign, like watchful guardians presiding over the landscape, either on their own, or in fields, like clusters of mushrooms. Others are bent over, as if kneeling. They reminded me of ice structures known as *pénitents* that I had once seen in the Andes. It was as if the land was warning me, reminding me once again of my mortality, demanding my atonement.

It felt as if time itself was at the end of its tether as, each morning we ventured out into the emptiness of this vast, indifferent landscape, sand drifts encroaching upon us like rivulets. Suns boiled, moons glowed. Winds came and went with different names – *Irifi, Ouahdj, Ghibli* – each more menacing than the last. The *Irifi* arrived in spirals like a detachment of tornadoes; the *Ouahdj* burned your skin with its rancour; the *Ghibli* shrieked like a banshee as she beat petulant grit into the eyes and mouth.

There was Suleyman, marching silently, and behind him Samir, like a white rabbit pulled from a magician's hat. There were the camels, stoical, patient. Still, there was no sign of the holy *marabout*. I thought of him now as a mirage, like all the other mirages that floated tantalizing on the shifting horizon.

❋ ❋ ❋

Imagine what it must be like to be permanently travelling. Richard Leakey once wrote, 'Given that thousands of generations of our ancestors were hunters and gatherers on the move, it may well be that this life is an indelible part of what makes us human.'

Industrial civilisation has existed for less than 300 years. Agriculture, a keystone of society, has been practised for just 10,000 years. Yet in the million or so years during which humans have inhabited the planet, the majority of people found ways of living on the go from what nature provides. Those who choose to live in this way today endure conditions we can hardly understand, often in great hardship. They work with the environment – hunting, gathering and tending livestock – rather than against it.

Quite apart from the estimated sixty million political and economic regufees spawned by the conflicts in Syria, Afghanistan and central Africa, born nomadism has shrunk dramatically in relation to so-called civilized society, pushed out to its periphery. It is not just the Tuareg who have suffered (although many of them are now sedentary), or even Australia's Aboriginal peoples. The same applies to the Inuit of the Arctic, the Mbuti rainforest pygmies of the Congo, the Amazonian Indians, the Gabra, and the Turkana cattle-herders of Uganda.

There are still some nomads who travel great distances. Every spring the Nenet reindeer-herding tribes of Russia make the 200-mile journey on caribou-drawn handmade sledges from the forests of western Siberia to the tundra of the Yamal Peninsula. In south Sudan the Dinka move their cattle away from their temporary camps in the savannah woodlands. In west Africa the Fulani move towards the bush. They travel in land, rather than through it. Their medium is space, not time.

But this is rare. The vast majority of people struggling through the vast inhospitable deserts of north Africa are obviously not there out of choice or tradition. They are escaping something which in their eyes is even worse.

A group of Eritreans, children travelling alone mostly, were crossing the Sahara in sandals and flip flops, with just a few dollars in their pockets. We sat among the rocks with them, and their story unfolded in such a matter-of-fact way that you might almost have missed the hopelessness of their journey. To get this far they had already gambled what little they had. Their promises had been long broken by people smugglers, those who had taken their hard-won money and abused them.

Awate, whose name meant victory, had never owned any pencils before. He could not read or write.

'But you can draw?' I asked him.

'Badly,' he grinned. His weary smile belied a truth that his eyes could not conceal.

I thought of children in Afghanistan I had known, and the unspeakable images of war in their drawings. This boy had the same look, that of death.

'And where are you heading?' I asked him. I searched for other questions, but they evaded me, because there were no answers.

'A normal country,' he said, and I asked him what he meant by that. 'One without killing,' he replied.

'But you endanger yourself travelling in this way?'

'It is better than being tortured.'

Awate was not alone. He was like all the other refugees who did not want to risk their lives walking through the scorching hot desert with no roads, but for whom there was no choice. His family had been murdered in the fighting and he was alone.

Awate stood, dusting himself down and bidding his farewells. He wondered if we could spare a camel. We almost gave him one. Vegetables and water are an inadequate offering when a whole new life is needed. We were all of us prisoners of circumstance and our limitation.

As we watched them go, heading nowhere, I folded myself into this alien geography, unsure if I would ever be able to reach out and grasp it. We were only a few miles from the border, but like all frontiers in this unforgiving, waterless continent they were invisible. Like the sand and the people, like the cusps of the dunes and the edge of the horizon, every line kept shifting.

The tide of the cursed and the wretched is not just flowing through Europe. The ocean of water is just a stopping point. Before they even reach those perilous, freezing waters and climb into makeshift, sinking boats, African refugees have another ocean to cross, the one of sand. That one is arguably fiercer and perhaps more hostile. No one is ever pulled from its dry waves. Its victims lie buried where they fall, their bodies entombed by the desert sands that drift over them for ever.

※ ※ ※

The air cooled, the light mellowed, the flames crackled. Finally the figures vanished, a flight without a vanishing point, driven on by the mere potential of escape.

Suleyman was nowhere to be seen again, and this time Samir had gone with him. Earlier, they had been speaking in Tamahaq, a deliberate habit when they didn't want me to understand what they were saying. What did they have to discuss that they couldn't say to my face? I couldn't help suspecting that they were talking about me.

Eyes closed, I sat reaching out towards the landscape. There was little I did not worry about. I worried for the women and wished they were with us. I worried for Fleabag. I worried for the Eritreans.

I must have nodded off there, under the bush, because I woke with a jerk, coming from such a deep place that it seemed I must have been having a nightmare. I sat up, gathering my wits.

Crouching to pick up some wood, fingers straying over the ground, at first I thought it was a leaf on the stick in my hand. The stick moved. It kept on moving, even after I had dropped it. I snatched for a larger stick and turned on my wind-up torch.

In the beam, about two metres away, was a yellow Saharan fat-tailed scorpion, pincers and tail raised.

Now I really was having a nightmare.

The scorpion was threatening me. It didn't seem to register that I was a giant.

In the white beam of the torch I saw red. I became lucid. I heard steps. I saw forms. Frost crisped on a drying shirt. A white fly froze on a grey stone. Shadows slid across the darkness. Were these emanations *djinn*? A lone jackal, perhaps. My voice was dry, rasping.

Samir appeared like a ghost. Side by side we stood, staring down. Samir listened with his eyes.

The shiny, bulbous armour was thicker about the trunk and darker than I had imagined. The tail was raised, the arms poised. It knew no fear.

But there was no time to think, because at that moment another shadow sprang, this one deft, feline. Suleyman's knife plunged, digging the tip into the gut and lancing it.

The creature fought back, writhing helplessly, jabbing at the air, but it was no match for Suleyman. The tail came off first, then the head. Bulbous, crab-like, the two pincers, disembodied on the sand, twitched slightly, as if possessed like devil's claws.

'*Allahu akbar*,' he said, clutching the quivering torso between thumb and forefinger. 'Nothing to cure this one.'

A detailed search with the torches could unearth no others. We still shook out our clothes, equipment and sleeping bags three times for good measure, glancing woefully at the kit for scorpion stings that I had brought with me. It was just as useless as that trusted Tuareg remedy for scorpion stings, the sap of the *alkhad* would have been.

The land itself was black and quiet, an absence rather than a presence, betraying no sign of its own ruthlessness. The camels slept like babies.

Suleyman boiled tea and afterwards he began to pray his thanks.

Samir edged a little nearer. 'You are blessed today,' he whispered, clasping to his breast his sacred *gri-gri* charm that in his mind had saved us. He was grateful it wasn't an *aqrba*, one of those scorpions of the wind that use the air to leap upon their victims, and whose poison women place on their nipples when breastfeeding as a vaccine to protect their children.

The tea glass was hot and the liquid was comforting as it slipped down my throat, 'as sweet as life' as the Tuareg say, but as we said goodnight there was no doubt in my mind what had saved me. It was a nomad's skill and good luck.

I went with the ardent wind

Addawegh ed-ahod

Dawn brought none of its usual light. A stark chill had descended. Sand swirled like ocean spray, its thick foam deleting the lines, contrasts and softening the horizon. Dust clouds churned in the sky, dulling everything into opacity, veiling it.

The desert in anger had found its voice. 'Go home, infidel!' it cried. 'This is no place for you!'

Nose to the tent flap, I shouted something back – and got a throat full. No wonder the desert people felt the hand of Allah behind the wind that commanded the desert.

Not far away a motionless shape took form. At first I thought it was Fleabag, but it might have been Agizul. Or perhaps it was Usem. It was impossible to tell whether it was a camel at all. I tried to wade over, but my limbs felt constrained, the effort of seeing too great. I was drowning. Only my skin kept me afloat. I was a sand grain myself.

The desert was blocking me, like a wall. I could make out a cloak, or at least I thought it was a cloak – and now, a camel nostril extended as if made of elastic, or perhaps it was just a sand swirl. If I shielded my eyes, I could make out hump shapes, or perhaps they were sand mounds.

And then everything fell into slow motion.

Squinting, hands over my eyes, I saw a figure melting away to one side. I thought it might be Samir, but suddenly there was Suleyman, *chèche* masking his face, furled expertly in his robes, his head and shoulders rising above the cloud as though he was swimming in a lake.

In this blankness of colour, line and texture, Samir was nowhere was to be seen. I had never been able to see him accurately. Now, like everything else, he was a blind spot.

At once, everything vanished in the whiteout. It felt like minutes rather than seconds before I heard someone calling. 'Over here!' The words came out of the vacuum, disjointed, as in an Alain Robbe-Grillet novel.

We made it just in time, before the density of sand became impenetrable, huddling under the cover of camel blankets propped up with tent poles.

Red-eyed, sand-blasted, lowering his *chèche*, Suleyman was spluttering almost as much as I was. This was a *Ghibli*, south-westerly in direction. We would have to wait it out.

By the light of a torch he pulled out his *guerba*. The water splashed water on his face and over his lips. Chest heaving, he coughed and coughed again. He thought it was good that I experienced the desert at its most powerful. The sand was so unpredictable in the wind's hands that it was lethal. It was a cruel, unrelenting monster. It could snap you in two like a twig, bury you for ever without trace. At other times it came slowly, creeping up on you like a snake.

Around the makeshift tent the storm raged. Inside, we clutched water bottles, the three of us, bunched up, legs crossed, thinking of the camels sitting outside.

Being British, I tried talking about the weather.

The curiosity and amazement didn't once ebb from their faces as I tried to explain what a blizzard was, but I could tell that I had failed to offer any inspiring description of a snowstorm, just as I was left to search for meaning as my companions described a dune sea.

After a while, Samir reached into his pocket and pulled our a cluster of particularly filthy-looking dates. He popped one in his mouth and offered me one.

'That's camel feed, isn't it? Why don't you wash it?' I croaked, shaking my head.

'Everything from Allah is clean. Sand is clean.'

'Snow is clean.'

'Snow is from the West.'

'Snow is from Allah too?'

'Sand is better than snow,' gasped Suleyman. Samir didn't appear to notice his father struggling for breath, and I couldn't bear arguing with either of them.

Thus we remained, our gazes still averted, as was customary, but also because we were each of us, even now, trying to decipher the code of each other's worlds, but our eyes betrayed our thoughts and feelings.

＊ ＊ ＊

As quickly as the storm arrived, the wind died down and the sand settled, our friend once again. From nowhere the sun came, lighting the sprinkles that drifted on the airwaves under the tarpaulin. We peered out, blinking, like survivors of a shipwreck.

The horizon felt wider than before, as if the storm had opened it up. Where there had been flat ground, there were now rock clusters; where there had been solitary rock trees, a canyon had appeared, and craters with jagged edges. Towards the south dunes ran on endlessly.

Everything close up had sunk. One or two girths and straps lay on the surface like snakes. A water trough floated like a lonely island and a canister drifting nearby seemed to want to join with it.

A few brave birds stalked the newly exposed areas – little desert sparrows and *moula moulas*, messenger birds, hopped over the sandbanks. Some yards off, one or two sand-encrusted mounds were stirring. A loud camel aria punctuated the air, a little like Puccini and filled with just as much melancholy as the original version. A hump, half-buried and wriggling, might have been mistaken for a piece of scenery. This Madame Butterfly was stuck.

I rolled up my sleeves and fed her a fig. Fleabag didn't care that it was sand-flavoured. She even sang me an encore, though I hadn't asked for one.

About ten yards off two intermingling profundo basso notes broke out simultaneously. Mozart's Don Giovanni had returned from sandstorm hell, it seemed. Or rather it was Usem, who, with the aid of his reluctant sidekick Leporello, otherwise known as Tlatig, was recounting his own experiences of visiting the underworld.

As I shovelled with my hands, Fleabag gave one of her more approving gurgles. Her eyes looked fine, with their bushy brows, double eyelashes and that clear inner eyelid designed specially to protect against sand blizzards; she also had hairs in her ears to stop the sand entering. She was in good shape. Her skin had healed and her nose injury was far behind her. She could even close her nose flaps.

The others, having finished singing their hearts out, munched freshly emerged bush twigs. Samir walked over to them, dusting off their flanks, collecting the juiciest branches and feeding them by hand.

'There are boats in your country?' he mused. With faraway eyes, he wondered what kept them afloat. He had read somewhere that they sank very easily and that there were no life jackets. He had never seen the sea, that unfathomable land that Allah had created, although he had known many who, fleeing their lands, as he put it, took their chances upon the great liquid desert that separated our countries, never to return.

'And waves? How are they? Do they move with the wind, as the sand grains?'

I reflected for a moment, wishing I could show them to him, that we might both watch fluffy white seahorses combing their waves towards the shoreline. I wondered how he would react to that other glorious uncharted landscape. A sense of awe and respect in the face of nature filled me. Such great expanses of sand and water defied definition.

'Yes,' I said, 'they are a little like drifts.'

'And what colour is the water around your country?' he asked, his tone now eager, excited even.

'It's grey a lot of the time,' I confessed.

Suleyman smiled. I could tell that for him the desert was deeper and more mysterious than the ocean could ever be. He brushed himself down, took out his pipe and sat on a chair-shaped rock that had appeared.

'Are you all right, *haj*?' I asked.

'I'm allergic to sand.' He coughed as he inhaled.

Samir wasn't listening. He was unearthing the cooking equipment, sniffing an open jar of a somewhat grainy-looking tomato purée.

The storm winds had made other things resurface too – above all, my worries. A *torha* shrub had been nibbled bare, a telltale sign of wild camels.

Suleyman had finished his cigarette and had recovered slightly. Now he was busy supervising. Despite our mass of luggage we appeared to have omitted the one vital piece of equipment: a shovel. He wandered over to Usem and rubbed the sand from his neck, whispering to him.

The other bulls protested. Were they jealous? I wasn't sure. Agizul seemed the most restless. He refused to be tied and issued a high-pitched squeak like an alarm call.

I had a feeling it was one.

The fire didn't take long to get going. The weather had unearthed plenty of dry sticks, although we took care in handling them because, according to Suleyman, they were *torha* twigs, and their sap would cause blindness.

Vegetables, shrivelled with the heat and covered in sand, were rubbed in yet more sand to 'cleanse' them, and cooked in gritty water because Samir decided they needed salt. He proceeded to heap a handful of what looked very much like sand into the cooking pot.

The water bubbled but my worries had reached boiling point. Without wishing to cause any further confrontation between us than there already had been, I could not help but air my concerns. 'Agizul seems slightly nervous,' I said light-heartedly. The indirect approach was a widely known military tactic. It worked well for soldiers. Perhaps it might work for me.

Samir was employing his own military strategy, his usual one – evasion. 'I think we're out of onions,' he said. Past the knowing grimaces of Tlatig, he walked over to a rock and sat down on the other side.

'Well, we have plenty of carrots,' I called out, feigning withdrawal.

Suleyman strode off. I caught a waft of whisky. Perhaps a more direct approach was required. I tried once again. 'Are you absolutely sure it isn't the rutting season? I heard that there are wild camels in the Sahara.'

Usem howled. Agizul squeaked. The others glanced about like submarine periscopes.

'Where did you hear that?' Samir walked back. 'It's not the rutting season and there no wild camels in this region. Even if they appear wild a shepherd will not be far away. Why do I have to keep repeating myself?' He adjusted his veil higher. He stood, legs apart in that way men do when they are trying hard to assert their authority.

The bread, having been left out during the sandstorm, had a decidedly crunchy texture. I chewed determinedly. 'But if there *had* been and if it *was* the rutting season, perhaps they might leave a bit of evidence?' I said, hoping to disarm him.

'Allah reveals all,' he said defiantly.

In my experience, Allah concealed it.

And so I decided it was time for the attention-grabbing shock tactic: 'What about this *torha* branch then?' I waggled the pathetic, chewed-up twig in front of him.

'Don't do that! You are touching *torha* blood!'

He leapt back, cowering. He seemed genuinely scared.

But the full-frontal assault had backfired.

'You never listen. You do not pray. You like snow. You hate rain. You are strange.' Having spoken his mind, Samir snapped shut.

Fleabag had it covered, immediately implementing her own SOS. She had learned how to bellow.

Suleyman had returned. He smelt of whisky and urine. 'I'm too old for this,' he said adamantly.

It was a typical Parthian shot and I saluted him, but it did nothing to quell the feeling that we were spiralling out of our depth into another as yet undisclosed tempest.

Having established that feral herds existed in my imagination, we headed towards the dunes on the basis that on rare occasions 'lost' camels avoided the less 'woody' areas, and with the promise that there were no scorpions. Dusk would cover our tracks and the full moon would light our path.

Of one thing only I could be sure. One landscape had definitely shifted. It was our own.

There is no certainty
Ibas tilla adutten

In 1927 Werner Heisenberg stated, 'The more precisely the position of something is determined, the less precisely its momentum can be known.' Unlike Isaac Newton's clockwork universe where everything follows clear, pre-established laws and patterns, Heisenberg believed that nature suffers from an inherent fuzziness. He suggested the more we know exactly where something is, the less sure we can be of how fast it is moving.

I tried this by studying Fleabag. I could see where she was and how she seemed motionless – at least she certainly seemed fuzzy, whereas with the *marabout* it was more a question of guesswork.

It was soundless in the dunes except for the tinkling of camel bells and the wind – which, having risen again, groaned periodically through the pockets in the sandbanks – and the noise emanating from Suleyman, who had dozed off on camelback. His loud, rhythmic snoring could be heard several dunes away.

Now that they were upon us, the term 'sea' did not seem a wholly accurate description for the shapes made by the sand. They certainly undulated, but they did not wave.

The impression of waves in a dune sea is just that, a sand ripple, a superficial build up of mass, a disturbance brought about by wind movement. True dunes are different from drifts, which are shaped like windbreaks, with one much sharper edge, and do not conform to an exact pattern. Dunes are perfect in form, sculpted according to sand volume and wind strength. They are also gregarious by nature, huddling in great families, communities even.

Samir thought the curves flowed like poetry. They reminded him of the women he had known, an uphill struggle with great big breasts.

Feet gliding effortlessly, the camels seemed to be in their element. Small flutters shaved fractions from the ridges as their feet skimmed the sand. Out in front, Usem strode confidently. Winaruz brought up the rear. Between them, Tlatig and Agizul held steady. Fleabag walked in the middle. She found her footing well. Only occasionally did she lose balance and veer suddenly, splashing the grains in fountains. Her eyes still followed Samir.

Dusk drew out life from the sands. Animals had adapted to a largely nocturnal existence, sloping off to their holes to sleep during the day and waiting for the shadows before resuming the hunt. Often I caught glimpses of sand beetles scuttling, leaving hieroglyphic imprints in their wake.

I was relieved that we were simply skirting the dunes.

Walking in the desert in full moonlight is a completely different experience to being in sunlight. Patience and stamina are needed to traverse dunes at an angle that is consistent. In theory, shallow sides of dunes face north-east, but crossing them can be disorienting. It is necessary to be at the top of a dune to see the others properly. Right-handed walkers tend to go around in circles because they take longer strides with their right legs. Left-handed travellers have the opposite problem.

In daylight, there is no danger of stabbing your shin against a slightly darker patch of sand that turns out to be a rock. It is easy to see the ground, and you know you won't twist an ankle; plus there is a skyline, however distorted by the heat haze.

In a dune sea at night, even in bright moonlight, there is no skyline. It is necessary to take extra care.

We had decided to turn east. At least I thought it was east, and the equipment certainly indicated east, but Samir and Suleyman distrusted compasses. They swore on the Qur'an that we had turned west.

Above, the sky swirled in divine spirals, as if the gods had left footprints. I watched their lights like the trails of my past. I wondered what they would leave behind when they had fallen.

Another dune came, then another and another. There was a rock, a turn, a passage, now another rock. I was aware that it took great skill to negotiate the *gassis*, the paths that wound between the peaks, those places where even shadows became confused by their own darkness, and where, according to the Tuareg, the *djinn* and Kel Essuf lay waiting.

As we stalled once again, I became suspicious. There seemed something peculiarly familiar about the steep, sloping peak that loomed ahead of us. It had an identical-looking grass tuft on the left face to one I had seen earlier.

It was obvious that something was wrong, and not just because Fleabag had obeyed me.

Samir caught up. We gathered around the compass, arguing.

'Well,' I said, shining my torch on it, 'I think Mertoutek is that way.' My finger was pointing directly at a void.

'Yes, but the route takes us through Tazrouk.'

'That is the first I heard of it,' I said.

'You weren't listening.'

'Perhaps we should go back?' I had let slip my true feelings. Samir frowned. He kicked sand in the air.

From out in front Suleyman cleared his lungs. 'I swear by God we are less than two kilometres away at most,' he hollered.

'That can't be true,' I called back. 'Bearing in mind we cover fifteen kilometres a day, it must be more than that? It's more than twenty kilometres from Tazrouk?'

He halted the camels and wound back to us. 'Did Samir tell you that?' he gasped.

'No. You did.'

'I did not. It must have been my son.'

Samir drew down his veil. 'In Allah's name I never said that, father. You know I do not lie. God knows.'

'Suleyman?'

'I say again, my son said that, not I.'

'I think you did mention it, as I recall,' I said.

The two men stood apart. Raising a forefinger and putting it on his heart, Samir swore to God that he was honesty itself, renowned throughout the Kel Ahaggar for his straight-talking truthfulness. His father protested his own integrity, renowned throughout the entire Sahara.

Now they were lapsing into Tamahaq again. Items were being hurled – a bag of tea, a glass, a kettle.

Suleyman lobbed a sugar cone. '*Hader full erafin!* I swear by my head!'

'*Hader full eri-in!* I swear by my neck!' cried his son.

'*Iver-ka tilrant ta teggaret eyhiod!* The misery of the donkey should come to you!' cried Suleyman.

'*Igged-kai yalla dar temsi!* God will fry you in hell!'

They could shout all they wanted, but it made no difference.

Samir's chin was trembling, eyes pink and watery as a laboratory rabbit's. I wanted to put my arms around him, to make it better, but it was nonsense. I was not his mother.

'*Io.* Come,' I said.

Suleyman's veil had dropped. 'By God, Samir is correct,' he whispered. Glancing heavenwards, he muttered names, as if he saw faces in the constellations. He spoke of places as if they were stars, transient echoes mapped on the galaxy of his own fragile memory.

'Suleyman, you are the only one who knows the way, don't you remember?'

He did not look at me. He was in another place, a memory. He opened his eyes again and saw a tamarisk, which was, in reality, a twig. 'I remembered it so well – once, the *ghaf* trees, the *jisrif*.'

'There are no trees here, Suleyman,' I said.

We continued on our way. Or what we thought might be our way.

'Watch out!' Samir jumped. '*Djinn* have hollow backs,' he said, as if they were listening. 'It is hard to see them coming. They like to hide around corners. We have to be alert to catch them.'

'It isn't anything to do with the *djinn*,' I sighed. 'In fact, I am perfectly ready to punch one if it ever declares itself.'

'*Ya Rab*. Oh Lord,' implored Suleyman. He uttered a prayer. Afterwards, we were still lost.

I looked up at the capsized stars of the Plough falling on the horizon, and the black holes stared back at me with their warped space and time, casting their shadows, and it felt as if I had been sucked into their vortexes.

'Father!' Samir buried his face in his hands, astonished that the man who had taught him everything he knew was unable to provide an answer to our predicament. He sat down beside Suleyman. He was unable to speak and I could do or say nothing that might have comforted him.

At that moment, a soft, furry cheek appeared, rubbing against my earlobe. I took hold of the muzzle and felt the soft fur. I whispered the words of endearment audible only to her, and she turned to me, lifting her nose and swishing her tail.

A light breeze whipped the sand. It played through the pathways with a sound like a sigh, but there was nothing to be said. It was not Samir's fault, he who had tried to make things work. He meant well and, whatever complaints I had, we were all dogged by fatigue.

Nor could I blame his father, when I myself had so long ceased to be sure of my own past, when the images that had surfaced in my memory undermined rather than reinforced any certainty. We were curators, he and I, of our relics. We both of us pushed our homeless thoughts across borders like refugees, and neither of us found the answers.

Samir did not kick up too much of a fuss. There was no point. But things did not look good. If a Tuareg made a mistake, it was normally serious. Nomads did not believe in maps. Nothing led them to safety and water other than their gut instinct.

In vain, I tried not to panic. I told myself to be strong. I reminded myself that he must know where we were going because of centuries of tradition. I shut out all ideas of who might be watching, waiting for us to fail. I instructed myself to believe.

Dawn brought relief in the form of a few dusty dates and a packet of strawberry biscuits. With bulging cheeks, we discussed how to tackle the seemingly insurmountable mass of sand that lay in front of us and drank *bawre*, made of the leaves of the wild fig tree, for strength.

It would be much longer before Suleyman apologized for what he described as the extremely small detour. He had wanted to show me the scenic route, he said, in order to keep me entertained.

Radiance
Ahal

That high dune took half an hour to conquer. It was so tall and steep that we spent most of the time going backwards. But we were not to be defeated. Suleyman dragged Usem, groaning and moaning pitifully, while Tlatig and Winaruz staggered behind unwillingly. Hot on their heels, Samir tugged Fleabag, scrambling with difficulty, loose sand cascading with every step. The most reluctant animal of all came last – I didn't know it was possible to fall upwards.

Sweaty-browed, aching-limbed, the team lay collapsed at the base on the other side. Suleyman, chest heaving, mixed acacia honey with *ahzenan* root. Samir boiled tea. We deserved a morning off.

It was a beautiful day. Had I not been so scared or exhausted I might have revelled in its beauty. I needed space. I was thirsty for silence. And I needed to pee.

Were you to have asked me what my ideal path might have been, it would have been flat earth rather than sand, with palms shading intermittently. The sun would be gentle and there would be birdsong. Instead I trudged slowly and doggedly, through more sand deep enough to cover my ankles, the sun splintering on my head. I should have taken more care, for I had no water or compass.

On this occasion I had chosen a more accessible-looking incline to tackle. It was still tough going. Close up, it was possible to see how texture and surface varied enormously. Some edges were flat, smooth and silky, others pitted with ridges. Small stones twinkled like fireflies where the peak sloped, meeting the next rise about halfway down. At others, the contours fell more steeply, impervious as rock, hot from the hours of daylight when the high banks focused the heat into unbearable temperatures.

Life sheltered in the cooler sand just below the surface, where against all odds miniscule plants found moisture – strawberry cacti and little grasses that in the absence of rain had not blossomed for decades. Skinks slithered through the sand like fish. A white camel spider floated up the river of grains, struggled briefly and drowned. A translucent, waxy lizard popped its head out, astonished to be disturbed by such a strange creature.

From this vantage point, the scale of the dune sea was extraordinary. Vast accumulations of sand moved inexorably in regular formation, as it constantly strove to reinvent itself. *Sief* – literally 'sword' – dunes meandered over the desert floor like sand serpents. Those shaped like crescent moons, or *barchans*, solitary by nature, linked to form great chains, pushing against the wind, somehow retaining their form through constant shifting and realignment.

As the wind changed direction, it altered the landscape once again, moving the grains one way and then the other, forming them into starfish shapes when it whirled in circles. These sprang from nowhere on the tip of crests, especially upon moon crescents, where they contracted and expanded in infinite complexity.

The light was intense on the east sides, the sheen on the surfaces limpid. I sat on the slope in the sand, washed by nothing and hanging on. I had come to the edge. I could so easily fall off. I picked up some sand and the action seemed to activate something within. Sounds, scents, images flashed before my eyes like stills in a life picture, pixelating, fragmenting, falling. This time, the images were not vague, but sharp and defined. Detached from context, they followed a sequence, like skimming stones across a lake. There was just water, the water of light seeping into my bones.

Gradually I grew back and blinked. I was sitting under a blistering sun gazing out at an ocean of sand. And I had still not found a place to pee.

I pushed away from the sand wall and the sky moved edgeways. My tracks were already vanishing as I began down. Checking the path along a shortcut through two almost vertical slopes, in my head I drew a direct line, but even then I was thinking I should turn.

Something tipped my balance, a shoe jamming against stone. Sand in my eyes withdrew like smoke.

A huge wild camel had come to a stop no fewer than thirty yards away.

It was a well grown, strongly arched beast, and it was blowing froth. The fur of its hump lifted, as if held by an electric current; its back glimmered in the morning sun, showing off its curved haunches.

The stranger stepped back, as if startled.

It wasn't half as startled as I was.

My muscles knotted in tangled skeins. I thought about running. My legs were stuck.

The bull stood firm, immobile apart from its flaring nostrils, and I stood firm before it, flaring mine. My white knuckles clenched. The red had bled away. I told my hand to open again, managed to reach out my arm, just. I needed to prove that I had nothing to hide.

'It's all right,' I said. 'You can go now.'

That was as far as I got, because exactly at that moment somebody fired a gun.

Bang.

The air broke as if a cleaver had hewn it.

I remained fixed to the spot. I could not edge back, as I wished.

I was watching the camel.

It was watching me.

The sand was listening to both of us.

But it was the wind that made the first move.

Amid the explosion of sand particles the camel reacted violently. Mottle-gummed, dagger-toothed, it lashed the air, coiling and recoiling, extending its powerful neck.

Second bang.

The hind legs bucked higher, the contorted body rising and falling, a sand monster from the deep.

Noise twisted in the air, this time fading off. High screams and shrieks jarred with low thundering feet.

After that came fainter shouts. I saw flicker of light, a pink fingernail. I heard a distant thud.

The soundlessness took a long time to return. Only now did I feel some courage, and then it was tiny, ant-like in its proportions.

Rifle in hand, Samir strode towards me. I was glad he had aimed high.

As he climbed, he called out. 'The *djinn* are not done with us yet,' he said.

That was the first time I wondered if I could love him.

We walked back to chaos: packs, fruit and vegetables, dislodged equipment, rugs and water cans scattered over a wide area.

Suleyman fell to his knees, cupping his hands and facing towards the east.

This time, I knelt silently with him.

Sunset
Almaz

+ · ∴ · ꞉ · ‖ +

Searching for freedom

Eswadagh y el houria

Sometimes it is so easy to give up. How do we know how to find our way? For how long do we have to walk before we let go of our lost dreams? Somehow we must find in ourselves the strength to keep going. Winston Churchill put it much better. 'Success is not final. Failure is not fatal: it is the courage to continue that really counts,' he said.

Samir's outline was hunched, angular, constrained, an isosceles triangle of a young man. Beside him his father slumped cross-legged on the sand, dishevelled, breathing heavily, camel-hair blanket draped around his shoulders. There was something didactic in his tone that set me on edge. His professions of reassurance made me suspect the opposite. He was less patronising than usual.

To lose a camel on flat ground was a mistake. To lose two in the dunes was a disaster.

Even now, the smell of dung and camel sweat lingered upon me and the shrieks rang in my ears. I could still hear them streaking past, the long legs moving so fast they seemed frozen, like wheel spokes.

Suggestions were fired, followed swiftly by criticisms shooting them down again. Suleyman offered me *takokiat* bark as a stomach remedy. It didn't work.

Gathering belongings we searched for clues in the sand, pondering over toe prints with more slightly lifted hearts. Tracks led out towards the plateau. If they had run deeper into the dune sea, we would have been lost.

In a surge of pragmatism, I switched on the equipment,

sent an SOS signal via the EPIRB, charged the satellite phone and waited. I kept the miniflare in reserve. I knew I had been right to bring it.

It made sense for Suleyman to stay back. Someone had to guard the equipment, although from whom, I did not wish to ask. There was more to this decision than age or despondency, a sense of things needing to be proved, repudiated. As he coughed again, mopping his brow with his sleeve, I felt helpless to find him a plant or root. He had long finished the antibiotics I had given him.

By eight-fifteen, Winaruz was saddled and roped and waiting to put himself at my service. He uttered a wild belly-call and, by the lift of his head, I knew he longed for freedom. Usem couched. Samir secured the saddle and climbed on.

The camel stood with his usual fierce jolting.

Twenty minutes later we were riding across a dead area stretching towards the horizon, around us an alien landscape of huge plains and rocks of twisted stone. This was the maze of Titeras N'Elias, where rectangular faults in the sandstone had been widened by the wind and eroded.

Winaruz moved faster than I expected, his head high and proud, his eyes piercing and intelligent. A warm breeze lingered, of flowers, old rubber and rot. Dust swirls ran along the crests of the drifts. The flies here were fearless. They had never known swatting.

Patterns lay carved into the rocks as if a carving knife had inflicted wounds upon the earth. Lines crossed over and re-crossed, primary blocks in a Mondrian painting that had no end in sight. Over and over again we came across lonely tracks littered with warning signs. Ridges and gorges cut into the land with their uneasy edges.

Anyone could be hiding in them.

The wind made the sand sing. What was it trying to say? Was it a warning? A curse, perhaps? Sand really does have the ability to sing. Conditions have to be right for the whistling or barking sound it produces when wind passes over its surface or when footsteps incite it. Sometimes it can be a tiny squeak, at others a loud boom. There are various theories as to how and why this happens. Some believe it is to do with the vibrations related to the thickness of dry grains.

I felt comforted by Samir, but I knew he could not protect me. I was anyone's fair game – as I had always been.

As noon drew near the wind abated. We found ourselves climbing a low ridge alongside a gorge. Far below swifts wheeled out between boulders. One twittered and shifted its loose feathers, half-hidden in the dry leaves. It didn't want to fly, for there was no other greenery around for miles.

Samir tugged at Usem's shoulder to slow him down. Suddenly this confident young man seemed taken aback.

'You are not afraid, are you?' I said.

My voice echoed among the rocks.

I knew by now not to expect an answer.

The afternoon wore on. Shadows came to rest. Light and dark appeared so perfectly balanced they might have been a mirror image of each other.

We circled the area several times before skirting prickly patches called *zayyat*. Beyond the low level of the plain and canyons a steep incline could be seen. Below lay an *oued*, where volcanic rocks loomed like old giants. Acacias grew horizontally with juicy leaves and tasty *jujubes*, a feast for any hungry camel.

High on the ridge, standing in the undergrowth, saddle about his belly, stood Agizul. Fleabag was hiding behind his hump. About fifty yards off a mature wild bull was feeding. I wondered if it was the same camel I had met earlier, but it was too far off to be sure.

A symphony of camel greeting began, the long cries bouncing off the rocks, as if Agizul and Fleabag were broadcasting news updates.

'How did they get up there?' Samir pulled a face.

Staring at the slope I gave a short laugh. How would they get down again was the question we should have been asking ourselves.

Still lingering at the edge, we wondered what to do.

Our errant camels had stopped munching. Their heads were up and there were stalks sticking out from between their jaws. Fleabag was motionless. There was a tautness about her frame, as if she was listening. No doubt she had seen the stranger.

'I thought there weren't wild bulls in the Sahara?' I said

'Must have escaped.' A smell of dung hovered around Samir. It had a whiff of frankincense about it. Of course, there was no odour of any apology.

The bull lifted its head. It had smelled our presence too. It paused. Then, lowering its neck again, it carried on feeding, apparently unbothered.

I glanced at Samir. 'What did I tell you?'

'It's not the season,' he said, and indeed, I had not seen the *dulaa*, the fleshy pink tongue that protrudes from the mouth of male camels looking to mate.

The bull was an outline against the shoulder of the hill, feeding. It turned to stare at us again, sniffing the air as if to discover the feelings it found there.

Apparently they were unrequited, since Fleabag herself did nothing to acknowledge the handsome suitor, even as a shrill toot pierced the silence. Perhaps it was because her heart still lay elsewhere.

Samir knew how to whistle.

With a flick of the head the bull had gone. So much for conquest. I thought male camels were supposed to fight for their females.

'What if he comes back?' I said.

'Don't…' Samir was busily securing Usem and I was attempting to tie up Winaruz, without much success.

I did not want to climb. The sun was hard, broken through the rock. Spangles tinkled in my eyes like fairy dust. I listened to the fate of small stones cast off by my scrabbling hands, chest pounding. It was more by luck than hard work that finally I made it up to the ridge. Or perhaps it was the *qat* that Samir had given me to chew; it tasted like a tobacco plant, but made me move like a rocket.

Agizul was already hobbled by the time I reached him and by then my legs did not feel my own. Fleabag, still grazing, had her back to us, as if pleading ignorance. Samir crept slowly towards her rear and slid the rope around her neck. She complained, but accepted it. She had submitted.

A camel love song sounds a bit like a toilet flushing – on a good day.

'Catch this.' Samir threw the rope.

He was just gradually easing Fleabag forward when in a split second she lost confidence. Leaping from the undergrowth towards the edge of the slope, she stumbled on her hind legs and whirled. With a long groan, not of love this time but of fear, she managed to regain her footing. Trembling but uninjured, she didn't falter as I approached. Nor did she sweat, as I did.

I played with her little camel bell. I stroked her. She leaned towards me. As she closed her eyes, I could swear she winked at me. I smoothed her hump and she rubbed me so hard that I almost fell over.

There were no carrots in my pocket.

It was a miracle that we managed to get down that slope in one piece. Samir tugged his rope and set off, leading with Usem. Winaruz followed behind, and then Agizul, dribbling a little. He didn't object to the rope. He knew his place.

Fleabag couched without my asking.

I laid the blanket in position by her hump.

An ear twitched questioningly.

I stroked her neck. I *suf suf'd*.

She let me on.

As soon as we were up I tugged on the rope. As I dug in my heels, she walked.

By now the clouds had caught the sunset contours. The wind rippled over the sand like spun silk and there was less warmth in the sun's rays.

Fleabag liked the feel of the breeze. I turned her to face it, tasting the freshness.

Up ahead, Samir paused and the three camels under his command remained steady. 'Come on,' he cried, fastening his eyes on a distant row of palms.

Fleabag understood perfectly. Her entire body prepared itself, all sense of insecurity banished.

We took off instantly, she and I, and it was as if we flew on the wind. No longer did we lumber. We floated. We knew what to do. We had skills.

Anyone who says that camels cannot run is a fool.

A sea of rippling sand stretched out in my mind like green velvet, as if the landscape of my youth was suddenly before me and I could see it all so vividly; at last, like the dust between my fingers, it evaporated.

So this is it, I thought to myself as we were moving. This is happiness.

On the tip of a ridge Samir waited. For a split second, man and camels twisted into one, sculpted against the sky.

Without my asking, Fleabag slowed. She chose her tree and settled before it, searching with her mouth. Perhaps she remembered it from her recovery.

We began again, at a more leisurely pace. Still she needed no guiding. She twitched her nose, cooling the incoming air, condensing the moisture from her breath. I stroked her hump, told her she was adorable. It didn't matter that she was moulting all over me. Even her bushy eyebrows were sparser and finer-textured, as if someone had been tweezing them. Her eyelashes were still gorgeous, double-rowed and mascaraed with dust. Most women would kill for them, and this camel knew exactly how to flutter them.

She was also heartsick for freedom. That much I could tell, by the lift of her head, the way she turned and the new sounds she made. There were other feelings burning inside her too, although I could not fathom them yet.

A dark figure had come into view, in profile, like the sort of miniature portrait you might carry in your pocket. Nearby I could just make out two hump-shaped smudges, behind them a wave of golden-brown sugar mounds.

'You are late.' Suleyman's frown hardened at my approach. The sand seemed to have ingrained itself more deeply into his forehead since we had left.

'I didn't know we were on a schedule.'

'If the sun turns, you must return to camp immediately. It is in the *laws*.'

This was rich coming from a rule-breaker. 'I don't remember it being in the *laws*,' I said.

The anger left him as he gave Allah his thanks, but I had come to understand that neither Islam nor tradition but the desert formed his real religion, this great place that was as a father and mother, testing us while acting as our guardians. In Suleyman's eyes small things would always go wrong as we slept or were not thinking properly. Armies of ants might invade, jackals could wander in. Scorpions would creep up on us. But when something major went awry it was because the desert itself had decided. Either it was angry, doling out sandstorms. Or it was asleep and not paying attention to us. When this happened there was only one option: to wake it up and shake it by the scruff of the neck. This we would achieve by resourcefulness, wisdom and persistence – not to mention a cunning that ran deep in the veins of those brave ancestors of theirs who raided caravans and took the rich pickings.

We feasted like kings on the dates we had picked, fussing the camels like children. They in turn lapped up the attention like the vast quantities of water they consumed. Suleyman began to sing, not pausing for a moment in his boisterous rendition as it built towards a crescendo. This time even his son didn't object, and as the wailing subsided he took the rags away that had been plugging his ears and we laughed. All the laws were out of the window bar one.

There is no law like the law of attraction.

At last the tune faded. Suleyman's eyes glazed and he blew his nose on his ragged blue sleeve. It wasn't just the sand that could sing with longing.

It was much easier than might have been expected to teach Samir how to waltz. Tuareg men do not dance. It is considered undignified, too physical, too dangerous.

Fleabag didn't object. She even seemed to like it when I hummed the tunes. There was the triple-time American smooth, Peggy Lee and Benny Goodman and Fats Waller. It didn't matter that I had forgotten the reverse Fleckerl. We made it up.

His father, turning a blind eye to that which his elders would have thought shameful, lit his pipe. He knew all about improvisation.

'It's all about the groove… the beat, the swing. You either have it or you don't.'

Samir scratched his head. He had never heard of Paul Whiteman. He had never danced.

He slid his arm around my back as if it were unnoticed, as if we were standing some distance away from each other, and we spun around on our golden dance floor, the sand sprinkling away from our feet like the dregs of yesterday, surrounded by the time we had created.

In dancing like this, I may have thought I was holding back something from time and culture, rescuing it in the manner of childhood fairy tales; although the journey had been no fairy tale, and Samir was not quite the knight I had longed for. It made no difference. In those few moments a cultural gulf was closed and I did not feel I had taken the wrong path. That night there was a clear light over the desert that seemed to radiate downwards. The past was just a cloud dwindling upon the horizon.

Fleabag had blown it away.

'So, be honest, when exactly is the rutting season?' I asked, when we were all sitting around the fire again.

Suleyman hung his head. 'It's always the bloody rutting season,' he muttered.

That man

Ahales waday

'Peace be with you. *Salaam aleikum. Al chair.*'
  'And you. *Wa aleikum salaam. Al chair.*'
  '*Ma toled?* How are you?
  '*Alkher, ghas.* Fine, thanks.'
  '*Ennek manewinnesen?* And your family?'
  '*Teggit, tanammert.* Very well, thanks.'
  '*Manewin ullinnem?* And your goats?'
  '*Teggit, tanammert.* Very well, thanks.'
  '*Mattulid d'asikel?* How was your journey?'
  '*Alkher, ghas.* Fine, thanks.'
  '*Isalan?* News?'
  '*Elwan.* Plenty.'
  '*Ane tkked?* Where are you heading?'
  'Mertoutek.'
  '*Manefin amagur ennek?* And is everything going well
with your camels?'
  '*Ayoh aha, massinagh.* Yes, thank God.'
  '*Massinagh.* Thank God.'

It was a typical exchange with a passer-by, peppered
with the expected pleasantries in Tamahaq. Such meetings
between nomads were always transitory, opportunities to
exchange information and news.

The three men squatted, drawing signals in the sand
with sticks and without eye contact, just as generations
before them had done. Tiny finger movements indicated
small variations in the terrain ahead; a shake of the wrist
was used for more drastic changes.

But this meeting made me nervous. I didn't say much, but I felt awkward and uncertain. I had no idea what this nomad had said. I did not know his tribe or what his intentions were. His occasional glances in my direction had not helped. They reminded me that I had no inkling of where we were going.

My confused heart was partly of my own making. I shouldn't have drunk so much whisky. The others didn't appear to have hangovers at all. I needed coffee. Instead there was 'sand tea', because we were rationing sugar.

The men said their farewells. Suleyman bought olives. He looked forward to meeting him again; I hoped that was the last we would ever see of him.

'Who was he?' I asked after he had left.

Samir leaned over and whispered, 'He is one of the *ikhlan*.' For once, his eyes met mine with no attempt to divert their gaze.

'You are not serious?' I drew back, away from the uncomfortable sentence I had not wanted to hear. I had heard this word *ikhlan* before. It had an Arabic meaning: 'to be black'. It alluded to slave-keepers.

Once again I was aware I was at the mercy of the desert and her people, whoever they were. Suleyman made no effort whatsoever to condemn the practice of slavery. He was a noble and, whatever happened in the contemporary world, nobles still inherited swords, robes, religious amulets – and people. They looked down on the dark-skinned tribes who did not have their pale complexions and, in his view, superior birth.

It is well known that the Tuareg once kept slaves and had vassal classes – they have been universally vilified for the custom. Officially slavery was abolished long ago, but I was astonished to learn that in some places it persists.

'What exactly are you saying?' I asked Samir.

'He is a carrier, a fixer. He helps people.'

'Across the desert?'

'Over borders.'

'Women?'

'Sometimes.'

'And what happens to them?'

He refused to answer that. Instead, he muttered, 'He is going to help us over the zone.'

His father rolled an olive in his mouth. He spat out the stone to one side. As to which zone and where it was, he wouldn't be drawn.

I was playing chess in my head again, only this time everyone was making the wrong moves. Perhaps I should not have been so taken aback. People are being trafficked in every corner of the world while others profit.

'I don't think it would be wise to go with him,' I said.

I wanted to return to the previous night's dance, but the moment for dancing had passed. Now it was time to face the music.

He turned away, *chèche* high as the Thames barrier, but I had already seen the expression in those pale, red-rimmed eyes, as if he were heroic like his early ancestors, a warrior blazing a trail towards greatness. They belonged to another place, those eyes, that secret landscape of matters unspoken, not to the real, grim, modern world of people trafficking.

Fleabag was neck flicking. The flies were taunting her, and the *agar* balm Suleyman had mixed for her eyes and ears had the effect of attracting rather than deterring them.

Usem seemed better at tolerating them, or perhaps it was resignation. As if to show solidarity, he delivered a targeted line of pellets, then opened his mouth and let out a self-congratulatory honk. The others remained sitting in the cool shade of an *abaka* tree, where they were ripping apart some vicious-looking thorns.

Samir took a breath. 'Are you all right?' he said, his face still covered.

'I'm fine,' I said. I nodded and smiled, but they were glancing at me oddly now, the two of them, and there was something strange about their voices. Perhaps it was because finally they were telling the truth.

Our visitor moved into the light and grew colourless, nothing but a shadow in the breath of the sun. The only sound was our beating hearts.

I gathered up the olive stones into my pocket.

'Are you sure there is nothing wrong?' Samir looked concerned. He brushed my hand, as if he wanted to dance again too. My impulse was to wrap my arms around him, cling on to him like a lifeline. Maybe I could pretend to faint because of dehydration.

The sky was soft and pale as we pressed on, and the horizon leaked like wet blotting paper, though its ink was invisible. The day felt empty, as if everything had vacated it, as though there was nothing more to come. Like its co-conspirator the land, it colluded in the mask of serenity.

I drew comfort from Fleabag, walking silently beside her. She seemed glad of the lighter packs we had given her to carry, which held my tent and sleeping bag. From time to time she swung her neck round to nose them. I felt proud she was not rejecting them. And she did not once try to break into the vegetable sacks in Winaruz's baskets.

That afternoon there were more breaks – double the usual for the distance, in addition to our siesta. It gave me time to think, to doubt. The desert has this effect. Suleyman lamented my 'madness' about slaves. I must have been suffering from *afa*, he said, or heatstroke. He had a remedy for me – brake fluid mixed with the leaves of the *tichghar* tree, because it was said many good spirits sheltered there.

The dance was already consigned to distant memory, but my frustration at Samir had gone, along with the edgy tension we had felt in the early days of our journey. What remained was uncertainty, or rather a duality, a crescendo, and simultaneously a diminuendo. These two opposing forces formed their own tensions.

In one of our shorter pauses I sat beneath a *tagar* and tried to clear my head, but meditation was more daydream than release. I saw my feelings for Samir as an interrupted cadence. Each of its notes was independent. Put together, they did not cancel each other out. They were errant and disobedient. They did not blend. They did not resolve. They remained separated from each other, like the words uttered by the nomad and the signals he made with his hands. They were music at a party, a party with a closed door that I was unable to open.

All the time I quelled the rising fear that I did not know him after all – that for all our closeness last night, we were further away than we had ever been. Step by step, inch by inch, I had the creeping feeling that something bad was coming, and that it had nothing to do with getting lost. I was already lost. I always had been.

The long, hot track eventually came to an end, the flat line of the horizon now a paper-cut silhouette. We wound through an inhospitable valley littered with rusting tin drums. A military drone flew overhead. I had grown used to their hushed flights above us.

There were no trees to speak of, only a solitary *afalo* or an *etafi* here and there. A cluster of buildings had turned gold, as if an unseen master had been preparing them for later, when they would emerge from the oven crisp, brown and perfectly roasted. I am not sure why I assumed they were military.

Some way off, a small cluster of tents had been erected, their outline fragile, indistinct, as if it might collapse under the sheer weight of the red sky that bore down on them.

A figure stepped forward against the light. I recognized it immediately. It was the nomad we had met earlier.

❋ ❋ ❋

Tangerine cloth covered the walls and ceilings inside the tent. There were animal skins, camel blankets and a few large crates, containing what I did not want to know.

Heads held high, wearing wraparound sunglasses and digital watches, men stared. Worry had not abandoned their faces; it had been passed down from generation to generation like their tools. Their hands were rough, hard-working instruments, their feet bare mostly, leathery and thin. More men stooped through the entrance, slipping off their sandals.

Cheese arrived in walnut-sized balls. I took a tiny one and passed them on.

The nomad, who was called Hassan, seemed jovial, much too jovial in the circumstances. Regarding him again now, there was nothing out of the ordinary about him. He bore the same world-weary, weather-beaten features as everyone we encountered. He asked no questions. He talked of his life indirectly. He had five sons and four daughters, all with the same wife. His brother and sister lived in the next tent, with their own families of six sons and five daughters. Hassan had been a soldier once, but nomads did not make good soldiers because they didn't like taking orders. They were better off as farmers.

He was well acquainted with the underground water sources. As a young man, he had been a well-cleaner; the *rtass*, as they called it, was a respected profession in the desert. Many of those who now cleaned wells began their careers as well-diggers, a job fraught with danger and accidents. Most of those who had trained as diggers had turned to working for the oil companies, drilling oil with machines. The only thing Hassan was interested in digging now, he added, was his exit. He was working his way north towards Europe.

I sat amid strange voices speaking unknown tongues in hushed tones. Whatever I said felt wrong, as if I was sitting outside a walled room where decisions were being made that I did not understand.

'And what does he have to do with us?' I whispered to Samir, when Hassan wasn't listening.

'He is going to arrange our undercover manoeuvre,' said Samir, with his mouth full.

'What undercover manoeuvre?'

'Over the zone, of course.'

'I thought we had decided we weren't going that way?'

'We have no choice.'

'Why?'

'Because we are taking something.'

'Fleabag?'

'Not exactly.' He paused for a moment. 'There is nothing to worry about,' he said, and, of course, that gave me more reason to worry.

The bag of weapons we were carrying rolled into the forefront of my mind. That detour in the dunes must have been deliberate. What a fool I had been. That was how they afforded their shiny Land Cruisers. I felt the sweat seep out of my skin. It drizzled down my neck in thick globules.

'Samir,' I hissed. 'It's the weapons... isn't it?'

At first, he tried to ignore me. I wanted to dance. I wanted oak trees. But the bubble of my ignorance had ruptured.

'What do you mean?' He looked away. He knew he wasn't going to get away with it.

As he told me straight out, I almost choked on my cheeseball.

Bread was broken and passed around the group, but a new ingredient had been added to the air already sweet with the aroma of goat's milk.

It was the scent of disillusion.

A spectrum of jagged flashes appeared before my eyes. My chest hammered. We were not just carrying weapons. We were selling them.

Calmly, Hassan went through what he saw as the 'nuances' of the situation, which were hazy. Then he ran through our options which appeared to be just the one. He couldn't help mentioning that there would be a few other travellers crossing the zone as well, although he wouldn't say who they were.

Suleyman stood up and walked out.

Samir pulled me back. He spoke in Tamahaq. '*Awahla?* Is there a problem?'

'*Kia bo.* No.'

Darkness fell. The men prayed to Allah to grant us a safe passage. I longed for sleep, but the day was not over.

Death is here
Tamatant tilay

Fear is a place that can halt time and close up distance. Its spiky, thorny edges cut to the bone. I recognised its dark venom of old. Now it reached back to me, this terror, from out of my past. It slunk silently out of my muscles and sinews and stalked me.

I felt it. I smelt it. I knew I was its prey.

There was a group crossing the *zone interdite* that night, but in the dark it was hard to tell exactly how many. There may have been fifteen or twenty of us, excluding camels, plus a few sheep. I could make out children and babies carried in slings. Tucked into the warmth and rhythm of their mothers' bodies, they made no sound. They learned from the beginning about danger.

Who was afraid? Did they see my fear? Did they hide theirs from me? It was but another shadow. It was buried in the drifts and folds around those dark eyes I sensed watching me that saw more than mine. It rung in those ears that heard the sounds that flew past my own.

Hassan whispered instructions, his breath making swirls in the cold air. We had to move silently and quickly, so as not to draw attention to ourselves. We had to follow in his footsteps because around us there were landmines and *djinn*. We had to stay on guard in case the soldiers at the army posts spotted us.

I nodded. I couldn't see any army posts, but then again, I couldn't really see anything. I wasn't brought up to see in the dark like he was.

A hill-shaped outline appeared silhouetted against the moon, then another and another, but these curves were not land features. The camels seemed scared too, but after a little urging they were loaded without too much fuss. They led on unquestioningly, despite the hour and the freezing temperature. Fleabag started off slowly, but Samir was careful to hold the rope short in case she started.

Suleyman led, his robe twinkling as if someone had cut out a piece of the sky and clothed him in it. Samir walked behind him and I followed them both, with my beating heart and my too-loud breathing.

In the blue-tinged starlight the path looked surreal. Insects flicked and purred like metronomes. Small cries echoed in the undergrowth, as if strange beasts lurked there. In the sheltering rocks I felt eyes watching us, though it was too dark to be sure. There were only shadows, so elusive by nature that it might be argued that even they had shadows. Some appeared soft, others hard-edged. Patterned areas mottled the distance which might have been rocks, their surfaces radiating and blurring, and lighter areas of what I guessed might be grass, twitching slightly when touched by the cold air. Or perhaps it was my flickering vision that made them alternate.

I stalked my shadow and it stalked me. Still, neither of us could catch each other.

Fleabag shivered, her dark outline so black that her mystery seemed unfathomable. I laid my hand on her shoulder to comfort her.

Together, as a team, light and dark slowly took form. Stones became sharper, gathering around our feet, as if the rock itself had awoken and was coming to get us.

A latticework grew out of nothing, a fence, although the varying light exaggerated its distortions, as if someone had lost interest when erecting it. It was about fifteen-feet high. Along the sides were holes and dips where the metal had eroded, or where someone had cut through. A large rock concealed a cloth. Under it, a hole had been tunnelled in the sand. About twenty yards off, a section had been pulled down entirely. Perhaps Hassan had removed it by himself somehow.

Part of me wanted to cry out, but the fear remained inside. Silence was easier. No one else spoke. There was no sound from the babies, only the angry buzz of midnight insects.

Signalling to Suleyman, Samir took over Usem's rope, leading him across to the other side. The other camels followed obediently. They knew how to stay quiet when it was important. They were braver than I.

That thought was premature, because precisely in that split second Fleabag emitted a loud sound that defied any translation. Tlatig bucked. Usem tore at his rope. Agizul kicked out. Something had unnerved them. Others had smelt it too. '*Alfo! Ek!* Yuk!' The abominable stench was everywhere. It was worse than fear itself.

Slowly, the camels settled. They trusted their master, bowed to him. I wished I could have had the same blind faith.

'*Io*! come on!' urged Samir. 'We have to go quickly...'

But Suleyman knelt. Someone trained a torch and all of us stared down. Suddenly, I saw perfectly.

The face of what once had been a camel had long gone. The eye sockets, now hollow, were cavities, the teeth gritted in a ghoulish grin. The hide was intact on the flanks, but some of the body appeared to have been eaten. Parts of the leg bones lay scattered, as if they did not belong to it. The ribcage was visible, draped with muslin-fine skin.

The neck lay stretched like a long, thin rope, as if struggling to reconnect the head that had become detached.

The men cast up their palms, invoking the Kel Essuf spirits to lend peace to its soul.

'Did it die naturally?' I wondered.

'Probably. It was a bull,' said Samir.

'Was it the one we saw earlier, in the dunes?'

'I don't think so.'

'Did a jackal attack it?'

'Perhaps, though it would have been picked clean by now.'

Suleyman frowned. As he lifted his veil. I looked at his face and examined the strain upon it. His chest heaved and he coughed painfully. 'It is a *gri-gri,* a changed one,' he said, gathering himself.

He meant it would bring bad luck.

We walked on, and this time the silence was greater, deeper. Sometimes the air was filled with the rumble of a camel, at others the tick-tick of an insect, but that was all. As dawn broke the flashing lights in my head mingled with the brightening sky, but I hadn't even noticed my migraine.

It was another hundred yards or so before Hassan gave the all-clear. He stepped forward and we shook hands. '*Yetkel yalla full-ak turna- ta-rer.* May God take away your disease,' he said, and I assumed he was speaking of my foreignness. He smiled with his deceptive teeth and then he left us, as quietly as if the wind had taken him and the dollar notes that Suleyman had dropped into his fist.

Against the stumps of greenery and the animal tracks winding between the wrinkled rocks, the line of the group straggled away. None of them knew where they were being led. I did not know where I was going either.

❋ ❋ ❋

Just as people have an aura, places carry an atmosphere. It is as if the ground itself has the ability to absorb energy generated by those who live on it or pass through, and to reflect it back like an echo. In a war zone, or anywhere that has witnessed tragedy, violence stamps its mark on to the landscape, in twisted bodies in roadside ditches, in bullet-riddled buildings. When it rains it is as if the sky is shedding tears. As dust becomes mud, it is as if the earth is bleeding.

It is important such places are not forgotten, not just so that we may pay homage to those who have suffered there, but because through the act of witnessing them maybe we can alter their tune. Perhaps only then can there be healing.

In the cold light before dawn the recollection of the trauma still not yet clear was becoming obvious. Death was no stranger to this place. I could sense it. I could smell it.

On the ground lay pipes, a burnt pathway where the land was raw, distressed and porous. There were no trees or plants here, no healing herbs, barks or roots. The land was like burnt skin, healed over, but forever scarred.

In the misty half-light, crystals glistened in the sand. In some places the rock had retained a little of its original character. In other places it had melted entirely and was coagulated. Sulphur and rust and neon green glistened on the ground. Any natural hues had been obliterated.

Suleyman paused often. The air into which he exhaled his cigarette smoke was already hot. It had a poisonous quality that lingered long before he had lit up. He knew what went on there, but he did not wish to speak of it. No one ever spoke of what had caused this devastation, the day the sky caught fire. But that day was burnt for ever in the memories of everyone who knew, however much they wanted to forget. I did not give it a voice either, although I had heard the rumours of the nuclear tests carried out by the French in the years before I was born.

For decades the military zone in In Eker has been out of bounds. Today it lies in the blind glare of the hottest sunlight on the planet, but it is a place of shadows. There are no residents. Only flies make their homes here – and smugglers. Even the rock underfoot has melted, so that everything feels detached, as if the earth's surface is in exile. It is a rejected place, where no tree survives. A realm of *djinn*, the only beings who can sneak past the security clearances are invisible.

The bitter, sick land faded from sight. Half a mile on, Suleyman hobbled the camels and sprinkled down oats for their breakfast. They did not want to drink.

Bone-weary, we clambered inside our tents, I, resigned to an unknown fate that I assumed would be worse than death, the two men laughing about what Samir described as our escape from Medina.

☀ ☀ ☀

As the jeep purred to a halt all I could think of was how new it looked and how smoothly the brakes were running. Two well-fed, balding, crisply-uniformed soldiers stepped out, designer sunglasses flashing in the sunlight.

Boldly, Samir walked forward, the colour flooding in his face. Suleyman was right behind him. A waft of *eau d'urine* hung in the air, but it was not his own. Not for the first time he had been drinking camel pee. The Prophet Mohammad prescribed it as medicine.

'You have permission to be here?' said the first soldier,

straightening his belt. He had slanting, sleepy eyes and his front teeth were uneven. His head glistened in the sunlight.

'*Bien sûr.*' Samir gave a sharp guffaw. I couldn't be sure, but I had a feeling he knew them. He didn't say so. He acted as if they were strangers. Casually he handed over the stained piece of paper, torn at the edges.

In the distance I heard Fleabag call ruefully. There was excitement in that noise as well.

'There is no date on this document,' said the officer, glancing at it, although deliberately not at Suleyman who gave a short, swift response: 'They didn't put one.'

Sensible questions echoed around the rocks. Did we know there were bandits around here? Suleyman played dumb. Did we know it was dangerous? I played dumber.

As Samir handed over another tatty document I was grateful he interceded for me. Perhaps they had every right to be suspicious of the pale foreign woman making strange expressions as she explained disjointedly in their language that she was was taking a camel to a *marabout*. There was no reason to take her seriously. She was a fool.

'I don't think the *marabout* is in Mertoutek these days,' said the first officer, whose slanty eyes now looked as if they were closing with boredom.

The other soldier looked marginally more interested. His eyes were kind, fiery. I wanted to believe him. 'What makes you think that?' I said.

'We saw him.'

'Really?'

'Yes,' interjected the other one. 'Everyone knows he has a house in Tazat.'

'Tazat?' Samir scratched his chin.

'What if we called?'

'There are no phones.'

'Not even satellite ones?'

'You know they are illegal.'

Having established that we were in possession of one, the radio equipment was searched twice, and after that my lotions, balms and underwear, but it was my mascara that raised an eyebrow because was not kohl. Next they turned their attention to the food supplies, eyeing the small volume of Tennyson with particular disdain. No one took any notice of the guns.

'They will take what they like before they let us leave,' whispered Samir behind their backs.

He was partly right. It was my Agent Provocateur perfume that got me off the hook. The officer took it for his wife.

Waving, they purred away in their pussycat engine. 'They are *akzew*,' said Samir, glancing around furtively – those shameless oppressors who commandeered their camels, took water from their wells and made whores of their women folk.

It was only much later that he confessed that they belonged to the 'secret police', and then, with the greatest reluctance, Suleyman told me that he had paid them.

'Do I owe you?' I said.

He shook his head. He wouldn't say how the deal was made either, only that camel wee was a *baraka* where baldness was concerned. He wasn't joking.

Samir was equally tight-lipped. 'You mustn't say to people where we are going or why,' he said only.

'Why not? You said yourself it was secure.'

'It's very political,' was all I got out of him.

'*Et le document?*'

'*Le mirage de la photocopie.*'

A prisoner of the present
El waqqen high anukmamnen

A sound was floating in my head. It had a sort of throaty, grating quality. There it was again, reedy, questioning. A cramped sensation overcame me, a feeling of warmth and, at the same time, of constriction. As the thought flashed in my head, something drifted past my nose. That's funny, I thought to myself. Dreams don't usually stink of ammonia. It must have been one of my nightmares.

I turned over and snuggled up to my teddy bear. Then I opened my eyes.

'Get off, Fleabag!'

Around me the tent lay collapsed in a crumpled heap. The pegs had been uprooted. A solitary pole kept what remained of its support structure from my face – that was, of course, apart from Fleabag's hairy beard. Somehow she had managed to manoeuvre herself into my tent, except she hadn't really moved 'in'; she had simply asserted her authority upon it – or tried to.

Her body was beside me, head hovering above mine. There were a lot of teeth. She didn't shift when I asked her politely. She simply gurgled. Nonchalantly she chewed her cud. There was a relaxed, warm, fuzzy look about her. It said, 'Now I have decided to act friendly.'

'Fleabag… you are on my sleeping bag!' I really wasn't in the mood. Nor, considering the state of that breath, was I ever going to be. 'Get out!'

She sidled a little closer. Hastily, I reached for a plastic bag… just in case.

What was it with camels, anyway? One minute they didn't want to know you – spent months playing hard to get and vomited on you – and then the next minute they were all over you with their killer Satan breath.

She shot me another look. It said, 'Whatever.'

She carried on chomping.

I lifted the collapsed tarpaulin and peeked out. The sun hung menacingly, as if planning today's onslaught, but there was no sign of the men. What were they up to this time? The hour for dawn prayers had long gone, and I could see no *atise* or *tichghar* to collect bark or roots.

Still sitting in my sleeping bag, I pulled on my sweater. The trousers required more wriggling. Perhaps it was a good thing they were not there. At least the two of them wouldn't have to witness my foul language.

Now that there wasn't a tent in the way, I was afforded an uninterrupted view of the sky and an excellent one of the desert. On the lower slopes of the Atakor, and even right up in the peaks, darker patches lay like playing cards amid the expanses of boulders, scrub and isolated trees. I imagined they were gardens where plants and vegetables were cultivated.

In the foreground a tall, wavy line was working its way around the boulders. The line grew bolder, paused and waved. It was Samir.

Fleabag's tail swished contentedly. She appeared to be enjoying her predicament. Or maybe it was because she had spotted him.

He looked good as he walked over. He was without his *chèche* and his stride was bold and strong. He seemed more confident somehow. There was no hint of the cosmic worlds that separated us. I wanted to dance with him again there and then, but there was a problem.

A camel was sitting on my tent.

'What happened?' he gasped, trying to coax Fleabag up.

'She just sort of... invited herself in,' I said.

'She could have squashed you!'

'I know.' Death by camel suffocation wasn't exactly what I had had in mind either.

He sat down on the sand beside me. My veil was off and he was gazing at my hair.

'I am sorry,' he said sheepishly. 'I must have forgotten to hobble her properly.' His gaze had deepened from within and he had become more insistent, as if wishing in this moment to be understood, but with no words sufficient in any of our crossover languages.

'It is I who needs to be forgiven,' I said, after a few moments.

I shouldn't have asked him about the guns. I should have acted dumb. It was usually best to play the fool, especially in a world you did not understand and which did not understand you.

Fleabag rose from her new domain with the utmost reluctance. The other camels remained aloof, tents having lost their thrall long ago. We were still picking up the pieces when Suleyman returned from his 'walk'. He looked a little more dishevelled than usual. He smelt of camel pee.

'How are you, Suleyman?' I said. I did not wait for an answer. I knew it would not be forthcoming. Hastily, I grabbed a scarf and wound it around my head.

He smiled his unsettling smile. His breath was uneven, his brow moist. 'How are *you*?' he asked. 'It is very dangerous to allow a camel...'

'But...'

He did not wait for an answer. Camels were the least of our worries.

Over tea we reassessed our situation, Fleabag still sitting near my half-dismantled tent along with Winaruz, who had loped over to watch. Suleyman patted his forehead using his sleeve. Once again we discussed the vagaries of hunting down the lesser-spotted *marabout*. Was he still living in Mertoutek? Maybe he had moved on to Tazat, as the secret police maintained?

Holy men in north Africa often move around, giving blessings and receiving alms. There were other villages he could be visiting. He might just as well have been in Tahifet, Tarhaouhaout or Tin Tarabine. Or perhaps he had journeyed south-west to Iglene, Otoul or Amsel, or to the flat expanse of Tanezrouft?

More likely, he did not exist.

'Of course he does!' Samir tried not to scowl. 'He is in Mertoutek, as I said many times. You just don't *listen*.'

'I do not *listen* when I do not like what I hear,' I said.

Suleyman refereed with a camel bell. 'There is just a very small place that I would like you to see. Really. It is on the way.'

'How small?' In all honesty, I didn't really care.

'Tiny.'

Against a big red sun, Suleyman paced. According to his estimation, it was going to take two days to reach the *sebkha*. I understood by this that he meant about four, since he was so prone to underplaying everything. Given the inevitable delays waiting for what he loosely described as authorization, that would bring it to ten, and that was without the unforeseen setbacks. I thought this was to be a short trip. I hadn't counted it up, but if my map was anything to go by, we had more than 30 kilometres still to go. Some terrain was impassable, but there was a small, spindly-looking track leading part of the way.

'Why don't we hire another truck and drive? Fleabag is much better about travelling these days. She may not even need a sedative. We can keep the truck for our return journey?' It meant a journey of hours rather than days and I was shattered. Another blister on my heel was agony.

'You don't like walking with us?' Suleyman looked offended, as if shocked I might not like the idea of walking along an exposed track in the heart of an area well known to be dodgy.

'I do like walking with you, but…'

'You don't want to see more of beautiful Algeria, lovely sunshine, Allah's chosen land?' said Samir.

'The route is dangerous,' I said.

'We know the dangers,' he quipped.

'But it's the unknown ones I'm worried about,' I said, addressing both of them.

'We are resourceful,' said Suleyman, popping a camel spider into his mouth and crunching.

'But the road is notorious,' I winced.

'It is safe.'

'But it isn't safe, is it? It never has been.'

'The mountains are our allies. They will not harm us,' insisted Samir.

'But we are not going into the mountains, are we?'

'Only to the foothills.'

'And is that where the guns are going?'

He did not answer this. He looked away, withdrawing snail-like into his shell again. I had upset him.

'OK, let's do it,' I said reluctantly. There was nothing else I could say. I had no control in this predicament and I had brought it on myself.

✹ ✹ ✹

A few hours later, our supplies had been restocked, a truck had been arranged and the camels given their sedatives. By some strange fluke I wasn't too far out on the timing.

Ours was not the only vehicle heading along the mountain road that night. A few trucks carrying passengers met us head on, causing some treacherous reversing to avoid hitting the sand drifts. The trucks passed by, and in the wing mirror I watched their headlights petering out in the distance of my mind. The immigrants I had known had become emigrants. They were no longer strangers. They were people.

The plateau looked surreal in the sunset, like a lost land. A Rothko red sunrise was being painted, its halo a pink wash. Two small clouds bobbed above the horizon. There were no drones flying that evening; this time they were real clouds.

The region of Atakor is startling in its emptiness, of things, of people. The only features are mellow boulder fields. The peaks appear not to belong to this earth at all. Sections of rock fit together like dovetail joints in a fine table, their ochre hues more intense than the sand winding between them. Everything has shrivelled – riverbeds, the vegetation. They are like strange air-dried skeletons of their previous forms.

My head reeled, not just from the heat, but from all the activity that was going on in it. We had been arguing again, Samir and I, badly, about the route, about the camels, about many things. Or rather, he had been evading my questions. He was silent as he negotiated the track. I glanced over at his father and saw that his head had fallen sideways. His eyes had closed.

Hot on the heels of our heated discussion about the route, another argument about Islam had followed, this time about *jihad*. Regarding matters of unity and the caliphate, this was the first moment Samir had given any indication of being delusional and irrational. His insistence and my caution blended to create a *froideur* in the hottest place on earth imaginable.

He had begun quoting verses from the Qur'an about the Day of Judgement 'when the sun shall be folded up and the stars shall fall, and the mountains set in motion... and the seas shall boil'. That day was still to come and, as far as he was concerned, America and the West were making it happen.

I, being Western myself, refuted this.

'Look,' he insisted. 'There are varying opinions.'

'Varying opinions? You mean black and white terms. You cannot possibly sympathise with Isis?' I found it almost impossible to believe that he could support the violence and human rights abuses that were happening in Syria.

'Of course not,' he said, adding more quietly, 'Not entirely.'

'How do you mean?'

'Syria used to be a stable country. It was repressed but it was safe. Your bombing has made it one of the worst places on the planet.'

This particular viewpoint proved unarguable, and he had not convinced me he would not take up arms there if it was asked of him.

We settled on one matter at least: that we had to stop people turning to Isis as a solution.

Or, as Samir said, 'It is *your own* fault that people are flocking to Isis.'

I didn't dignify that comment with an answer. I bet Tuareg women never had to put up with this rubbish.

Instead I countered, 'It cannot be the only reason,' at which he shook his head in disgust. I felt at pains to appease him, worrying that I had upset him, caught between respecting his views and wishing to put across my own. But there was no reasoning with him. I wondered if this was far enough, this uncharted border that I had now reached with him. Something had been aired that was fundamental and it was much larger than our own haphazard, contradictory interactions. This was the edge, the final point.

There was no option other than to back down.

'Please don't be cross. I thought we had agreed to put politics behind us?' I said.

He didn't answer. He was concentrating, his foot on the accelerator. He was intent on watching the road, anticipating drifts. I decided not to press him. There was no point struggling on. We knew each other too well.

In the back of the truck even the camels were silent. I wished I was sitting with them. I envied their state of sedation. Nothing could ever be as soundless as our own yawning silence.

Thankfully, the journey passed without alarm and the camels slept for its duration. Fleabag was still sleepy. She retained a fear of vehicles, but she had recovered a great deal from the angst of those early days. She ambled down the ramp with quick, strong steps, drank her water with the others and began grazing with few protests. I couldn't see her, but I moved about her and sensed her muzzle.

A thin mist shielded the sky and concealed the land in its mystery. The men took out their rugs. In the beam of the headlights, they touched their foreheads to the ground in gratitude to Allah for delivering us safely and, in Samir's case, for delivering us from ourselves.

With weary steps, I wandered over towards the camels, shining my torch in case of scorpions. I could feel my heartbeat, the fast blood surging through my veins. My muscles prickled. I was heavy as a tree, though a little squidgy in the middle.

But it was too dark to turn inwards, that place where the darkness had ruled me, where it had governed me in occupation for so long, oppressing me, waging its war. I wondered if this crazy trip was just an excuse, a distraction. Perhaps the veil of our own shadows is in reality a comfort blanket. Perhaps it is a disguise.

In searching for the truth, so often we find ourselves at a loss. Our minds compensate for the shortfall.

René Descartes once wrote, 'If you really want to know truth, at least once in your life you must allow yourself to doubt everything you thought you knew.'

My mother always used to remind me of this. My love for her now, laid bare, was visceral, as if somehow the invisible umbilical cord between us lingered. How selfish I had been to abandon her.

Profound quiet followed, the deep silence of the plain as infinite as the stars. I switched off the torch and the light disappeared. Night eyes glittered in the bushes. For now they remained watchful.

Other things beyond my imagination moved there too. I guessed they were the monsters of my fears.

My heart cries out still

Ihal falas oulhin

We rose and set off before sunrise with mixed emotions. Suleyman said he knew what he was doing. His manner was self-assured. He had done it many times, he said, and with camels. Samir was confident too. We were not walking *across* a salt lake so much as *around* it, although it cannot have been said there was exactly a pathway.

Around us the brutal, inhospitable land felt unbounded. The wind blew sand, but apart from that, nothing stirred except the flies. They were out in force, laying siege to our hands and the tips of our noses, buzzing around the camels' heads, crawling on their eyelashes.

The region of Tanezrouft is known locally as the 'Land of Terror', 'the nothing in the nothing'. For centuries it has been regarded as one of the harshest environments in the Sahara. In 1809 the corpses of 2,000 caravaneers and 1,800 camels were discovered not far away. It encompasses several stretches of land suffused with salt deposits, including the Sebkha Mekerghene and its small family of equally hostile patches. We were entering only the periphery, although knowing this didn't make it any easier.

It was astonishing to think that there was once water here, that pomegranates and watermelons grew, birds drank and fish swam. Oak, walnut, cedar and elm had originally flourished in this parched, arid place, when the expanses of the Sahara had been woodland and savannah, lush grasslands and forests. An immense inland sea reached to the Niger River and extended south right down towards the Bight of

Benin. At around 2,000 BC the weather suddenly changed. The rains stopped falling on the lowlands, the lakes and rivers dried up and the change of climate altered the landscape irrevocably.

Today, strange curled shrubberies the colour of crystallite and mineral growths poke out of the cracked crust where evaporating water has left deposits.

Samir picked one up. He folded his fear into a perfect rose and handed it to me.

It wasn't a rose exactly, and yet it did look a little like one, its fragile petals meeting at the heart as if a flower had been formed from the desert. I had seen something similar in Mexico, a crystal rosette formed out of sand inclusions. I couldn't imagine it had healing powers, although for many people the natural chemicals of desert roses hold a metaphysical meaning.

'Thank you,' I said, and slipped it into my pocket. It was too hot to be romantic.

He smiled as if he had forgotten our arguments, as if they meant nothing.

Ahead, the blurred rule of the horizon separated sky and land like two blank pieces of paper, forming an unbroken sheet of whiteness. You could have turned them upside down and been none the wiser.

Progress felt so slow that it was as if we weren't really moving at all. A halo hovered around the camels, a pulsing wave of their mortality. Occasionally, one of them jerked a little, as if pushing away unpleasant thoughts. I admired their resilience, their fearlessness. They took adversity and swallowed it.

Fleabag stood tall against the whiteness. In the light, her hide shone gold, her long tail swung to one side and then back again. Now and then she became motionless, her attention caught by some far-off sound or movement. Every line of her body utilised instinct. Every ounce of her conserved itself against the heat. Every sinew stretched itself to the limit.

Then all these visions, like the words between us, dissolved again, leaving just our small caravan wandering through the haze in silence. The sounds of our footsteps and loads were the only structures and patterns.

I saw this shimmering landscape like a mirror, stark in its intensity, a perfect image of all that lay above and below at a single equidistant horizontal in my life. There are moments in time in which a place reveals its soul to us. The layers are peeled back and we are allowed a glimpse of its essence. Now was such an instant.

My throat was dry, my lips like sandpaper. There was two of everything, one distinct and another filmy and translucent. Figures melted. Flies swam. Thoughts became wayward, selecting their own pathways.

Hold on to Fleabag. There, that's the girl.

Fleabag sat down with me. My white hands were over her neck. I pressed my head on her, breathed my troubled breath. I buried my hands into the side of her body, felt her heart. I took her in and felt her oxygen. And she shaded me from the intensity that poured down on us.

That was when the memory hit me, like a train. At first it was a sound. It entered my head as a loud, distressed wail; it was that one, the one that had stalked my sleep like a dark tyrant. Only the dazzling intensity of this place brought it to fruition.

There are things that no one should see, cries no one should hear, words that should never be written.

A minute was too long in that dark place. I took a breath, and another. Breathe out. Breathe in.

A cool hand was on my brow. 'Are you all right?' Samir's voice was distant.

'My legs just went. Sorry.' I forced my wobbling mouth into a smile shape.

We sat there, immobile, Fleabag shielding us, the only movement trembling. I heaved a sigh and half-closed my eyes. Opening them again, a long way up I saw Suleyman's large, kind face hovering over me.

'Breathe like the camels. Take the minimum of air in.' His voice was kind. Liquid trickled on my cheek, the only water for miles.

He opened a packet of dehydration salts and mixed it with water for me. He added a herb. He said a name. I breathed like a camel for England. A few minutes later I was ready to walk to In Guezzam bearing Fleabag on my back. Ahead, Usem, Winaruz, Tlatig and Agizul stood in line. They did not fidget or groan.

Fifty metres later Suleyman paused again. He gave three sharp taps with his stick. The ground held firm. He tested the other direction.

Crack. There she blows!

He bent down and with his fingers reached out. He scooped a few grains and touched his tongue with them.

'It must be the sea,' he said, as a small child in Christmas wonder might, stars in its eyes. 'It is just as you said.'

'Yes,' I said. 'Like the sea.'

'The *baraka*,' he whispered. 'There will be no more bad spirits.' He closed his eyes; when he opened them again, they were glassy.

I could tell he was charting the ocean of his mind. He was connecting the waves of his imagination.

※ ※ ※

The sun began to dim and a breeze lifted the air. Sand swept along the land like water ebbing sideways. It was still another merciless mile before set-down and, by then, the camels were straining, their humps depleted, eyes bulging a little. There was water in a rock *guelta*.

Only after we had watched our good friends drink did we fill our bellies with our own water bottles.

Suleyman drank as I had never seen anyone drink, glugging the liquid as it spilled over, letting it run down his chest as though his life depended on it. Afterwards he took out his pipe and lit it, and the water that had gone in flowed out again in memory.

It had started back in the 1960s, when French scientists conducted tests in the region, contaminating the desert and poisoning relations between France and Algeria. But that wasn't all that was poisoned.

France chose the abandoned place of In Eker in what was then a French colony to carry out nuclear explosions. Some say France deliberately exposed her soldiers to the blasts to study their effects on humans, but it was not only the soldiers who suffered. In some locations radiation is still twenty times higher than normal.

There was one day burnt into Suleyman's own history. On 1 May 1962 a test codenamed Beryl went wrong. Due to improper sealing of an underground shaft, a cloud of radioactive dust and rock was released into the atmosphere.

Almost half-a-century later, some of the truth has also leaked out. Its toxic legacy is one of environmental devastation and disease that has caused untold damage. Cancer has killed a great many local people, and infertility and cataracts are commonplace. Access to medical treatment in the area has always been scarce, but today it is even worse. To this day France refuses to deliver the archives to Algeria. No apology has been made to the people or any compensation awarded.

The French are building a power station in England.

Officially the irradiated area in Algeria has been sealed off. Unofficially it has not. Traffickers daily slip their cargo through, unhindered by the authorities. To those they are carrying, who are paying their life savings for the privilege, they play down the dangers. Most people are so desperate that they take the risk anyway. As do their children.

This was the dark zone we had passed through. The majority of people who have lived anywhere near it have become ill. Even camels have lost their lives. Back when it happened, everyone believed that a pregnant woman's anger caused birth defects and that adultery resulted in madness. But the locals were not stupid. No tree or plant could have saved them from the diseases that followed. Of course the authorities denied responsibility. No one was accountable.

Samir's grandmother was one of the first to fall ill the day the great *djinn* lit the sky. She was only twenty-four years old at the time. She lived for six more years. By then she had given birth to two sons and two daughters. Three of them had subsequently died young, including a daughter with 'the face of an angel and the body of a *houris*'.

She was Samir's mother.

Suleyman's pipe was trembling. It would not obey the fingers that held it. Watching him stare out into the great dark abyss of his past, it occurred to me that in seven days he had achieved a few more wrinkles. His *chèche* was low, eyebrows a little whiter and sparser. He had lost the glossy veneer that I used to see in him. Perhaps he had come to realize that he too was fallible.

And he still hadn't done up his trousers properly.

A band of cloud had formed as the golds of sunset swept across the peaks, filled with rose and amber. Across from me, sitting on the night-black rock, Suleyman's son, though silent, still moved and breathed. There was nothing I could think of that would comfort him.

He took up his pipe. As he abandoned himself to the moment, it was as if the explosion was happening all over again and he saw his beloved wife as a spirit standing before him, an all-embracing whiteness, like sunlight reflecting off sand, cascading over the mountains and opening out across the desert plains.

As soon as he described her he fell silent. The light faded from his eyes, as if her soul had been swept away on one of the shooting stars his people navigated by.

Regarding him, I wondered if perhaps everything we are stems back to one moment. If we could only go back in time and pinpoint it, we could access the key to our future, but we do not possess the power to turn back our clock in history. Only in our minds can we perform time travel. Only in our hearts can we find truth.

'And is that how you became ill, Suleyman?'

He did not stir at my question, and it was a very long time before he cleared his throat again. 'The desert makes everything dramatic,' he said.

Samir leaned forward. I could tell he wanted to touch me. 'They are mining plutonium over there,' he whispered.

I should have guessed. The oil rigs were never oil rigs at all. Now he confirmed it, swearing upon the Qur'an, I had to believe him.

There are uranium mines west of Tamanrasset. Senior nuclear scientists have bought houses in the desert. They are from Libya, North Korea, Russia and Pakistan. What if al Qa'eda is smuggling nuclear material from Mali and Libya via Algeria? Guns and drugs have an easy passage through the desert. Customs checks are lax and everyone knows, however well they conceal themselves, Isis support is well established in north Africa.

Suleyman wouldn't confirm any of it, but he would not deny it either. An elderly man might not see as well as he used to, but he enters into percipience.

As the sky began its usual display of glittering spirals, the camels nibbled *jujube* leaves. We sat for a while, gazing in wonder at the sea above our heads where a million grains of salt floated. This time, all our eyes were glassy.

Dusk
Takkawalt
· ‖ ⊐ · ⌗

I am ready to die

Edjegh iman-in taxya

It is a universally known fact that nuclear weapons emit thermal radiation. Energy is released as visible light waves, known as flash, and invisible heat waves. It is the expansion of this energy, through space and particles, that forms the heart of any nuclear blast – a fireball around 300,000°C in temperature, huge and bright as a devil's sun.

Fireballs take different forms, but their effects are always devastating. Immediate damage is mainly thermal injury. Shock waves generate pressure waves through the tissues of the body, causing embolisms or haemorrhaging.

Many effects are more gradual. Long-term devastation includes radiation poisoning, infertility, blood cancers and cataracts, plus an increase of subsidiary diseases including polio, TB, pneumonia, cholera, typhoid and dysentery.

In the face of all this, burnout can seem inevitable.

There was a renewed sense of purpose in Suleyman's footsteps that following morning. I hardly noticed him struggling for breath. He said nothing more about the tragedy that had taken his family from him and he did not mention the illness that had been slowly devouring him that he attributed to radiation.

Perhaps that was why he wanted to go to the *marabout* in the first place; he needed to be healed as much as Fleabag did. That he had poured out his heart after so long made me realize that I owed him something. He, too, had been walled in. Bravely he had kept it to himself. And nothing could be more painful than losing someone you loved in such horrific and avoidable circumstances.

As I glanced across from father to son, these two men I had spent so much time with and to whom I had entrusted myself, I saw how little I had really known of them. What had I still to discover? Were the weapons the worst of it? Or was there more?

That morning, as we offered alms to a *tiboraq*, believed to shelter good spirits, and started off towards Mertoutek, I banished all fears from my mind. I was fooling myself, but then I always had been.

Samir acted as scout, walking ahead, scanning the pathway. We had put all arguments behind us, but my feelings remained mixed. Now that I had discovered that he had lost his mother in such dreadful circumstances, feelings welled up in me that I could never have imagined. I felt seduced by his difference, drawn by it; but why reinforce his stereotype? I would throw my arms around him and he would make whatever use of me he wanted and prove himself right.

The camels walked stoically, haunches crinkling like pistons. They seemed alert to every sound on the breeze that cooled our cheeks. Tlatig, strong and muscular yet nimble-footed, was leading, negotiating the slope effortlessly. Behind Tlatig, Usem brought up the rear this time. He had adopted his superior face.

Fleabag held her head high. There was a new wisdom about her gaze. Her eyes were full of intelligence.

Beyond the dry lake of salt that smelt of rotting oceans the land began to rise. Gentle slopes and misty low valleys surrounded us now, the beginnings of yet another expanse of wilderness, this one extending over 2,150 square kilometres and named after the pommel of a Tuareg sword,

Occasionally small chessboard patches of worked land

could be spied. Farmers toil to cultivate land in the region, using irrigation by *fogarra*, or underground manmade wells. In Tidikelt and Taouat they run miles beneath the desert. Here in the mountains they are sometimes just a few metres down. Settlements such as Indeles and Tazrouk, Hirafok and Abalessa rely on nature's blessings to survive. The foothills generate their own microclimate. Around granite waterholes life flourishes, although rains are seasonal, and when they arrive, flash floods are a constant danger to those who dare to live here.

Viewed from this high position, the desert behind us had faded into a varied collection of impulses. Beneath our feet lay basalt, raw from the outpourings of ancient volcanoes. Ahead, rock formations staggered in geometric edifices or in eerie stoops and leanings. Spires and pipe organ structures rose in rock cathedrals. Not for the first time did I get the sense we were passing the end of the world, that what lay beyond was unchartered.

Along with the undulations of the path came relief. The heat had waned. A breeze beckoned us like a welcoming signal. Aristotle believed air to be hot and wet, like blood, occupying a place between fire and water in the elemental spheres. Here, it felt anything but that. It rushed into the lungs, gossamer-light.

Looking back, I saw my footprints as obstacles, imprints of the insignificant worries and irrelevant concerns and fears that I had been gripped by in the past – the longing for love, the security awarded by possessions. Those tracks had disappeared beneath the weight of Suleyman's story.

The first hint of the Atakor is offered by the light of the peaks, a light so luminous that it has a bleaching effect on the lower slopes. In the early morning the land rises in cool purples from a *sfumato* of mists. As they evaporate, all that is left is a blue-grey expanse and, in the foreground, the ochres and rusts of rock and the green of cultivated oasis gardens. These are interspersed again with barren areas. The peaks sweep down to where rough edges fall in smoother, gentler folds.

No wonder they call it the *terrain abandonné*. It is at once wonderful and terrifying, a landscape that appears to deny all human access. It has remained almost entirely undeveloped. In the past, thousands made excursions to Assekrem, the hermitage built by Charles de Foucauld where he spent most of his time at prayer. Thinking of him now, I wondered if perhaps his fate was my own. He was murdered by separatists.

For all its barrenness, there are people. Children here long for a future and old women wear drab clothes that were once gaudy. They make no attempt to wash hardship out of their faces. We passed a man carrying a kid slung over his back, women bearing panniers, bands around their foreheads, and others herding goats.

The sun had risen fast and was hovering menacingly, as if planning its daily onslaught. Behind us the exclusion zone felt stark and unyielding. It was towards trees that we headed, breaking late morning into a rock-filled valley, unloading the camels and feeding them their oats. Sheltering in the shade of a *tiboraq,* we did not dwell for long. Tuareg custom held that it was important not to impose on its branches.

Further up on the slope the light was less intense, glittering on a lacewing basking in its warmth, or glowing red in the latticework of branches. Suleyman's trees – the *adoua, jujubiers, yadin, anzenan, arounkoud, anizame* and *tezagh* – found sanctuary in sacred spaces imbued with *baraka*. The *agar*, the *afgag* and the *abaka*, those trees that held untold secrets sheltered good Kel Essuf spirits. Butterflies danced like confetti. Underfoot, locusts ticked like old hall clocks. From grass tufts, mantis stared with chinless faces. Sandy heads popped out from beneath isolated rocks. Small geckos stared with globular eyes, while absent-minded flies barged across the ground, unaware they were on the menu. To remain invisible, a chameleon altered its colour as it moved across stones.

What is the colour of love?

It is just as well camouflaged.

Treading carefully, I avoided going anywhere near the fearsome *tadan* tree that sheltered bad spirits and gave fruit. Instead I sought refuge under the *afgag*, which I was confident of not offending. I cracked open a pomegranate and in the glistening redness I saw a memory.

This time I did not shut it out. With the juice, I sucked out that memory. I faced it head on – this mangled roof of a London bus peeled back, the carnage of injuries that cut deep beyond any physical damage.

Samir was rumpled, unshaven as he sat down beside me. He did not see my pain. His look had a melancholy about it, as if he was re-living his own.

My veil was skewed and he rearranged it.

'You should wear it looser,' he said, twisting the material back and pulling it around my shoulder. He tucked in the bed sheet that he had draped me in. I stood still and allowed him to fold it how he liked.

He rose to his feet, placed me in the twilight of a myrtle, turned me and stood back a little. I no longer cared how he saw me. My hair was always sticking out anyway.

'Would you teach me English?' he asked suddenly.

He was closer than I felt comfortable with. I smelt the smell of his sunny skin. I felt like an old sock. I sensed he was boxing me up again, wrapping me in the straitjacket of his expectations. 'I'm not sure I am able,' I said. I didn't exactly know where my sudden reticence came from. It seemed rude.

'But you can try?'

'Of course.'

As I spoke the words, a vibration rattled in my sinus cavities and grew loud.

It was the roar of Fleabag's jealousy.

We packed up and pressed ahead, still ascending among the scant vegetation, until at last settling breathlessly in an uninhabited valley full of boulders.

It had been a hard walk that day for all of us, and now it became harder. The mountain air at night was far colder than in the desert. It cramped the fittest of bodies. As the light waned, a harsh wind swept grit into my eyes and nose. My teeth began to chatter. It didn't matter. The only thing that mattered was Fleabag. She was the only one that I could trust and that had any kind of constancy. I knew her past and how awful it had been, but we were fixing it slowly and there was hope. I clung on to her truth, her fear, her pain, as if they were my own.

Careful not to step near the *agar*, the tree that I now knew it would be unwise to sleep under, I walked over to her. I had no axe to hand to render its *djinn* harmless. The wind was bitter and I felt a deep chill over my legs, right up to my neck. I leaned against Fleabag's side and stayed there, letting her warm me.

Soon a soup, *chorba*, was on the boil and the cooking pot was simmering. Fleabag and the other camels were munching oats. Dipped in thyme honey, the locusts didn't taste too bad, but I won't try eating them again

Our conversation reverted to that familiar old topic.

Only seventeen days had passed since I had first heard of him, yet I had the impression that the *marabout* really did have the power to take or give life.

Something else had changed too. 'He is a powerful man, of influence.' There was, I detected, an undeniable hesitancy in Samir's tone. He spoke as if he himself had lost faith. Or maybe it was something more sinister.

'You are not scared of him, are you?' I said.

'The *marabout*?' He had stopped eating. A little oil dribbled down his chin. He turned his head away.

'Of course. Who else?'

'A little.'

'Is he dangerous?'

'Perhaps. Do you still want to go?'

I nodded. 'Of course I do. We've come this far. Fleabag deserves it. Anyway, now I want to find the *hantit*.'

He laughed a belly laugh that I had never thought possible of him.

Fleabag seemed to agree. Sitting beneath the *ebizgin*, that tree with sharp thorns that did not bother her as she munched them, she dribbled.

Suleyman remained seated, camel blanket wrapped around his shoulders, squinting into the distance. He did not laugh. He was miles away. Shifting his prayer beads, half-murmuring, he whispered words from the Qur'an almost inaudibly, fanning the mood of acceptance.

Even as I began speaking again, seriously this time, he did not appear to be listening. Nor did he lift his *chèche* as he always did when he felt uncomfortable. A stillness veiled him that I could not fathom.

It had been a very long time since I had lost my friend that day, when the destruction of the blast in Kabul had seemed so great that the air itself seemed to be ablaze. She had been killed outright. She had simply been in the wrong place at the wrong time.

Maryam was a young girl aged seventeen who had wanted to save the world. Convinced that education above all else is the way to solve the poverty and lack of understanding at the root of the conflict in our world, she had been training to be a school teacher. She had believed knowledge is the key to understanding.

It was she who had been the inspiration for my own work in Afghanistan, creating books for those children without hope, who could not afford schooling, who had no money even for food.

'*Ilm*,' said Samir.

I nodded, and a silence filled the air that felt very long.

'It is always extremely dangerous to meddle with situations that you cannot possibly understand,' said Suleyman eventually. There was no emotion in his voice.

'Yes, I know,' I said, gathering up my own veil above my nose. How well I knew. It is so easy to have the best of intentions but to make the gravest of errors. It had taken me a long time to learn that lesson.

Samir stood up and walked off. Suleyman went over to him. As the two of them began whispering, it was impossible to hear what they were saying. I knew I should never have told them.

Soon the peaks became shadows, the skies emptied of their usual glitter. In silence and with difficulty, the two men reached agreement. Together, they picked up the oversized camel-skin bag.

It was obvious which one that was.

Clunking and clanking, the contents poured out. There they all lay – enough to vanquish an army of terrorists: one pile of guns and ammunition, and another, smaller pile of modest-sized blades, all made out of brass, with wooden sheaths covered with tooled leather.

Samir began to sift through a cluster of small knives and long daggers he called *sheru*, most of which had been acquired on the black market. Those ones were 'secret'.

'*Ma-môs awa*? What is that?' I asked.

'That one is for decoration,' said Suleyman, handing me his prized possession, a large silver blade carved in detail. He seemed surprised that I had picked up some Tamahaq.

I admired it closely. It had the most exquisite leather sheath I had ever seen.

He delved into his robe, fished out his pipe and lit it. He coughed painfully. Misty-eyed, he spoke of old times, when his ancestors had carried the *coba*, the sword. He told of the *llagh*, the lance, and the *aghar*, the shield made of antelope skin, and of the times he had hunted jackal with a bow and arrow, the *amur* and *taganze*.

One of the swords, a *telek*, had a grip in the shape of a cross and a gold inlay studded with rubies. The base was made of brass, with green geometric patterns carved into it symbolizing tribal leadership. Another, diamond-shaped, had been hand-forged. The *ricasso* was particularly fetching, covered with decorative brass with triangular copper panels.

'It's very expensive. The best,' said Samir.

'*Io*. OK.' I handed it back.

Next he moved on to the rifles. There were about ten, battle-ready, as new.

'This is *your* weapon,' he said. 'Fast, efficient, used in the Second World War.'

He handed it to me and I handed it straight back. It was an MG3 and looked particularly dangerous. I wasn't sure if I should be holding such an object. Samir put it down.

'An F2000. Premium quality. Goes like a rocket.' It was

an assault rifle, produced by FN Herstal in Belgium. 'I got it from a businessman in Abu Dhabi.'

The Heckler & Koch 416, an updated edition of the American M4, looked particularly lethal, although the Heckler & Koch MG4, dating back to the 1990s, was known as an even deadlier killing machine. It never missed its target.

'Ah, those are from Gaddafi,' he whispered. It was a gold mine.

'How did you come by them?'

'Secret.'

There were several AK-47s that had also been travelling with us. Those ones I knew well, from when I was in Afghanistan. 'Did you get them in Russia?' I asked, putting on my wide-eyed expression.

'How did you know that?'

'Secret.'

Samir smiled benignly. Without realizing, I had been cradling the sabre.

Two sub-machine guns lay among others at the bottom of the heap: an Uzi, designed in Israel, and a Thompson MI921. 'It has astonishing accuracy,' he said.

The revelation that they were buying and selling arms was not a surprise, but the quantity and quality was almost overwhelming. We counted the main ones in Tamahaq... '*Iyet, essin, harad, okkoz, semmus, sedis, essa eham, tezza, meraou...*' There were more than a dozen in all.

'Everyone has weapons. How else are we expected to make ends meet?'

'Who are you selling them to exactly?' I said.

He pulled up his *chèche*, as if out of defiance. He would not look me in the eye.

At that moment a shrill yapping broke the silence, the

inimitable cry of the hunting she-jackal. The camels seemed undaunted. They knew it well. Even Fleabag didn't scream. Instead, she raised her head and cried back.

The truth, when it emerged, came gradually from his father's lips. Most of it is well known, although much of the information is not released. All manner of surplus ammunition and semi-automatic rifles are traded freely in the Sahara. Food and water is hard to come by, but the supply of weaponry is so liberal as to appear unlimited. Small pistols and AK-47s, often from Russia, have flooded into the region during the multiple wars of recent decades. They are easier to come by now than they ever were.

Drugs provide the funding, although it is not like in past decades, when drug barons such as Hadj Bettou or El Chelfaoui, known as the Pablo Escobar of Algeria, ruled over the drug trade in north Africa. Nowadays, terrorists and drug-dealers share the same shadowy territory. Groups such as GSPC, the GIA and Boko Haram control many of the established smuggling rackets. Arms purchased in Niger, Mali, the Ivory Coast, western Sahara and Libya are used to fight *jihad* in the Middle East.

Many that are traded are sold to Isis.

It is a sophisticated business and, of course, a global one. In the Sahara, where family and tribe form deep bonds, old loyalties hold strong. No one ever grasses on anyone. They know how to keep their promises because their very lives depend on it. For the right amount, anything – or, in my case, anyone – can be slipped through the desert with little effort. If someone wants access to a region for business, they just call the man from Aqim, or they fund a terrorist group long-term. They call it protection money. If a trafficker wishes to transport their 'cargo' across a territory, they call the police and do a deal.

'Last one. You're not concentrating. See,' said Suleyman, showing me a holder for extra bullets or magazines. 'Less time for refills.'

'Isn't it too risky, even for you, Suleyman, to carry weapons?'

Suleyman cast his eye towards the distant horizon. 'I know it is safe,' he said, 'because the spirits have told us their secrets.'

He smiled. I think he meant it as a reassurance.

'This was never about Fleabag, was it?'

He frowned, and a silvery droplet of sweat ran from his eyebrow. 'We never meant to deceive you,' he murmured. 'Only to keep our promise to you.'

Samir had disappeared up a slope. I hurried after him to the sound of the wind whirring. When he saw me, he spun around and took long strides back down towards me.

He stopped as if he wanted to ask something. Then he appeared to think better of it. As usual there was no sound save the echo of our thoughts.

Still he didn't openly ask me. He never made a move. I was giving him mixed signals.

I kissed his cheek – a light kiss, the shadow of a kiss, like a whisper.

'Don't go back,' he said.

We were both aware this was a pretence. I mean, as if I was going anywhere.

'I'm not,' I said. I felt seduced by his need. Only to think of it made me feel released, full, like the flesh of the pomegranate. He, I imagined, was seduced by what I could offer him, a new life maybe, a passport even. He might have deluded himself about it, but it was true.

He reached for his binoculars, fixing on a point almost directly at a quarter-turn. We were surrounded by rock, our breaths loud as we climbed the heavy path upwards.

'What is it?' I gasped.

He looked through the field glasses, trying to keep them steady. He passed them to me. 'See for yourself.'

'What?' It was so black I couldn't see anything. I would never be able to see in the dark. I handed them back.

'It is the village.'

The dog leaves the doghouse

Izajjar edi asanso-net

Sometimes it is as if the closer we appear to be to attaining our goal, the further it recedes. A chasm appears to open up before us. We ask ourselves, 'Where am I now, really?', even if that question feels meaningless. Perhaps it is so between all beginnings and endings, and all apparent opposites. For only when we stand at the brink do we become aware of the real distance between where we are and that for which we are searching.

I woke and slept, woke and slept. The denial inside me was like a wall, impermeable, unbreakable. I was standing at my own precipice, occupying a betwixt and between place, where sand had become blood. Its receding tide had washed a piece of the past at my ankles. I picked it up. That day I had had a meeting with the Taliban.

Nietzsche wrote, 'A man must have chaos yet within him to be able to give birth to a dancing star.' He also wrote, 'People don't want to know the truth because they don't want their illusions destroyed.'

We were carrying weapons and both men were still refusing to say where or with whom they were trading them. All along I had known we had them with us. From the start, I had deliberately put myself in a situation most people would have deemed suicidal. And they were right. Just like before, I was on my very own suicide mission.

I was grateful that Suleyman had told me the truth, but I knew he had not revealed all. We shared a new under-standing, but I still did not know if I could trust him. With

Samir it was different. Underneath I told myself I might be in love with him, though in the corners of my heart I knew it was not love.

Love is the greatest mirage of all.

With trembling fingers I took out the slim volume of Tennyson that had travelled every step with me over so many kilometres of hostile territory. I opened the page and the torn piece of paper I had slipped into the middle when I was in London, long before I had ever set out on my journey, dropped out.

I scribbled those words myself. They were not mine, not Tennyson's, but those of Edward Wilson. 'It makes me feel that if the end comes to me or hereabout,' he wrote from the base of Beardmore Glacier in 1911, 'all will be as it is meant to be.'

We ate our small breakfast, loaded up and set off. All was quiet except for the creaking of the equipment and the shuffling of camel feet. A brightness warmed the space between the shadows, and the air had a dewy smell. A little moisture had settled overnight, dampening the ground. Black twig-like structures littered the expanse behind us.

Ahead, new panoramas opened up. From a single vantage point I counted no fewer than eight peaks, divided, according to Tuareg custom, into males and females. The Tuareg give them names and characters, some grand, heroic and warlike, others submissive. It is said that some can even move position, while others with their heads in the clouds are able to alter shape.

Suleyman led in long, determined steps, but he was visibly struggling. His breathing was laboured, uncomfortable. His cough had worsened. Samir went next, while I staggered behind, with my sore, mooncrater feet. There is a fine line between stubbornness and determination.

The camels found it equally hard going, stumbling on the downhill slopes and having to be pulled and egged on uphill. Fleabag moved bravely. I felt uplifted by her. It was she who urged me on. It was she who gave me strength. She was under no illusion about anything.

It felt like an age before the next stretch of winding track lay behind us. Those shapes that had appeared murky and threatening in the darkness had become more defined, gradually resolving into their recognizable forms. The steep slopes, so mysterious in the haze, gave a sense of isolation, of abandonment. Some of the rocks had clawed indents, as if strange beasts had attacked them. The men called them wild dogs, foul-smelling and four-toed.

What had once been a lizard had transformed into a husk, a stick figure made of bones, tiny at its extremities, but as delicate as living tissue. The sun had burnt away every ounce of flesh. Perhaps it was my own.

Was the village an illusion as well? One or two small settlements seemed to waver, teetering on the rocks as though they might tumble and fall. I still had no idea which one of them was our destination, if any.

The wall inside me was collapsing. Confidence, fear, resistance, hope and frustration formed paradoxes, knotting into entanglements with no pathways towards resolution. What remained hidden from me that I did not yet fully comprehend? Were we going to the *marabout*? Had we ever been? I was blind, but there was nothing I could do about it. Ignorance clawed at my thoughts and my stomach like those wild dogs. Still, I felt resigned to my fate. Still, I was leading myself on.

Samir did not speak of his emotions. It was the Tuareg way, and perhaps a male one. To have given expression to his feelings would have shown only weakness. It made no difference. His forlorn look and manner said it all.

Suleyman knew. He was his father. He said nothing because it was not in his culture to do so – he understood only too well the perils of intervention.

※ ※ ※

It felt like everyone that inhabited the area had gathered to watch the spectacle of our arrival. Children in clothes too big for them petted the camels, while some way off a few auxiliary figures stared silently. They had every reason to be suspicious. Hardly any visitors came here, and those who did come always wanted something.

Standing at the gate, the first thing I noticed was the bucket – after that, the well. I glimpsed the man in his long, dark robes and dishevelled turban as an afterthought. He was sleeping in a sitting position, hunched back leaning against the well.

By then the dog's scent was in my nostrils. Initially it appeared to be benign, lying there on the ground, head resting on its front paws as any domestic dog might. But this was not a domestic dog. Fortunately the rope around its neck was not quite long enough to reach us, or to allow it to savage the few mangy chickens that clucked anxiously around the pathway.

At our approach, the dog's body stiffened. Its lip curled and its mouth began to drool. I shielded my ears, but my weak hands could not shut out its piercing yapping.

Of all the camels, Usem reacted the most violently. He pulled and fought against the rope. He shook his head and lifted his feet. The sudden lunge is always expressed in the same way with camels. The long neck extends and the head reaches out. It is a reflex, a capitulation. The action set off

Tlatig and Winaruz who, screaming and hollering, shifted nervously, so much so that their rope caught. They struck each other, humps wobbling on impact.

Fleabag, terrified, screamed. Rising in the air, I could see clearly her white gums. She was totally out of control, as if all the fear she had ever felt in her life had suddenly resurfaced and the ghosts of her past had reappeared before her to destroy her once and for all.

The look of implacable determination on Suleyman's face as he reached out to her did not pass me by.

Usem had moved so far forward that his baskets were almost dislodged. Being in front gave his forelegs more freedom and, by pulling at the rope, he forced himself free. This caused a flurry of plunges all round.

Nothing could placate Fleabag. She reared again. She let out a deathly wail. She strained her neck. She writhed.

At last, in one deft and surprising jolt, Tlatig twisted out and, as the dog nipped the back of his leg, wrestled free and struck back with his foot.

The hunched man's eyes flashed open. He scrambled to his feet. He took off his shoe and hurled it. Three sounds filled the air: the high-pitched screams, the flapping of chicken wings, the crunch of tooth upon leather.

The dog was airborne.

Suleyman acted fast. Samir took up the slack. I stood helplessly by.

Afterwards, the camels sat, sides heaving with breaths that were almost moans, in a tumbling of dominoes. Tlatig's head was the highest of them all. It was his finest hour, and he wallowed in it. He had proved his worth.

My eyes were on Fleabag. Her head had turned and Samir was whispering to her. I could tell she was listening. Saddles and baskets somehow intact, the others seemed to settle a little.

The dog slunk back to its resting place. As though seeking applause, it looked up and around, then resumed chewing, as if nothing had happened.

Still catching my breath, I too tried soothing Fleabag. It was an unfortunate incident, but not an unusual one. Dogs have a tough ride in Islamic societies. So often they are chained up and neglected, left to scavenge and pilloried with stones. At the heart of the issue is culture, which set its standards long before religion, although that too has a responsibility. Muhammad regarded cats as pure animals, but it is sad he taught that dogs are unclean, even if he did say they should be well cared for.

By now Suleyman and the hunched man had finished their greetings.

'We are hoping to buy some holy water, *s'il vous plait*,' ventured Suleyman. He cleared his throat.

Around us sheep bleated. The dog carried on chewing.

The hunched man responded. 'First-best quality or second-best quality?'

'First-best quality.'

The bargaining began cordially. Suleyman initiated proceedings with a compliment about dogs. The hunched man returned it with one about camels.

And then a price was named.

Suleyman looked stunned, at which the hunched man looked equally amazed, having been mortally offended by the paltry counter-offer. Suleyman protested again. The hunched man looked defensive. Suleyman shook his head.

And now a high mewl from the onlookers. A baby started crying.

At last Suleyman began digging out the notes he was prepared to sacrifice, wafting them in the expectant air. The hunched man raised his eyebrows for an instant, but seeing the amount swallowed hard, as if to divert attention from his disappointment. With a dejected glance, he slipped the money into his pocket. It had been a special price, he said, because it included a chance to meet the *marabout*.

We were not done yet. Just as I thought we were about to be let through, something stirred among the chickens. A small boy darted like a fly. A nod from his elder gave him the signal that he needed. He picked up the bucket that lay in the dust, lowered it down, then drew it up again. He scooped a little out into a cup.

Suleyman took it first and passed it to Samir. Samir handed it to me.

I stared at the murky, foul-smelling liquid, knowing the only gift it could possibly give me was dysentery. 'I shall keep it for later to fend off the *djinn*,' I said, reaching for my water bottle.

Everyone looked delighted.

'There is,' continued the hunched man as he poured in the last drop and handed the water bottle back to me, 'the very small matter of the intercessory commission.'

'The intercessory commission?' Samir and Suleyman exchanged looks.

'Five thousand dinar, please.'

'Five thousand dinar!'

Some way off a cow mooed, as if in sympathy.

'I'll pay,' I said. It seemed churlish to haggle when the service provider was Allah. Maybe it might encourage Him to answer our prayers.

'Perhaps you cannot count in our currency?'

I double-checked my wallet. Strangely, he seemed to have overlooked the one currency that mattered – that of decency. How much more to heal a camel? Were they more expensive than people, or less? What was the price of mending the pieces of a broken heart? Was it less than a stomach problem or more than a skin complaint? If I had enough, would Allah be able to cure Suleyman's cancer? How much money did it take to heal a country?

Samir stepped in sharpish. 'One thousand is good?'

'Good for you,' huffed the hunched man. 'Allah is bountiful, and one thousand is nothing for *her*.'

'For me?' I felt my cheeks burn.

'Yes, for you.'

'Surely Allah does not concern Himself with money?' I said in disbelief.

'You are right, but you need Him to protect you. You know there are bad people *everywhere*.'

Samir was so cross that he almost threw the money at him. Fleabag, who had by now recovered, gave her own opinion. She farted.

She runs to the house that is burning
Osul s'ehan iraqqan

Trust is a delicate thing. We put it in the hands of others every day of our lives. Sometimes the risk feels so small as to be negligible – when we buy our weekly groceries, for example. We hand over our beloved children to child-carers every day; we trust our partners to be faithful to us. And, of course, we trust our leaders to make decisions that affect the world we all live in.

But what if the trust we place in people is broken? What if that nuclear weapon, with all its interconnecting waves and particles, somehow falls into the wrong hands?

The Tuareg trust too, that the sun will rise and the stars will lead them home, wherever that is. And, of course, they trust in Allah.

I envied them that. Samir knew my trust was failing again, but it had not yet broken entirely. It co-existed simultaneously with mistrust. These two conflicting feelings were not mutually exclusive. They alternated.

Knowing this didn't change a thing.

The *marabout*'s house finally stood before us. In the pale, wan light it was surreal, a mirage. It had a listless air and a lingering smell of tobacco. At the same time, the stone from which it was constructed gave it a more solid aspect than any building we had encountered in the desert. Beside it, a little sunlight sprinkled into a courtyard where a range of goats, sheep and donkeys were tethered.

I had placed my trust in two men I hardly knew; my life depended upon them. I had not valued that life.

Trauma, a loss of hope, of love, a feeling of failure – all these things push us to make 180-degree turns that we never anticipated. They also allow others to label us foolish – worse, selfish. How foolish they are, because it is they who fail to understand.

Consider this: how much pain does someone have to suffer to throw their own life away? Soldiers, terrorists and others find courage in self-destruction. They place themselves deliberately in extreme situations where they are vulnerable and out of control, on behalf of a cause that even they themselves do not fully understand.

The door swung open and banged against the wall. Chips of adobe scattered over the dust. In the murky light I couldn't see much. We entered anyway, skimming past a pile of sandals and another of bags, rugs, blankets and weapons, moving in single file towards a large dark room that smelt of dung. There was not much light there either; the tiny window was covered with plastic sheeting. But the room was packed. Small children were crawling and screaming among the feet of the crowd.

'Who are they all?' I whispered.

'Just people,' said Samir.

I wanted to see what dangers lurked there, but the people seemed to be shepherds mostly, old and young, and their families, some with their livestock. Some waited with palms upturned. Some lay curled, having walked great distances to be here. Others, seated on tatty blankets, stared ahead in far-off contemplation, as if waiting for a miracle or, as Samir said, possessed by *djinn*.

'Who is she?' I heard someone whisper in Arabic.

'A foreigner?'

Samir turned around. 'She is no one.'

'Ignore them,' whispered Suleyman.

We squashed in, and I received another lesson from Suleyman on *marabout* etiquette: how to bow, how not to offend, how to blend in and keep a low profile.

We sat for some time before two teenage boys walked in, followed by a somewhat diminutive white-robed figure. Immediately a hush fell.

I peered expectantly, aware of faces around me doing the same.

The *marabout* carved his way across the room, the crowd parting before him like the waters of the Red Sea. Now the chorus of adulation and imploring started up, becoming ever more fervent. A few people prostrated themselves. Others fell to their knees and bowed their heads. Bleatings and brayings from the animals joined in the chorus.

If I craned my neck, I could just see his face. He was a hawkish man with a large hooked nose. He wore an immaculately folded turban. He was dressed entirely in white because, as Suleyman hastened to point out, white was a holy colour and if you happened to be a *marabout*, it was essential that you dressed correctly for the part.

I recalled a *burka* I had worn once, and smiled.

Slipping off his slippers, the *marabout* began speaking in a low, gravelly voice. All the while, the two boys sold amulets from stalls set up in the dingy shadows along the walls. Payment was negotiable. It depended on the ailment and whether an animal had to be slaughtered. Payment in livestock was also accepted.

Through the tiny window the light dimmed. A thick vapour coating the sky seemed to presage a rainstorm, although the men thought that unlikely. They hadn't seen rain for years.

The room began to empty. The sheep were led off. All at once it was our turn.

The *marabout* extended his hand and Suleyman dutifully kissed it: 'Your grace, your worshipfulness... It's such an honour.'

'So kind,' croaked the *marabout*.

'It is two long years since I last came to seek your advice,' said Suleyman.

'Too long,' sighed the *marabout*. He turned to me and added huskily, looking very pleased with himself, 'I knew you were coming. I saw it in the sands.'

'We have come for a blessing for our camel,' said Samir.

'A camel?' he rasped. 'You came all this way for a camel?'

A flurry of robes produced another, even smaller young boy, startling Suleyman so violently that he almost fell over. The boy was unfazed. He whispered something and Samir turned to me. 'He wants more money.'

'He's not getting any,' I said.

A few minutes later we were coming back down the hill. The sky had brightened a little, but my disillusion had not faded.

At the base of the slope, five humped shapes stood silhouetted against an *efiz* tree. This time there was no running, rearing up or bellowing.

A lamp swung and bobbed further up the path behind us, and I could see the white splash of the *marabout*, his entourage following him as they hurried to catch up with us. More boys were in attendance, lanky-limbed and almost bearded. I hardly dared think what their function was.

With cautious steps the *marabout* approached Fleabag. He looked over her earnestly and she looked down suspiciously at him.

'Gently...' Suleyman steadied her.

She turned her head. She looked unimpressed. She let

out a snort. Her eyes swept over the group and she shuddered. That new noise I had discovered in her was, I fancied, tolerance.

Usem was watching. His head was up, eyes wide open, his whole face showing curiosity while, being above it all, the others sang blah-blah-blahs.

The *marabout* rinsed his mouth and spat into his bowl. He had a habit of screwing his head to one side as he spoke, and of looking out of the corner of his eye.

Samir took a tighter grip on the rope holding Fleabag. Blankets and cloths were draped around her hump.

The *marabout* offered Fleabag a date. She went for it, lips slobbering all over his hand. She knew how to charm.

Now that everyone was on best terms, the blessing began. The *marabout* bent down in concentration, reciting hoarsely from the Qur'an, scribbling out an amulet, eyes half-closed in delirium. Behind him his entourage knelt, forming a scattering of little 'j' shapes.

One of the older boys, who could have been no more than eight, stepped forward and explained that the *marabout* would use the 'measuring' method of diagnosis.

A cloth was measured out. Three times the *marabout* spat on the material, then he began reading the verse. Afterwards, he spat again twice, just to be on the safe side, because he was unsure if he was treating both Evil Eye and mouth, or just one or the other.

Fleabag's neck was slumping. It gave her a spent look. Perhaps it was because she had just walked almost a hundred kilometres through some of the harshest terrain on earth. I stood beside her, gazing at the sky past the outline of the broken rock edges. I thought of my mother, how she had raised me, how she had never told me what to do with my life, how she had supported me. I wondered if I would ever see her again.

A sudden gust of wind disturbed the dust. The cloth ballooned up. With earnest mutterings the *marabout* caught it back. It was Allah's will.

The *marabout* continued, his eyes clouding over as if he had been transported somewhere, a far-off place where he was rich and Allah was happy. He rummaged around in his robes and drew out a pen. He started to write something down and I feared it was another *surat*.

Suleyman began helping. He seemed to know what to do, as if he was acting as an assistant.

Herbalists and holy men have always worked in tandem. A merger exists between those tribal beliefs predating Islam and the science of the Qur'an, whose verses are written on amulets and other objects said to bless or heal the wearer.

I slid my arm around Fleabag's side and whispered to her, and she turned her head to me. I put my hand to her side and listened to her heart. My heart slowed. Perhaps at last the Allah with closed ears had opened His heart to her.

Above, the cloud seemed to be passing, dispersed by the wind. One of the boys stated with pride that it was because the *marabout* had made it happen.

Darkness fell as the *marabout* and his entourage moved off. By then Suleyman had already accepted his invitation.

We stood and watched them go. Soon nothing could be seen but the lantern, and I followed its slow progress up the pathway.

'Who else is going to this supper?'

Samir shook his head. 'No one important.'

'Who is that exactly?'

'Scholars, philosophers, teachers, the usual.'

'Can they be trusted?'

'Of course,' he said. 'Those Dal Rag bumpkins are slow-witted.'

As Samir avoided my gaze, I knew that there was more to this than I could ever have guessed. He and his father looked genuinely offended at my questioning. Turning down the *marabout*'s invitation would only invite bad luck for the rest of their lives. There was no choice but to accept. They had agreed and, by default, so had I.

We gathered around the fire. In the darkness the flames flickered goblins on the sand. The *djinn* were back, but for tonight they were good ones.

Midnight
Ehad

⚇ ⁝ · V

I do not understand

War efhemer

Suleyman was coughing again. His chest sounded terrible. We had collected the cool leaves of the *ebizguin* tree – for colds, sore throats and blood illnesses – and I had pounded them in his *ten*, just like he did. I had made the tea on the fire, and he was sipping it, criticizing it for strength and asking for yet more sugar although there was already a ton in it. He needed a doctor, but there weren't any. In any case, he didn't care much for doctors. In his mind, they were vets.

He was thinking about the past, about the old days again. He had forgotten himself. He had even almost made eye contact as he offered me the impractical-seeming get-out clause. It involved a truck (which, naturally, could not access the steep mountain pathways), a specially commissioned helicopter and $5,000 of my (by now virtually non-existent) money.

As we turned on to the familiar track, there were no angry dogs lying in wait, just crumbling mud, rock and silence. I felt oddly calm. Not resigned or numb. Instead I was intensely, painfully alive. I remembered as a small child playing Pandora, unleashing all the evils of this world. I had never imagined back then that it might be a prophecy. Sometimes the places we end up in can seem like portals to the places we call home. It is as if the greater the distance, the more home draws us in.

We had settled the camels, Samir and I, and left them with our belongings. Suleyman was tired. He seemed paler, more subdued, but the heaving had died down. The tea appeared to be working.

The *marabout*'s house looked different without the crowds and felt eerie without the earlier bustle. Not far away a cluster of low goatskin and burlap tents had been erected. Already lanterns had been lit, yet only the squawk of a bird hinted at life under tarpaulin. The flaps were closed, the inhabitants unused to visitors – and seemingly hostile to them. Either that, or they were sealing themselves in, unwilling to witness our presence.

Samir's hesitant knock brought out a feathery-bearded, buck-toothed teenager whose sandals cut into his dirty feet. He ushered us in and then locked the door. My skin tingled. I wanted to be back out in the cool of the mountain air.

As we followed him into the dark passage, glancing over his shoulder, he offered smugly, 'She will have her *baraka*.' Samir's expression did not make me feel any better.

The long, dim corridor appeared to access a warren of rooms. Hand-woven carpets covered the floor in this section of the building. Wires threaded along the edges of the clay walls, but there was no electricity.

At the end of the passage, the teenager paused and opened the door to a sizeable courtyard where several donkeys were tethered. We crossed and went in at another entrance, entering a low-ceilinged room, where a group of people were standing and sitting. As we approached them the boy said to Suleyman, '*Haj*, your friends.'

It felt as if all eyes turned towards me. It was especially noticeable because no one had looked directly at me for so long that I felt as if I was being inspected. I felt exposed, scared. In the silence my heart thumped. A prickle ran up my neck. Had they set me up? Had it been their intention all along to betray me at the last hour? In the game of chess that I was manoeuvring in my mind, I was in the pole position of pawn.

The faces turned away and I breathed once more. Meat was roasting on the fire and an odour of scented soap filled the air. A tablecloth had been set on the floor. Places had been laid and glasses put out. Gas lamps burned at either end.

The village chief, a short man with dancing hands, came over to welcome us. Suleyman knew him. So did Samir. I wondered what histories had intertwined the three of them, and what rivalries. The chief looked delighted when Samir mentioned that I was from the Western hemisphere, although he had never heard of the place.

He didn't have to ask the others where they were from. He knew the unmistakable Kel Rela when he saw one. His own tribe, the Dag Rali, had lived in the Ahaggar since time immemorial, the proud descendants of the ancient Isbeten, who were there long before the Kel Ahem Mellen and the Tegehe Mellet, who they despised because they had brought camels into their goat territory.

Samir leaned over. 'Whatever you do, don't say you are British,' he murmured.

I couldn't have said anything. My mouth was as dry as the desert.

Reclining on a divan nearest the door, in the position of honour, was the *marabout*, face radiating benevolence. Around him sat lean-limbed, strong-featured men wearing turbans. It was hard to tell where they were from. There was a brightness in their young faces lit by the firelight and, at the same time, a gravity.

'Who are they?' I looked searchingly into Samir's eyes.

'The usual.' He still averted mine. His face seemed a little paler than usual and he kept glancing nervously towards his father. He had forced the response and it was vague. His behaviour did not help to quell the feeling of dread that began to seep through my veins. I wondered if he was as much out of his depth as I was, and if he too had no idea what was going on. At least that was what I began to convince myself.

A moment later he added, 'They are traders.' He said it with the air of a confession.

Traders of what exactly? I thought. I would be blessed if it was only weapons. My breath was quickening, my legs losing sensation. I could understand how Fleabag must have felt when we had found her at the market. As I collapsed on to the bright cushions silently, one of the boys offered tea and almonds.

I distracted myself sipping and eating. There were ten of us in all. There were no hints of unsettled scores and debts born of broken allegiances. These men were learned and intelligent, of that there was no doubt, dressed as they were in fine robes and clean white turbans. Their general demeanour was serious as they regarded each other every now and then with looks of puzzlement and expectation.

As he sat down beside me, Samir would not say how he knew them. Next to the *marabout* sat an elderly gentleman, a scholar and one of the *ulema*, immaculately dressed and well spoken, next to whom the village chief had taken his place. Suleyman sat down beside him.

Opposite, sat a coarse, heavily built man who seemed to note everything that was being said, although he himself said nothing. His darting eyes gave him the appearance of leering. His curled frame reminded me of a spider. Beside him sat another strong-nosed man in equally gloomy silence, whose large head, deep-set eyes and bushy black eyebrows made me think he might be armed, although I could see no gun or knife on him.

There was no outward sign of malice in the tall, thin-lipped gentleman who sat down on my other side. He uttered his Arabic gently and deliberately as he introduced himself. His robes were crisp and clean. He had a high forehead, kind, alert eyes and a slightly greying beard. He might have been about forty. His name was Abdul Kerim.

'*Assalaam 'alaykum.* Peace be upon you,' he said, apparently addressing the three of us.

'*Wa 'aleikum assalaam wa rahmat Allahu wa barakutah.* May the peace, mercy and blessings of Allah be upon you,' replied Samir.

'*Shhalkum? Shkhbarkum? Wayn sabiheen? Mnayan jaayeen*? How are you? What is your news? Where have you passed the night? From where have you come?'

Samir answered vaguely, saying casually that we had been staying in the desert and that we had been camping. This had a calming effect on my fraying nerves, but Abdul Kerim's following question, which ended the ritual courtesies, set them off again. '*Wayn mashiyeen*? Where are you going tomorrow?'

Samir looked away. 'God alone will decide,' he said.

The *marabout* waved his arms. One of his apprentices began going from person to person, proffering a tea kettle of warm water and a bowl for the washing ritual. This one was a teenager, pimpled and gangly, wearing jeans and a T-shirt. I extended my hands and let the warm water rush over them.

Out of earshot of the *marabout*, but within spitting distance of the chief, Samir whispered, 'By God, these Dag Rali mountain folk are sons of dogs. They have no ancestry. They are illiterates. The *marabout* writes from the Qur'an. He prides himself upon it. He is actually a Cheurfa by birth, descended from the Prophet.'

I was well aware of that fact.

'So what exactly are you doing in the area?' asked my neighbour. His expression was intense.

I looked up, immediately struck by the energy of his question.

'We have been seeking a blessing,' I said. Then, after a long pause, I added, 'For a camel.'

'A camel! And have you received it?'

I considered for a few seconds and said, 'It helps to have a faith.'

'And what faith might that be?' He seemed to be expecting more. I was still wondering how to reply when Samir dug me in the ribs.

By now Suleyman and the village chief were deep in conversation. Samir was also attentive to the *marabout*, but could not help being seduced by the platter full of lamb, falling upon it with the energy of a starving man who had spent two weeks in the desert, mainly eating soup.

'*Bismillah*,' pronounced the *marabout*, before everyone chorused back, '*Bismillah*.'

Abdul Kerim was not to be put off. 'Sunni? Shi'a?' he persisted.

Before I could answer, or Samir could nudge me again, there walked into the room a large gentleman, rather lame in one leg, who supported himself on a thick stick. He was dressed in long brown robes. Sitting down with difficulty, he muttered in a growling, discontented voice, 'English.'

Samir stopped chatting to his neighbour. So did his father. Even the chief fell silent.

'Berber,' said Suleyman. It seemed a ridiculous thing to say, although I recalled he had said it before when we had first met, and it was apparently not as strange as it seemed, since Berbers were often fair-skinned, red-haired even.

317

For a moment, the entire room was quiet, apart from the gnawing of cartilage.

Abdul Kerim let it go.

A bearded teen in flip-flops and a fluorescent green top offered around bread. Meat arrived with it, steaming upon a platter, and vegetables, where flies had settled. I took a little.

'It might be thought your life would be easier now with the secret trades, Abdul Kerim?' I assumed Suleyman ventured this as a distraction.

'The secret trades? You mean the profitable ones.' The chief, sitting diagonally from me, grinned broadly.

'You should know, Suleyman,' croaked the *marabout*, mouth open, cheeks bulging. 'You are the most profitable one of all!'

At this, peals of uncontrollable laughter broke out. The spider, sitting opposite, kohl smeared on his eyelids, leered at me.

'That man loves pale women... just a little,' said Abdul Kerim, leaning forward. Some gristle slipped between his greasy fingers. 'May I speak freely?'

'*Inshallah*' seemed to be the only word available to me.

'Then I shall tell you,' he said.

You can kill me or let me live
Atat djanegh kud hi tennam

Abdul Kerim began speaking, eloquently and without pausing for breath, as if the past was suddenly upon him. Fondly, he remembered the times as a boy he would steal goat butter, devour it and make himself ill.

He remembered his father, who had taught him to behave like a good Muslim, how to walk with his eyes down, never to look at a woman above the neck, how to wear clothes with no cloth below the ankle and to cover his head to ward off the devil. Then he remembered his brother, who taught him how to stand when praying, with his feet close together, not to look at his feet when he knelt and to focus on the spot where he had to lie down. At last, he remembered his mother who taught him good manners, how to laugh and how to be kind to strangers.

The foreigner who never listened was all ears. 'Your mother sounds like a fine woman,' I said. My throat was constricting and my appetite had dwindled. I was nibbling on what I suspected was a decorative banana leaf, and which felt just as inedible.

'A mother is blessed who can take pride in her sons,' said the large elderly gentleman, who had been listening in.

'I am sure if the world was made up of mothers, the violence we see today would not be so great,' I said, thinking of my own.

'My mother is dead.' Abdul Kerim had stopped eating.

He flashed a doubtful glance towards the men sitting opposite us, and I diverted my own gaze.

'I'm sorry,' I said, and put the banana leaf down. My hands were trembling. I hoped no one had noticed. The man who looked like a spider blew me a kiss.

Across the tablecloth Suleyman sighed. Samir slumped back on to his cushion and murmured something, but my heartbeat was so loud I could not hear it. Was it an expression of solidarity, some small show of reassurance, or a betrayal? It was impossible to tell.

'Who is she really?' asked Abdul Kerim, attributing the question to the group.

'*Hader elkattaben ku tet azzayer.* I swear on the Book I don't know her,' answered Samir in Tamahaq. He was not joking. He sounded aggrieved. This was hurtful. Why was he was doing it? Perhaps he had his own plan. If so, he had not confided in me.

'*Yermer kay yalla.* God bless you,' responded one of the two elderly scholars sitting diagonally opposite me. He seemed to be rather enjoying the exchange, it being less boring than usual.

Kerim turned, and Samir shot me a wary look as he disowned me yet again. '*Messiner ikkes i dar amadal ku-tet neyer.* God take me if I saw her.'

'*E alla, kay yer mer.* God bless you,' said Abdul Kerim, licking his fine, long fingers. He began again, this time recounting the experiences that had influenced his thinking in Arabic. He did not raise his voice and I did not interrupt. No one did.

I listened with an open mind, even as, harking back to his early years, he began airing the grievances I had heard on so many occasions previously. It did not surprise me that as a boy, he had watched interviews with Russian soldiers and had learned about Ahmed Shah Massoud and Gulbuddin Hekmatyar, who fought against the Soviets in the Eighties. He had learned about Westerners such as Hitler and his camps, and how the Americans had slaughtered the Koreans and Vietnamese.

As a young man he had read about Hiroshima and Nagasaki, the carpet bombings at the end of the Second World War and, in more recent times, about the injustices inflicted on so many Muslims in the wars in Bosnia and Afghanistan, not to mention, he said, the horrors the Israelis had carried out in Palestine, Iraq and now in Syria.

Hearing all this had made him consider the war in Algeria. The Groupe Islamique Armée had broken Islamic law, murdering innocent civilians. He had thought long and hard about the 1.6 billion Muslims worldwide who felt humiliated and let down by the arrogance of the West, those infidels who destroyed everything and anything that did not agree with them. It was for this reason he had decided to become a warrior.

Grradually, as he spoke, his voice so controlled, so measured, his words began to blur. At first, almost by instinct, I shut them out. I did not want to comprehend the dark threats conveyed in his explanation. I had often heard stories about what went on in the camps in the Hindu Kush and I expected this was no different.

He continued listing his achievements as proudly as if he was reeling off his curriculum vitae, which, in a sense, he was. In Khaldan training camp, Afghanistan, he had first studied the Qur'an with Tajiks, Uzbeks, Saudis and Chechens. He had trained in surveillance tactics, how to signal at night, how to ambush in cities, how to kill. With brothers from Yemen, Saudi and Morocco, he had been taught about explosives, absorbing everything there was to know about TNT, dynamite and Semtex, which was almost entirely undetectable, making mines and laying minefields.

After that he had been to university in Berlin.

'Berlin?' Samir suddenly sat up. He leaned forward, and for one second it felt as if he might save me. The subject would be changed and the conversation would revert to something else. Anything else. But just as I thought this, he fell silent again.

Abdul Kerim did not react. He was still turned towards me, and he was waiting for my response. I imagined the dreadful crimes he must have committed to warrant his need of *baraka*, and all I could muster was a crestfallen, feeble, 'That is very interesting.'

Where is the resolution we must find in ourselves when it is most needed? I asked myself. Where does it reside? Is it in the head or in the heart? Perhaps it is not courage, after all, since it is not a thought, but a reflex, an instinct even. Whatever it is, it had deserted me. I was beyond out-of-my-depth. It would be a miracle if I saw the sunshine bearing down on the desert again.

At this point another teen, this one in sandals and a white gown, came to my rescue. 'That is enough. The *marabout* does not want to hear you talk politics.'

Abdul Kerim waved him away. The two old fellows rose from their places and, crouching over the fire, held out their withered hands to catch the heat. The flame threw a ghastly light on their shrivelled faces.

Beside me, Samir was still tense. We were inches away, but miles apart. What was he playing at? Certainly not being my hero.

'And what do you think about Afghanistan and Syria?' ventured my inquisitor.

'Muslims are using Western weapons,' replied Samir on my behalf. Perhaps he meant to diffuse the atmosphere, but it did not work.

All eyes around the table swivelled towards him –
Abdul Kerim's especially keenly, but then his gaze
gradually became distracted and he seemed lost in thought,
perhaps unsure whether to be relieved or disappointed by
Samir's remark. Still no one spoke as Abdul Kerim
continued to devour his lamb. He took out a handkerchief
and wiped the fat from his chin.

'It doesn't matter whose weapons they are,' said
Suleyman at last.

'They are the enemy's and he forgot to take them
home with them,' said the chief.

Suleyman abstained from responding to this. The chief
was cunning enough. Immediately he saw that an
opportunity had opened for a more lucrative exchange of
a commodity he had long yearned for, that of weapons.
Hastily turning to the *marabout*, he whispered in the
venerable man's ear.

Abdul Kerim continued, his soft voice beginning to
rise. 'In Afghanistan I learned how important it was to fight
for the right reasons: for God, not for material gain or
politics. We had righteousness on our side, and we fought
to preserve God's creation – humanity. The deeper my
faith, the greater my ability to do God's work, the greater
the *baraka*. I would willingly give my life in exchange for
an eternity in Paradise. We must show courage and not flee
from battle, even in the face of certain death. Any man who
turns his back on the infidels and runs incurs God's severe
punishment. His final resting place is the fire.'

I thought of all the horrific crimes committed in God's
name, and that of many religions. I thought of the weapons
that were being developed by nations that were power-
hungry, greed-filled and who could not be trusted. Even as
my heart drummed and I dug my nails into my palm, I

seized my chance. 'And you, an educated man, who has been to university in Europe and has benefited from all that society has given you, believe this?' I said.

Somehow I kept in check my anger, even as he uttered his next, predictable statement.

'One day, all of Europe will be Muslim. The *kufar* will be wiped out.'

As I held my glass in my hand, I willed it not to shake. Taking another breath, I ventured, 'There have been just as many deaths in the name of Islam as against it.'

His face reddened. The meat bone in his own hand shook uncontrollably as he gripped it even tighter.

In that instant it hit me where I was – in his world, not mine. It was not my place to question. I put my empty tea glass down. My hand was no longer able to grasp it. I had spent two weeks in the desert worrying about dehydration. This time my saliva really had dried up.

Of all the people sitting around, it was Suleyman who came to my aid and who, while juggling the occasional reverence towards the *marabout* with his conversation with the village chief, was also managing to listen to ours. He casually mentioned something about rain.

A cry rang around the tablecloth. 'Rain! *Alhamdulillah*! Rain!'

Rain. The thought was inconceivable.

I dried my hands and, to everyone's relief, Abdul Kerim said, '*Inshallah*. If Allah wills it.'

'You are on speaking terms with Him?' said one of the elderly scholars.

'He speaks to me through prayer,' said Abdul Kerim. He looked very pleased with himself at this answer.

Hearing this, the *marabout*, who thought this treatment of the matter an unjust attempt at diminishing his own position, answered, 'God decides everything.' With a puff of his pipe he added, 'As soon as I hear from Him, I will let you know.'

'*Ya Rab!* Praise be to Allah!' muttered the chief, and everyone else joined in.

'He gives us chosen ones *baraka*, in our land and its riches. He comforts us in our suffering,' said Abdul Kerim.

'*Allah azza wa jal.* May He be glorified.' Samir nodded his head vigorously.

Buoyed up by Suleyman's support, I felt a sudden strength, at the same time a knowing, almost as the words began to leave my mouth, that I was sealing my own fate.

'But what about the victims' suffering? Are they not innocent? Do you not believe God loves them, each and every one, no matter what their faith?' I said.

Suleyman was searching for his pipe, perhaps in the vain hope that the smoke might provide a screen.

'Look,' said Abdul Kerim, 'you condemn our battles on America, the attacks on French land and the London bombings on British soil. But how about the millions killed on Muslim soil? Our losses have been untold. Our sacrifices have been countless.'

'So have ours,' I said. 'So why not stop?'

Samir squirmed on his cushion. He was sweating. 'I am as horrified as any man,' he said, 'but it is not surprising there is a reaction. The West *started* it.'

It was the same logic Islamic terrorists had used to excuse the cold-blooded slaughter of so many innocent people throughout the world. I felt bereft. He was letting me down when I most needed him. I was astonished and cross with him.

'And do you blame the West's many innocent people, Samir?' I was desperate to know what he really thought, although the possibility that logic, reason or justice might prevail now seemed remote.

'Sacrifice is complicated,' he said.

With each word I felt him withdraw further from me, the long, arduous journey we had taken together all but turned to dust.

'You are right,' said Abdul Kerim. 'But there are no innocents any more. Everyone is at war. Everyone is fair game. You worship ideas – success, power, money. You all see God in your own image.'

'I do not worship those things. Why do you accuse all of us when you do not know us? We are not all the same,' I said.

'You cannot change yourselves. Look in the mirror. Look at our women and children who have no food. Look at how we have been treated. Then tell us we have to change.' Abdul Kerim remained calm; he did not raise his voice or appear angry. He was working on me.

I remembered the children I had known who had been maimed or lost their lives, and families destroyed by Western violence. I remembered those I had met without shelter or medical care, who mixed mud with filthy water to fill their bellies, and the wealthy foreign governments who ignored them. After that, I remembered the very rich people who had pretended to help my charity, but who had in reality masqueraded as philanthropists while serving their own ends. Finally, I remembered those who had called themselves my friends but left me on my own in my hour of need.

'I think I know what you mean,' I said quietly.

Glances were being exchanged. Now I was cargo. Now I was a spy. What was I to do? I had no friends here.

Abdul Kerim was still studying me, as if he was in the

process of conversion, or as if he was trying to hypnotize me, but the time had long gone to look down or stay silent. I broke off his grasp.

'In Islam there are *rules,*' I said. 'The *sunnah* are very clear. No women, no children and no old people. You must not kill innocents.'

'The enemy has no laws. They kill indiscriminately. They kill women, children and old people and call it collateral damage.' Abdul Kerim's eyes sparkled.

'An eye for an eye,' piped up one of the elderly scholars, at which everyone uttered more Qur'anic invocations.

Abdul Kerim had glazed over. He was trying things out in his head, deciding. I couldn't read the look in his eyes. But now I had started, I couldn't help myself. I hardly noticed my hands shaking any more. I barely noticed my dry mouth. It was on its own journey.

I put it to him straight. 'The Qur'an says that you should repay evil with what is better. Then he who was your enemy will become your intimate friend. Physical fighting is permitted only until the enemy seeks peace, then it must stop. If they seek peace, then you seek peace.'

'But they never do,' he said bluntly.

'But what if they did?'

'What does it say in the *Shahada*?' replied an elderly scholar rhetorically.

Strength, fortitude, those things that, as the Tuareg put it, were on the winds and flew into our hearts, seemed immaterial. All I could think of was those I had seen suffer. I hardly knew what I was doing. I scarcely remembered the words. But I still cleared my throat and recited it, loudly and without hesitation.

'An infidel quoting from the Qur'an!' They glanced at each other with expressions of amazement. Even the *marabout* looked surprised. Smiling hideously, he said that if I studied hard and applied myself to the *sunnah* and the *hadith*, we could all be very good friends yet, and maybe, if I was lucky, even more.

At this, everyone reverted to concentrating on the fruit. I became aware of faces twitchy and swollen, and more lamb than could be eaten by the throng who had been here earlier.

Someone put forward another quotation from the Qur'an.

I countered with another.

The two elderly scholars, chiming together, began pouring out piteous lamentations upon my soul, which was, in their view, too doomed to be salvaged from its state of affliction. No *baraka* on earth could fix the plight of the Western woman.

Enough, I felt, was enough. How could they possibly argue that *baraka* could explain away – forgive, no less – the horrors we had seen happening all over the world in the name of freedom, justice, honour and, above all, God himself? Of course, this was not a question they could answer – or perhaps not one that they wanted to.

The boys were clearing the dishes. Suleyman turned his face away from me, adjusted his cushion and said, 'If I were able to predict the future as you are, most holy one…'

'I am not a fortune teller,' replied the *marabout*, settling himself once again and sipping his tea.

'No, no, my friend,' assented Suleyman, letting his head slump, and towelling away at his two hands, 'but let us say, you might receive inspiration…'

'Yes…'

'Do you feel there can be peace?'

'Praise be to God, there must be peace.'

A round of clapping descended like rainfall.

Of course, there was no mention the uranium, the testing, the smuggling of nuclear materials or other weapons.

The conversation was over. There was nowhere left to go. They had their views and they regarded my questioning as impertinent and misguided.

The *marabout*, the chief and Suleyman conversed in low voices. Nothing of the conversation was distinguishable beyond a few disjointed words. Anyone might have thought Suleyman was defending himself and that the chief was in a state of irritation. They talked intensely for a considerable length of time, all the while casting furtive glances towards me, before the *marabout*, who also appeared familiar with the subject, nodded. Something was going on beyond what I could comprehend.

I had been so absorbed talking to the others that I had not noticed something more sinister taking place.

The *marabout* licked his lips, and the chief began smoking a cigar. The thought occurred to me once again that I might not make it out. Droplets of sweat trickled down my spine and the room began to spin. It was not the rights and wrongs in the world that were being discussed. It was me.

It was only now, at what I believed to be my end, that I felt it, this edge I had been seeking all along. When fear takes over a body, the mind can do nothing to prevent the chain reaction. The pulse races, the heart pounds, the limbs crumble – and then all at once everything freezes.

I was in a place I had never been, but which I had imagined so often. The reality was different to how I had expected it to be. All notions of hugging the monster, feeling the fear and doing it anyway were off the mark. There was no heroism, no exhilaration, no strength in this place, only cowardice. There was an irony to this situation, for having come so far half-expecting I was going to die, and having gone to such trouble preparing myself for it, now that I was actually experiencing it – I wanted to live.

I felt the urge to laugh, gripped by a feeling so over-whelming that for an instant I was, literally, paralysed. Samir pressed against my knee, but as I pressed back he pulled away. Had I danced with my enemy in the desert? My mouth would not move, but my mind ran away with me.

Faces became animated. Eyes darted from one to the other. Chins were stroked. Voices lowered. There was a rapid exchange and hand signals that appeared to indicate some form of agreement, and at last it became clear that some goal had been reached.

Suleyman had struck a deal.

Peeling his orange, Abdul Kerim said, 'You are fortunate to be here tonight of all nights.'

'I am?' I croaked.

'*Inshallah*. You are blessed.'

'How?'

'It is a special night.'

'It is?'

'You do not know?'

The *marabout* nodded. The elderly scholars nodded, and another round of nodding began.

I managed to stand. Suleyman and Samir stood too and we made our excuses. I forced an unconvincing smile.

The chief stood up too. 'When can I find you again?' He looked searchingly into Suleyman's eyes.

'Tomorrow.'

'Where?'

'Here.'

'It is a promise?'

'You have my word.'

The spider and his friend, who remained seated, began to confer. I half-expected them to draw pistols.

'We shall meet again in Paradise, *inshallah*.' Abdul Kerim bowed to me.

'*Inshallah*.' My eyes were on the door.

'*Inshallah*,' added the scholars.

'*Inshallah*.' The spider stood up. Now I was his fly. Now I was in his web.

Suleyman gave me a signal. I stumbled after him, feeling the eyes of the men on the floor boring into my back, but only the *marabout* accompanied us, aided by his boys. He tottered along the passageway and through the courtyard, muttering something holy.

He paused for breath. 'Take this.' He handed something to Samir, although I couldn't see what it was, and Samir hid it beneath the folds of his robe.

Still airing his opinions about mothers, the feathery-bearded, buck-toothed boy took a long time rattling and banging with the lock before the door swung open.

The *marabout* said very little, only that he would pray for our safety and the health of all the camels, although he could not guarantee that Allah would not bless the goats instead.

I was too scared to consider what I would take with me this time. At best, a chance to live – and a set of keys to his four-wheel drive, to take us away from here as fast as possible, a *baraka* indeed. Above all, the blessing of good timing, because it was a holy night, the 15 of Shaban, the Laylat al Bara'ah – the night, it was said, that gave freedom from fire.

Afterwards
Darat

We crept like mice into the night's freezing clutches. Samir checked ahead, listening and watching, scanning the land as if trying to make sense of the shapes scattered there, though there wasn't enough light to see anything clearly. Indistinct outlines came and went, floating and shadowy. I could make out the textures in the shadows.

Fear was the only definite, the need to flee urgent, but I did not feel despair. How could I with Suleyman and Samir at my side? Despite our differences, we had been able to get along and survive each other – and ourselves.

Now there was black. Snatches of images went by – the sharp edge of a rock, the glistening backs of beetles... In his *Philosophical Investigations*, Wittgenstein wrote of beetles and of boxes in the same breath. Imagine, he said, that everyone has a small box in which they keep a beetle. However, no one is allowed to look in anyone else's box, only their own.

With his soft voice and indefatigable conviction, Abdul Kerim heralded a new age of terrorism. On one level it is inevitable that, united by the disastrous phrase 'the war on terror', millions of disaffected Muslims – many highly educated – dream of the promise of immortality offered by dying for the Islamic cause. Wars and invasions of their territories have simply exacerbated the situation.

In Abdul Kerim's eyes, the present battle is the most important that any *mujahid* can fight in his life, just as the *jihad* against the Hindus – those idolaters who worship the cow – or the struggle of Moses against the golden calf. In his opinion, open, global confrontation is inevitable, rather than the tacit, underhand conflict that has been waged for decades under our noses.

Reflecting upon what he had said, I felt convinced that we face a struggle which at its core does not concern race, colour or creed, but which is even more fundamental. It is about the very nature of who we are and wish to be as a global society. At the heart of faith lies understanding, but even if we do not believe, are we going to allow the past to mess everything up?

However wrong we feel the decisions taken by our politicians, however scared we may be by what the media tells us, let us set aside our differences and unite. It is up to us, ordinary people, to stand up for what we truly believe in. Evey one of us has a promise to keep to our descendants – and this must never be ignored. As long as there are shared values, surely there is hope. We have a future to be won and a peace to be fought for.

At the base of the valley the camels stood bunched and on guard. Heads lifted, noses higher than usual, they smelt that smell that wafted in the wind. They knew danger.

Fleabag saw me first. At my approach her neck came round. A mile or so off a jackal cried out. She heard it and turned her head in its direction. She appeared to appraise the importance of it, then to dismiss it. Her head lifted, and then all the camels stirred, their own heads lifted and their tails flicked sideways.

The pregnant sky had finally reached breaking point. Suleyman tightened the camel ropes as the first drops of rain began to fall, cutting into the ground like polka dots. A river ran past our feet.

Samir stood as the water floated over his wet sandals, tracing the line where dark sand met light. He seemed mesmerized by the drops dancing, as if he was seeing rain for the first time, as if the water itself was a concept alien to him. He let out a cry so shrill it was as though the heart of the sky itself had been broken. It was as if he wanted to tell me something.

Wrestling with tarpaulin took time. Dust quickly became mud, the wind a creature let loose from its chains. Then, standing up, it blew into our faces and slammed the tent down. 'How dare you enter my territory?' it seemed to howl.

'Because I can,' replied the darkness with a thunderclap. It did not scare me. Its reign over me had ceased.

This time we didn't argue over the plan. I remember little of the detail, just familiar assurances.

'We must get you out.'

The only movement was the rain falling through the still air. Everything paused – the camels huddling – the dead rocks rising up from the slippery ground. I cannot recall how long we cowered there like little swallows, half-wondering if we would be washed away together. Outside the tent we could hear cries. I made myself believe they were the movements of camels. I must have dropped off through exhaustion, for I woke with a start, the crackle of flames loud in my ears, the smoke thick in my nostrils. I felt the soft, damp sludge between my toes like *papier mâché*, and hurried to pack up.

As soon as the fire had dried our clothes, we were ready. Fleabag knew. The noises she made were of unease. She hadn't discarded those she knew of old, but they had a different timbre, as if indecision and confusion had left her. No longer the voice of the little one. Instead a mighty roar.

'Let her go.' Suleyman struggled for breath, pulling up the camel-hair blanket around his shoulders.

With that she was off, a shadow who had left to merge with all the other degrees of nightshade.

But this was no time to dwell. Rushed words flew in whispers. Someone had to stay with the camels, and we all knew that it would be Suleyman.

Strong yet fragile, he was by my side.

'Here, take this. It is my *ilm*. It contains everything you need to remember me by.' He slipped the insignificant-looking object into my hand. It was not heavy. I worked my fingers around the smoothness and found a surprise. One of the edges was rough, and when I tumbled it around there was something that drew the finger there, like an ulcer in the mouth where the tongue returns. I wondered if it was a tool, perhaps from the Iron Age, or even earlier.

I took out my touchstone, turned it in my fingers, weighed it in my palm. It was my own stone, and I wanted him to have it, for it contained my *ilm*. Perhaps it might help him to find gold, just as, in a way, I had done.

As I placed it in his palm, he looked upon the small, dark pebble with curiosity, peering at it, trying to see it, as if trying to work out its meaning.

'*Ma môs awa?* What is this?' His veil fell and we grasped each other's hands a little too long.

'*Yosa tamanyasat.* I shall return.' The words fell from my mouth. I could not look at him either.

That was the last time I ever saw Suleyman.

Samir began down the path and I followed him.

It was almost daylight, fresh and hope-filled. The stars were not how or where I used to think they were. Theirs was a older, wiser light than I had understood, a memory, and they were waiting to guide us.

Dawn
Tifawt

+ ⵣ ⵀ · : +

I touched incandescence
Kalla eknegh

It is an old Tuareg saying that *amam imam*. Water is life. Nowhere is water more treasured than in a hot country, but perhaps its allure lies in its weakness, its fluidity; its strength lies in its density, in the power of floods and in its persistence. After all, water by itself can move mountains. It is the only element that can overcome fire.

The first strands of light appeared behind the peaks and a greenish glow spread upwards. In this, the death of night rather than the birth of day, everything felt different. It was nothing you could put your finger on; neither a mystical or spiritual experience. It was anything but that. It rose from the stomach, from the gut.

Now that the danger had passed, it felt comforting to feel the soft ground underfoot. Further down, the path sloped more steeply, flattening before opening out again into a kind of rock amphitheatre in multiple strata. The Kel Ahaggar have their own form of Stonehenge. Tall slabs stand like regal beings. Chambers lie guarded by ancient kings.

A *guelta* had formed, born of the downpour. It was as if the rock had turned green from the enchantment of water. Small eddies whirled here and birds thronged – bee-eaters, rollers and the desert *dioch*. If you looked closely, you could just make out the shadowy forms of the rocks below the surface. The rain had persuaded strange plants to peek out. Shoots were pushing up, and small, round green pods had appeared. In the nooks and crannies of the rocks small tufts of vegetation poked out their noses – yellow-flowered, gauze-like fishing nets, small pink cacti, bulbous as coral, and a bush named *hero*, after the Greek for water, roots deep below the surface. Flecks of colour sprang vividly into being, the splash of an iris violent against the beige. Wild leeks and alliums dormant for years now sprang into bloom for tiny lifespans. The *jujubes*, normally bent and cruel, sprouted juicy leaflets.

Samir paused, his light robe dark with the mud that had stiffened its folds. We stood watching the water, which was as new and enchanting for both of us.

'Thank you for keeping your promise,' I said.

'This was about *ettebel*,' he said, and I nodded, for, as we both knew, it is an ancient Tuareg tradition that a promise made is a promise kept.

Nothing has altered the old feudal hierarchies and concepts governing Tuareg society, whatever other changes have been brought by the modern age. Suleyman and Samir would never have broken their promise to me.

There were core values at play. Above all, the concept of *temazayt*, literally setting aside a share, and which refers to the 'contract of possession' given by Tuareg nobles to their vassals, who have neither camels nor swords. In the past, nobles offered protection and, in return, they gained control over access, to land or to goat products. Suleyman had offered Hassan his protection that night we had crossed the forbidden zone; but there was more to it even than that. There were other secret oaths being kept. The village chief of the Dag Rali was bound to Suleyman by *khamast*.

Even as I feared for my life I had been safer than I might ever have imagined.

'As a matter of interest, how many guns was I worth exactly?'

Samir's voice echoed among the rocks. 'All of them.'

I had kept my own weapons concealed – the shield of my denial, the mask of my innocence, the sword of my knowledge of the Qur'an, but had they helped?

'And Abdul Kerim?'

'No harm would ever have come to you. I told you. A true Imohug would never allow anyone to hurt a woman. We respect them as much as our camels.'

I think he meant it as a joke.

'Then why did you disown me yesterday?' I couldn't help myself.

He did not answer at first. Then he said, 'We each have our different ways of coping.'

He hung his head.

After some moments, he said softly, 'It was not my father who brought you to danger. He would never have abandoned you.'

There was no doubt in my mind as to Suleyman's integrity, but as soon as Samir said that, something began to click. The words of Hassan, the old nomad, came back to me as if he was standing with us, and I could see him in his robes, carving patterns in the sand.

It was Hassan who must have spread the word. Much more likely, he had sold the information that a foreign woman was travelling, an advertisement to any criminal or terrorist who happened to be in the area and wanted to cash in. It was not for our benefit that he had carved directions in the sand, but for his own.

'Hassan betrayed us?'

Samir frowned. 'He was acting for himself.'

It was not the first time I had heard this as an excuse.

We sat for a while and allowed time to wash over us. 'Remember when we first met?' he said.

My picture of it was indistinct, like the shifting sands.

'And what about Fleabag?'

'It was you we wanted to see the *marabout*. *You* needed healing.'

'Yes.' I smiled. He was right.

'You do not have to leave.' He brushed the dust from his palms.

I didn't answer right away. I wondered if I could answer at all.

He lowered his head, as if unable to look at me, and this time it was not through any cultural nicety that he said, 'Why don't we go to Europe?'

I lowered my head too, unable to look back at him. What he really meant was, he would like a passport. I forgave him for this completely. We both knew it would never work. He would be dispossessed, of his beliefs, of the desert and of himself. He didn't want that. Neither did I. I wanted him to be him.

Twixt rock and sand we lingered in a state of in-between, like the interim in our conversation. A minute's pause, and with a small tilt of the chin he too showed he had recovered. I was grateful he didn't press me.

I did feel for him, but it was a different kind of love, the sort you *wanted* to believe in; the sort you felt when caught up in the moment, that you did not understand at the time because you didn't know what was happening; the sort that came with trust and mistrust, with excitement and danger and, with all that, ignorance. It was an adolescent love.

It might have been Samir, or anyone. I had put myself into an extreme position of vulnerability to see if someone would rescue me – only to understand that the only one who could really save me was myself.

Samir did not speak of his feelings. For a Tuareg man to do so would be regarded as a sign of weakness. It is what you do that matters. Still, as he took my hand, and I left it there in his grasp, it felt reassuring.

'Can you ever forgive us for taking advantage of your great generosity?' he said.

It had never been about money, and now that it came to it, he refused to take any.

'Of course, but can you ever forgive me for taking advantage of your honour?'

In reality, it was I who was in his debt. I owed him my life, and how can you place a value upon that?

'You are certainly not the typical Western woman,' he said at last.

'And you are not exactly a typical Eastern man.'

In unison, we burst out laughing. Neither of us had expected that we would respect each other.

He was happy. He had an epic to tell that he could add to his vast repertoire of stories, just like those recounted by the elders of his tribe. In the years to come he would be able to tell his children and grandchildren how we came within a camel's hair of death and survived against all odds. He would be sure to emphasize the role of the hapless foreign woman and how he protected her from the scorpions, snakes and jackals – but most of all from the one that had been her greatest enemy – herself.

'Stay.'

I swayed towards him, far away from the earth. Yes would have been so easy.

It was just as I was weighing things up in my mind, listening to the voice there, that I was caught off guard.

A rustling broke the silence. Two furry ears appeared, and teeth. She must have followed us down.

I flung my arms around Fleabag's neck and she roared in my face her fearless roar. Gently, I stroked her ears and whispered to her words I would never tell anyone, and she rubbed me. It wasn't exactly clear what difference, if any, the *marabout* had made. She was the same adorable Fleabag she had always been – without the sores and the ticks and all those other diseases that Suleyman had cured. The flying of the liver problem had vanished; the spirits of the wind that cause illness had long gone. But perhaps, if I was honest, something had changed in her.

We walked a little more together, the three of us, as the cool mountain breeze whirled around our bodies. Be happy, it seemed to be saying.

How could we not be? We had survived.

'*Ayr emir iyen.* Until the next time.' His eyes were looking into my eyes.

I looked straight back into them. '*Ewalla dab.* Yes.'

We had gone about two hundred metres when the *marabout*'s immaculate-looking Nissan finally came into view, its green bonnet luminous in the sunlight.

Beyond, two long stripes stretched out – a dark narrow ridge and another somewhat paler, fading upwards. That one was the road, filled with a disarray of cracked rock and rubble. It was impossible for a camel to walk on those sharp stones. Her feet would be shredded.

We didn't say goodbye, she and I, even then. It was as if she knew. She turned, swished her tail and wandered towards a *tichghar* tree, the tree with leaves most beloved of all camels and with which no human could compete.

Samir and I didn't speak again either. There was little point in making more promises.

When finally I turned, he was no longer there. Only a young, robed Tuareg man receded into the distance. Beside him a tall, elegant dromedary strode, a fine beauty, with long legs, lush lashes and alluring eyes. The desert was just a desert. The sky was just a sky. I knew they would be all right. There were no metaphors to describe the two of them. The landscape was empty of all that had filled it.

※ ※ ※

I began home alone. The ground passed my feet almost unnoticed, as if I was sailing, or walking on air. A jerboa hopped ahead of me. He had fed recently and he wasn't used to being in the light. He preferred the security of the night. Looking a little startled, he hopped off, disappearing behind a Joshua tree.

Lazily, I sat for a while on a rock, enjoying the feeling of breathing. I was not afraid of getting lost or running out of petrol, not even of being bitten by a snake or dying of thirst. I was just being.

A little wild *acheb* had blossomed in the rain. I gazed into the slow whirl of its atoms and saw the miniscule flaws of its interstitials, vacant, sparse places within its crystal structure. I saw infinite bulbs, waves and patterns.

One by one I took those fragments of my past, noble and dissolute, in my palm, and buried them in the sand, where they belonged. And then I made my peace with the God who didn't answer prayers.

In His own way, He had done.

The flash of emerald had become a block. I had the keys. I was moving faster. I still had blisters, but I hardly noticed the stones as they cut into my soles. Somehow, I had managed to overcome that small problem called pain. I was even singing. It didn't seem to matter that the words were a little hazy. I had written them such a long time ago. How far I had walked since then. I hardly recognized that young party girl.

By now I knew just a little more about that flame in our hearts we call love, that landscape as tough and unending as any desert, as great as any winds that blow there and bright as any sun. It burns our very souls to ashes and causes war itself, but it is worth the risk. Because love is who we are, the meeting point of truth and ecstasy, the highest form of the human spirit. Whatever joys or sadnesses it awards us, it shows we have given fully of ourselves to others and we have done it properly.

It is a testament we have lived.

I took one last look at the desert trees – the *ebizguin*, the *tichghar*, the *hagar*, the *hantit,* the *akakou*, the *arankat*, the *tedene*, the *tegar* and the *agar*, each with their different healing powers, spirits and foibles, and thanked them.

As I glanced back at the immensity of where I had been, I felt the white-hot certitude of a life lived without fear. For the first time in my life I was dancing with light.

I do not forget
Wer hintatwegh

I returned to England just as a chill was numbing the streets and the air made smoke of the breath. With my Brillo-pad hair and neon nose, falling-apart shoes and too-thin, tatty cotton clothes, I stuck out like a foreigner. I didn't fit in anywhere any more, but I was happy. Would others be happy to see me? They were. There were warm hugs, joyful tears and a very relieved mother.

With the passing of days the desert fell away, scattering like the snowflakes that dappled umbrellas. The sand dreams left me and instead of a white expanse I saw green. I had missed the land where it was fine to talk about the weather.

Once I had been a tortoise, now I lapsed into a sloth. My body was a feathery quilt in which I lay swathed. Small things brought comfort – a bed, clean underwear, a bath, children playing, a kind word, a thoughtful gesture – above all, the absence of flies.

Firstly something had to be put right. Only now did I learn that my mother had sold her house to help me, just one of the many sacrifices she had made. With what we had left I bought a cheap flat on a busy road opposite a building site. It was rented out and rats were laying siege to the front stairwell, but it was mine. I camped with relatives and passed the income to my mother.

Samir did not write. I began to think that something dreadful had happened to Fleabag, that I had not helped to banish her suffering, but only to perpetuate the cruelty. At night I lay awake thinking of her. I saw her long legs stretched forward, hump rounded and proud, as if all was well. For a moment my heart sang. I imagined I could touch her face, swish away the flies that irritated her eyes, put my own cheek against her soft nose.

Spring kept its promise to return, teasing life into the open. Orange-tipped butterflies spiralled around apple blossom, tawny owls nested, marsh harriers hovered and grebes courted. Fresh buds appeared on the rose bushes.

I revisited the oak trees and saw the economy of beauty in these natural forms as I had never done, as windows into our past, enduring everything life has thrown at them, bearing witness to our deepest sorrows and our greatest joys.

When I finally heard from Algeria, the leaves were beginning to fall again. This time I picked up a telephone call. Three long months had passed since Suleyman had died. Samir had been there at the end, when his father's eyes had begun to sparkle. Or, as Samir put it, as he saw the all-embracing whiteness he had talked about when we had been together that night at the salt lake.

It was as if he had seen a light that became brighter, like sunlight reflecting off sand, a whiteness that cascaded over the mountains and opened out across the desert plains. Then, as that same light began to fade from his eyes, with one last engulfing breath, he had gone. It was as though his soul had been carried away on one of those shooting stars he used to navigate by.

Only now did the scales fall from my own eyes, along with the water that poured so freely from them. Suleyman had always known he hadn't long to live when he had taken us to find the *marabout*; he must have been in terrible pain those times he disappeared. The family had not grieved, for it was said that when a true nomad died there was no need to mourn. His grains evaporated like rain and his soul became a cloud, one that for a day could blot out the sun. At that time his spirit soared and became joined with the sun, whose rays were each soul we had loved who had gone there before. Then the land and sky fell in remembrance.

I like to think that is how it is for all those loved ones I have lost.

Samir had other news. He had taken a wife. He had wooed Rhaicha with Western dancing styles. He put his luck down to the *baraka*-filled amulet he had purchased from the *marabout*. They were thinking of travelling with Hassan to Europe – the land, it was said, that was carpeted with pure gold.

It did not surprise me that Amina had taken charge of the camels. Her husband was not with her. He had given $2,000 to Hassan to take him to Libya. From there his plan was to catch a boat and travel to Italy.

And what of Fleabag, my camel, my belle of the desert, my queen of the sands? For a start she had been given a new name, a Tuareg one, which meant the most beautiful. She loved it.

I missed her deeply. She was that rare breed that fitted into no box. Her independent spirit gave her a haughty and superior air, but she was also vulnerable and her aristocratic demeanour hid a delicate heart. She was witty and playful, and she was also diligent, patient and stoical. And if she happened to pick you out for special attention, you truly were blessed, for when she gave her heart, she gave it completely, with a love that knew no bounds. I felt I would see her again, because if our meeting had confirmed nothing else, it was that events never take place in isolation. We just need to find our connections.

When the tenants left I renovated the small flat by the building site, banished the rodents and a short time later it was sold. With the proceeds I bought my mother the house I owed her and enrolled at the Royal Academy of Dramatic Art; it might have been argued I was well practised in the art of dressing up and playing parts. And then I handed over my charity to the Afghans. I had nothing more to give.

I thought of the Sahara as an old friend who had taken me by the scruff of the neck and forced me to know everything there was to know about myself. Whatever it had communicated to me was part of a process. I was merely a distillation of my experience of it, cleansed of my baggage. It had taken thousands of footsteps and hundreds of miles in space and time for me to discover these things. In the process I had crashed down to earth and made myself poor – but I had been afforded a priceless education.

Christmas brought brand new boxes. The old sealed ones came out of storage, and other possessions reappeared as if sand had unearthed them. A cast-iron roll-top bath that had sat in four different gardens. Five thousand books that had languished in seven separate storage locations returned to me. Looking at them now I could see how they all fitted together, how they displaced a small part of the air around them like rocks among sand.

On this occasion there was a breath of hesitancy before unwrapping. Then I tore them open. There were no tears, just happy forgotten treasures brimming with love and joy from childhood – and a new box, the one with the curious barks, roots and dry leaves, a desert rose, and a little camel bell that I would keep always.

This box stood out among all the rest, because it shone so brightly. It was filled with illumination.

Epilogue

Deserts come in many forms. Their arid spaces occupy not just land, but the heart and the soul. In them we are all wanderers, refugees going past things, returning or escaping.

There are no maps to guide us. Nor are there borders. Where we are reveals itself in small ways – in the tiny area of earth where our feet touch the ground, in the fractions of air we breathe, and in the cracks of our broken hearts.

Apparently unending in their barrenness, their stifling heat has the ability to suffocate us, to drag us down like quicksand. Their sandstorms turn our world upside down and bury those things which are real and important to us, sweeping aside all that should be laid to rest.

But deserts also allow us to breathe. They inspire us. No haze can disguise their brilliant luminosity. For this reason, we must all of us have the courage to cross them. Their deep chasms may divide us at our core, but their blinding light and bitter darkness teach us that a connection exists between all opposites, whether snow and sand, love and hate, East and West.

And they present us with a choice. We can either dwell in the shadows or step towards a light filled with radiant footsteps, the explorers of our own uncharted territories.

The fire is within us.

Glossary

Tamahaq / Arabic / English

abaraqqa / massar راسم / piste
ach / hleeb حليب / milk
achaersh/chèche / el-shesh الشّاش / man's head covering
adiaw / majmoo'at jimal جموعة جمال / camel group
adki / salam سلام / peace
aghmam / dhabab alharara ضباب الحرارة / heat haze
ajjen / mo'askar معسكر / camp
ahal / – / courtship ceremony
akerbai / – / loose Tuareg trousers
akel / mafqood مفقود / lost
akhle / – / haphazard dunes
akzew / waghd وغد / bastard
alakwas / urq mutawassit عرق متوسّط / medium dune
alkhad / nabta نبتة / plant
alaqen / dhakira ذاكرة / memory
alcher / mleeh مليح / good
amadal / mafqood مفقود / lost
amagur / jmel arbi جمل عربي / dromedary
amassakoul / musafir مسافر / traveller
amellulaw / ish'aa'a إشعاع / radiance
amensi / asha'a عشاء / supper
amidi / sahib صاحب / friend
anella / hinna'a حنّاء / henna
anaiwak / awqat jayyida أوقات جيّدة / one on one
aqrba / akrab عقرب / scorpion

351

areg / erg قرع / dune sea
asawad / arwah al-hulum أرواح الحلم / dream spirits
ashaqq / honour
asr / dhaheera ظهيرة / noon
asrir / rahba رحبة / flat terrain
atri / najm نجم / star
ayo / hassanan حسنا / OK
azeleuzelau / ghosn غصن / twig

djinn / el-djen الجن / Qur'anic spirits

edehi / raml naa'im رمل ناعم / fine sand
edeien / mliss مليس / flat, smooth land
edderut / huzn حزن / sadness
edewi / yarboo'a يربوع / jerboa
eghajira / - / Tuareg dish
eheder / nasr نسر / eagle
eihhed / hmar حمار / donkey
ekahi / djaja دجاجة / chicken
ekeuez / rimal adheema رمال عظيمة / bulky sand
elchemer / kuhool كحول / alcohol
elfikiet / khadrawat خضراوات / vegetable
elhennet / firdaws فردوس / paradise
ellelu / shaja'àa شجاعة / courage
elu / feel فيل / elephant
ennetti / bidaya بداية / beginning
erir / kubba zarq'aa قبة زرقاء / firmament
essem / hadeeya هدية / gift
essenari / jazara جزرة / carrot
esshak moni / karama كرامة / dignity

galabiyya / djellaba / robe
ghibli / el-qebli القبلي / south-westerly wind

352

golama / yteem يتيم / orphan
ibedni / - / guardians of emptiness
imohar / horr حر / free man
imohug / - / Tuareg noble
imojagh / karamah / dignity

Kel Essuf / - / spirits of the wild
karambaza / marad alma'ida مرض المعدة / stomach disease

lubaan / shahjarat el-luban شجرة اللبان / frankincense
tree

marabout / el-mrabet المرابط / holy man, saint
mask/adrar/tadrart / jabal جبل / mountain
mehal / mushkila مشكلة / trouble

orar / dhahab ذهب / gold
oued / wed داو / dry riverbed

shirgi / el-shergi الشرقي / dry, easterly desert wind
sira / surah سورة / Qur'anic verse

tagayt / nakhla نخلة / palm tree
tagelmust / - / Tuareg head covering
tagimgimt / ftoor فطور / breakfast
tahargit / hulum حلم / dream
tahel / ittijah اتجاه / direction
tahulet / shajaa'a شجاعة / courage
takamart / jubn جبن / cheese
takokiat / khaleet nubah خليط نباح / bark mixture
taflest / thika ثقة / trust
tamrennant / hadeeth حديث / discussion
tan daman / - / Tuareg sung poem/rite

tannamert / shokran شكرا / thank you
tanuflait / sa'aada سعادة / happiness
tarahamt / manzil منزل / house
tarebbirt / athar kadam أثر قدم / footstep
taremt / balda sagheera بلدة صغيرة / small town
tarek / sirj سرج / saddle
tariwen / hob حب / love
taschilt / hnesh حنش / snake
tasmit / hidaad حداد / mourning
tassili / hadaba هضبة / plateau
tehedit / urq sgheer عرق صغير / small dune
tehot / al ayn al hassood العين الحسود / the Evil Eye
temekelkelt / sileeyah سحلية / zard
tende / tabl طبل / drum
tende n'goumaten / – / Tuareg healing ceremony
teserseq / shou'aa' ashams شعاع الشمس / sunbeam
tesunfat / inbilaaj انبلاج / break
tetant / nissyaan نسيان / forgetting
tidat / hakeeka حقيقة / truth
tuksada / khawf خوف / fear

zeriba / el-zreebah الزريبة / palm hut

Acknowledgments

I am indebted to all those who read the manuscript for this book and for their kind, perceptive comments. In some ways words are like footsteps, and in particular Mr John Edward Macdonald encouraged me along the long, arduous piste of writing.

In giving me the John C. Laurence Award, the Society of Authors made it happen. Heartfelt thanks are due to Vanessa de Haan, for her patience and diligence and for making this a much better book than it would have otherwise have been. I am also very grateful to Deborah Adams, Orlando Hamilton and Helen Nelson for reading the proofs; and to Steve Crisp and Ian Hughes for making it look so nice.

To Amina R – who taught me to read and write Tifinagh, the written version of Tamahaq and so much else – I owe a great debt.

My grandparents always reminded me that as John Milton said, 'a good book is the precious life-blood of the master spirit' and that education is the key above all else. I will never forget their protection and inspiration. Most of all, thanks are due to my long-suffering mother, my very own *baraka*.

My iPod was the unsung hero of the trip, and in particular I am grateful to the following artists, and especially to J.S. Bach and Muse, who kept me going.

Part I: Muse *Endlessly, Butterflies and Hurricanes*; Chopin *Prelude in E Minor (Opus 28, No. 4);* Rachmaninov *Symphony No. 2 in E Minor;* Alice in Chains *Man in the Box*;

Carlo Gesualdo *Tenebrae Responsoria*; Royal Blood *Out of the Black*; Queen *I Want to Break Free*; Monteverdi *Vespro della Beata Vergine*; Muse *New Born*.

Part II: Rachmaninov *Piano Concerto No 2. (Opus 18)*; Queen *I'm Going Slightly Mad*; Ockeghem *Deo Gratias*; Hamza el Din *Escalay (The Water Wheel)*; Rage against the Machine *Killing in the Name, Sleep Now in the Fire*; Muse *Origin of Symmetry, Falling Away with You*; Guillaume Dufay *Ecclesie Militantis*; Deep Purple *Perfect Strangers*; Harvey and the Wallbangers *Allez Bananes, Shine*; Billy Idol *Rebel Yell*.

Part III: Kinks *You Really Got Me*; Tinariwen *Clear Achel*; Muse *Madness, Psycho*; Arctic Monkeys *Do I Wanna Know?*; Supertamp *Cannonball*; George Friedrich Handel '*De torrente in via bibet*', *Dixit Dominus*; Heitor Villa-Lobos *Preludes*; Queen *Innuendo*; J.S. Bach *Cello Suites*; Rolling Stones *Let It Bleed*; Guillaume de Machaut *Messe de Nostre Dame;* Jimi Hendrix *Voodoo Chile;* Tinariwen *Tassili*.

Part IV: Tinariwen *Imidiwan*; Jordi Savall *The Song of the Sibyl*; Muse *Sunburn, Supremacy, Uno, Follow Me*; Royal Blood *Figure It Out*; Dire Straits *Love Over Gold*; Josquin des Prez *Miserere mei Deus*; Ludwig van Beethoven *String Quartets No. 12 in E Flat (Opus 127), No. 13 in B Flat (Opus 130), No. 16 in F Major (Opus 135);* Iggy Pop *Passenger;* George Gershwin *Songs;* Cosmic Gate *Exploration*; Stevie Wonder *Superstitious.*

Part V: The Who *I Can See for Miles*; Red Hot Chili Peppers *Can't Stop, Snow*; J.S. Bach *Mass in B Minor;* The Divine Comedy *The Certainty of Chance*; Supertramp *Brother Where You Bound*; Muse *Starlight, Madness, Supermassive Black Hole*; Richard Strauss *Presentation of the Rose and Trio, Der Rosenkavalier;* Isaac Albinez *Asturias, Leyanda*; Joaquin Rodrigo *Concierto de Aranjuez*; John Lee Hooker *House of the Blues*; Alice Deejay *Better Off Alone;* Nirvana *Smells Like Teen Spirit.*

Part VI: Muse *Space Dimentia, The Resistance*; Rolling Stones *Beggar's Banquet*; Tamikrest *Chatma*; The Rhythm Boys *Happy Feet*; Irving Berlin *Songs*; Ella Fitzgerald *Swings Lightly*; The Ink Spots *The Java Jive*; David Bowie *Hunky Dory, Heroes*; Queen *Another One Bites the Dust;* Amina Annabi *Atamé, Dis-moi Pourquoi;* The Doors *The End, Riders on the Storm.*

Part VII–X: Rolling Stones *Play with Fire*; Muse *Time Is Running Out*, Thomás Luis de Victoria *Requiem Mass*; Olivier Messiaen *Dieu Parmi Nous*; Avo Pärt *Passio*; Muse *Absolution*; Henryk Mikolaj Górecki *Symphony No. 3 (Opus 36)*. Scorpions *Under the Same Sun*; J.S. Bach *Magnificat in D Major*; Richard Strauss *Four Last Songs*; Stan Getz *Over the Rainbow*; Miles Davis *Flamenco Sketches;* John Woolrich *Ulysses Awakes;* Muse *Unintended.*

About the author

Magsie Hamilton Little is a writer, academic and translator. She is the author of the acclaimed *Dancing with Darkness: Life, Death and Hope in Afghanistan* and *The Thing About Islam* and has been an expert contributor to several books about the Middle East, including *Afghanistan Revealed* and *The Rise and Fall of the Persian Empire*. She has also written for *The Times*, the *Daily Telegraph*, the *Daily Beast* and *The Lady*.